*Praise for Son of Southern Illinois*

"Southern Illinois is in Glenn Poshard's DNA. My friend and former colleague, Glenn made a life of politics and public service: soldier, state senator, congressman, candidate for governor and president of Southern Illinois University. Every step of the way he was faithful to his values and his heritage even at the cost of popular support. More than any person I know, Glenn Poshard has given a life of commitment to the families of Southern Illinois. When the political mapmakers carved up this unique part of our state, he refused to be any part of dividing the land of his birth. Now at a time when our nation is so bitterly divided, Glenn Poshard showed us that you can be true to your beliefs and still be respectful of your political adversaries. The voters, even when they disagreed with him, knew he was an honest, caring man in a world desperately searching for public servants to believe in. He and his wife Jo continue their lifelong commitment to those who need a helping hand with their Poshard Foundation for Children."

—**Senator Dick Durbin**

"Nobody represents the quintessential great American success story better than Glenn Poshard, and nobody represented Southern and central Illinois in the halls of power better than Poshard. From his birth and growing up in a hard-working blue-collar family in White County to a career in education and a second career in public service, progressing from Southern Illinois to Springfield, and then Washington, and back to southern Illinois Poshard compiled a distinguished career in both fields. Very few, if any, biographies of prominent politicians are this candid, resulting in a unique and important political biography."

—**John S. Jackson**, editor of *Southern Illinois University at 150 Years*

"I first met Glenn Poshard in 1982, two years before he was elected to the Illinois Senate. Glenn was the first senator from Southern Illinois to chair the Illinois Senate Labor Committee. Glenn's tireless dedication to working men and women and their unions has not wavered in the forty years I have known him. One example of his lasting impact on our region is the thousands of union jobs created by the construction of the Olmsted Locks and Dam, the largest project ever completed by the U.S. Army Corps of Engineers. These union jobs, a total of more than 45 million labor hours, were the direct result of Glenn's efforts."

—**Edward M. Smith**, president and CEO of Ullico

"It is difficult to estimate the influence of Glenn's life on vulnerable and 'faceless' children whose lives have been dignified and enriched through his vision, love, and service. His early experience with the orphaned children of post-war Korea was a defining step toward placing him on a firm path to serving similarly vulnerable children back home. I arrived at the Song Jook Orphanage shortly after Glenn left Korea, but the pattern of service he and his colleagues established continued to bless us children and other soldiers who volunteered their time and gave of their heart. I am grateful that decades later, our lives intersected again and I am able to celebrate and deeply admire his life-long example. His life is truly a testament that those who grow through service are magnified, and humble hearts combined with genuine love can lead to great accomplishments."

—**Jini Roby**, professor emeritus of social work, Brigham Young University

SON OF SOUTHERN ILLINOIS

# SON OF SOUTHERN ILLINOIS

## GLENN POSHARD'S LIFE IN POLITICS AND EDUCATION

Carl Walworth with Glenn Poshard

Southern Illinois University Press
Carbondale

Southern Illinois University Press
www.siupress.com


Printed in the United States of America

26 25 24 23 4 3 2 1

*Jacket/Cover illustration*: Glenn Poshard at Heralds Prairie Township Polling Place in White County, IL. Photo by Byron Hetzler.

Library of Congress Cataloging-in-Publication Data
Names: Walworth, Carl, 1961– author. | Poshard, Glenn, 1945– author.
Title: Son of Southern Illinois : Glen Poshard's life in politics and education / Carl Walworth, with Glen Poshard.
Identifiers: LCCN 2023013345 (print) | LCCN 2023013346 (ebook) | ISBN 9780809339181 (paperback : alk. paper) | ISBN 9780809339198 (cloth : alk. paper) | ISBN 9780809339204 (ebook)
Subjects: LCSH: Poshard, Glenn, 1945– | College presidents—Illinois—Biography. | Southern Illinois University (System)—History. | Public universities and colleges—Illinois—History. | United States. Congress. House—Biography. | Legislators—Illinois--Biography. | Philanthropists—Illinois—Biography.
Classification: LCC LD5101.S363 W3 2023 (print) | LCC LD5101.S363 (ebook) | DDC 378.773/994092 [B]—dc23 /eng/20230407
LC record available at https://lccn.loc.gov/2023013345
LC ebook record available at https://lccn.loc.gov/2023013346

Printed on recycled paper ♲

SIU
Southern Illinois University System

CONTENTS

## Part 4. Southern Illinois University Leadership



## Part 5. Returning to Roots

# PREFACE

As I pull in my driveway on a spring day in 2017, a call comes from Glenn Poshard. It has been nearly twenty years since Poshard served as Illinois' Nineteenth District congressman, three years since he served as president of Southern Illinois University, and eighteen years since he and his wife Jo launched the Poshard Foundation, a nonprofit focused on helping abused children. Poshard's unexpected call came a few months after I was in southern Illinois on an assignment, had a slot spot open in my schedule, and called Poshard about meeting for lunch to reminisce.

Over pizza and salad in the fall of 2016, Poshard had asked about my writing. In the two years since I retired from my work as publisher and editor of the *Journal Gazette and Times-Courier*, I had turned my attention to freelance writing, self-publishing a memoir (*The Mayor of Moultrie Avenue*), and writing a history of a nearby lake and feature-length stories on issues such as disappearing grocery stores across rural Illinois.

I first interacted with Poshard in the 1990s during my tenure as city editor for the *Journal Gazette and Times-Courier* newspaper in Coles County, when Poshard met with our editorial staff, when he hosted town hall meetings in our area, and when he was a source for articles I wrote about projects in our part of his congressional district. So when Poshard and I sat down for lunch in downtown Carterville, we could be characterized as a public political figure and a journalist/freelance writer, as men of faith, as fathers, as sports fans, and as Illinois and U.S. citizens who care deeply about our country and have a desire to make a positive difference in people's lives.

In the follow-up phone call on this sunny Saturday, my car facing the cornfield across the road from my home in Mattoon, Poshard said, "We've known each other for a good while. Do you think my life and career are worthy of a book? And would you consider writing it?"

The answer to the first question was an immediate yes, but the answer to the second question required more thought. As I walked in the front door, considering the Poshard project, I thought of my mother. She'd been raised during the Great Depression on an eighty-acre farm about thirty miles from where Poshard grew up in the hills of White County. I welcomed the opportunity to deepen my understanding of the history, politics, and culture of southern Illinois.

Poshard, born October 30, 1945, was raised with the same family values, fiscal frugality, and work ethic that I had experienced in my own family. Researching and writing a biography of Poshard, I knew, would require a simultaneous focus on his career and on the people and places that shaped him—the economic, environmental, geographic, and political dynamics of Illinois, specifically rural southern Illinois. I welcomed the challenge.

Little did I know that the process of research and writing would span more than five years and include more than a hundred hours of conversations with Glenn, his wife Jo and many others who knew of their work. I rode with Glenn in his minivan, passing places of his youth, including the Chapman Grove Baptist Church and the site of his two-room elementary school, now a small museum. His family prepared a delicious lunch. Later that day, we visited Jim Endicott, his high school history teacher then in his midnineties, who had instilled a love of history and government into generations of Carmi Township High School students.

In the first year of research and writing, I began interviewing Poshard in Mt. Vernon, Illinois, about halfway between our two homes. Together, we reviewed news clippings, handwritten notes, and brochures from the many banker's boxes of materials he loaned me. Over the next several years, I would continue gathering information and revisiting stories, shifting locations as Glenn, Jo, and about twenty-five people personally interviewed made time for this project in the midst of busy lives. The quotes from Poshard in this book stem from these conversations, email exchanges, and multiple Zoom calls. I have not cited each quote to a specific interview.

Sorting out the intricacies of Poshard's multifaceted career, what to include, how to connect things, has been a challenge. Many issues raised in the book resonate as much today as they did years ago. One such issue is what it means to be a Democrat. Poshard is now and always has been a Democrat. He also was conservative on many social issues and some economic ones, like a balanced budget. Poshard remembers discussing, in the Illinois Senate, what it means to be a Democrat with Penny Severns, a more liberal state senator. The following paragraphs typify ways Poshard in his own words describes key points in his life throughout this book.

"Many times at the end of a long day's session, we would sit and talk, and the discussion was almost always on what it meant to be a Democrat. What were the principles in which we believed? I still have a copy of the list we agreed on. First, balance the budget, don't borrow and spend on the backs of our children. If you feel the state needs something, then pay for it as you go even if it requires raising some taxes. Don't borrow the money just so you can escape the political consequences in the next election.

"Second, equal educational opportunity for every child no matter where they live. Neither one of us agreed that property taxes should be the basis for funding public education.

"Third, equal justice before the law. No matter a person's socioeconomic status in life, every person coming before our system of jurisprudence deserves equal and fair treatment.

"Fourth, stand firm for union rights. We both felt the unions built the great middle class of America, and without the wages and benefits they provided, the middle class would begin to disappear. Today, union membership stands at one of the lowest rates in our history, and the middle class is diminishing every year.

"Fifth, we must protect the most vulnerable among us. As Vice President Hubert Humphrey stated many times, 'The moral test of government is how that government treats those who are in the dawn of life, the children; those who are in the twilight of life, the elderly; and those who are in the shadows of life, the sick, the needy, and the handicapped.' We agreed, that, as Democrats, we would always try to uphold those principles."

I wonder what principles would emerge should there be a similar conversation in 2023. Could there even be such a conversation? Southern Illinois communities that voted Democratic in Poshard's youth now are solidly Republican.

While Poshard served as a Democratic congressman and ran for governor of Illinois as a Democrat, his approach to politics and civic life models deeply held American values—cultivation and respect for independent critical thinking, vigorous and respectful debate, standing up for what you believe in, and working with others (even those whose values you do not share) on common goals for the common good. In these hyperpartisan times, this book will resonate with readers who are strong advocates on both sides of the aisle, readers seeking strategies and models to help them understand and participate in values-laden and often contentious civic work in their home communities as members of local school boards, as church and business leaders, as young people participating in their first political campaigns, and even as consumers making daily decisions about whether and what to post on Facebook and how to respond to a neighbor or fellow parishioner with whom they strongly disagree.

This book goes beyond politics. Many issues that arose in Poshard's life are relatable to today's world. The role of mental health is one example. The book includes a life-changing mental health issue that Poshard talks about publicly for the first time. The importance of teacher mentors is another. The spiritual nature of life, yet another. One thing readers may find surprising is the role poetry plays in key life turning points.

This is an authorized biography in which Poshard participated throughout. As the story progressed, I drafted chapters, shared them with Glenn and Jo, revised with their feedback. We followed up with phone conversations. The book is very much Poshard telling his story with insights from those he worked with closely. While they had input, I am responsible for any factual or interpretive errors.

As I traveled for this story, meeting and listening to dozens of people, I discovered much about Glenn Poshard, about southern Illinois, about living a full, adventurous life focused on making a difference. Readers interested in a thoughtful, passionate, personal approach to tackling important matters that improve our relationships and our world will relate to this story. The approaches shown here underline that we can create a better, fairer world.

*Carl Walworth, January 1, 2023*

# WALWORTH'S ACKNOWLEDGMENTS

Many people contributed to this book, including those who were interviewed, those who provided feedback at various stages, editor Wayne Larsen, and SIU Press. This product reflects their skill and professionalism.

I offer special recognition to the following:

- My wife Kathie lovingly supported me throughout. Through many hours, some at unconventional times, not once did she object. I love you.
- Glenn and Jo Poshard, who trusted me to help tell their story, all the while living a fast-paced life of service focused on enhancing lives.
- My sister Candace, for her encouragement and counsel through this and other writing projects.
- To the memory of my mother, Eula, raised on an 80-acre southeastern Illinois farm in Wayne County during the Depression. Economically poor while rich in relationships, her family dealt with a mental health issue and difficult loss of family members. She and others used hard work, persistence, education, and personal integrity to make life better, opening the door for a better world for people like me. Her story resonated with me throughout this process. I think other families will relate as well to both the hardships and the joys. Here's to family stories that help fuel understanding.

# POSHARD'S ACKNOWLEDGMENTS

I want to thank my wife, Jo, who has blessed my life as we have shared this journey together, along with my children, Dennis and Kristen, and our grandchildren—Maddie, America, Tucker, Harrison, Maverick, Lydia, Sterling, Stuart, Nevaeh, and Noah.

Many thanks to my father and mother, Louis Ezra and Cleatus Rose Poshard, who struggled mightily to provide for their children, to my brother, Ed, and his wife, Phyllis, and my sister, Madeline, and her husband, John, who provided the affirmation and spiritual support I needed along the way.

If I have accomplished anything over the years as a state senator and a member of Congress, it is because of the work of my dedicated and professional staff. They are (Senate) Judy Hampton, Betty Davis, Victor Turner, Nancy Smolak, Roland Brown, and Susan Hannaman. (Congress) Beth Pierce, Dave Stricklin, Judy Hampton, David Gillies, Regina Hendrickson, Nina Christostomo, Steve Ball, Bernadette Laniac, Darrin Johnson, Sara Shumard, Nola Hanson, Kristin Nicholson, Karen Spencer, Betty Davis, Tim Martin, Vic Turner, Louise Nolen, Teresa Caliper, Denise Ryan, Pat Dawson, Robin Young, Sam Medernach, Anita Holman, Lisa Chaplin, Don Rumsey, Jim Kirkpatrick, Shirley Stevenson, Patti Henry, Phyllis McKenzie, Shane Rogers, Paul Black, Gary Rowley, John Alongi, Karl Maple, Ed Quaglia, Susan Ryan, and James Wilson.

My joy at being a student and administrator at my beloved SIU was made complete by the finest professional higher education staff with whom I could ever have hoped to work. Vice President Duane Stucky, Vice President John Haller, Vice President Paul Sarvela, General Counsels Jerry Blakemore, Jeff McLellan, and Luke Crater, Dave Gross, John Davis, Brian Chapman, Tina Galik, Dave Uffleman, Katie Houdek, Penny Moon, Martha Poiter, Laura Pind, Marilyn Piper, Erin Troue, and the glue that held us all together, my Executive Assistant Paula Keith, were the very best at accomplishing our shared goals for the SIU system.

SON OF SOUTHERN ILLINOIS

# PART 1

# SOUTHERN ILLINOIS ROOTS

CHAPTER 1

# White County Hills

About eight paces wide and sixteen paces deep, the block building rests on a corner lot in Herald, Illinois, 140 miles southeast of St. Louis. It has a simple white front door. The outhouse in the rear is original, a reminder of days with no plumbing, nor running water, nor electricity. The window air conditioner represents a modern convenience.

The two-line sign says simply:

Polling Place
Heralds Prairie 22

Heralds Prairie is a township with fifty-four square miles and about 650 people. It is rich in natural beauty but poor in financial wealth, save for rich deposits of oil and coal. Glenn Poshard recognizes his home area as a window to American democracy, a place he spent many boyhood evenings in his bib overalls with his father, Ezra "Lib" Poshard, and the men of what the locals call the White County Hill Country. "Right here," Poshard says, "I learned politics from my dad. I learned the value of voting."

The politics of Poshard's youth now are labeled retail politics: chicken dinners, chatter at the general store, connecting people to power, attending family events like weddings and funerals, doing personal favors, ensuring neighbors make it to the polls.

Lib Poshard had but a third-grade education. In local politics, his knowledge was expert. Aside from life's basic necessities, one of the few things in which Lib invested financially was a one-dollar wager on the hottest local race, which was usually for road commissioner. As a precinct committeeman, Lib interacted with residents throughout the year. He promoted attendance at political events in the local village of Herald, some of which attracted candidates for countywide races like sheriff. Occasionally, as in 1952, a state representative candidate stopped by to stump. "That," Glenn Poshard remembers, "was a big deal."

By age seven, Glenn not only was present on election night but also understood political nuances. As the polls closed, Republican and Democratic election judges began examining each hand-marked ballot. A vote was supposed to be a clearly marked X within the box opposite a candidate's name. Even a slight stray outside the lines often generated a hot debate about a vote's validity among the election judges.

From the beginning, politics and Glenn Poshard were a match, starting at the grassroots level but not stopping there. He followed events around the country and the world on the radio. On trips into the White County seat of Carmi, about a fourteen-mile drive, Poshard picked up recordings and transcripts of speeches by presidents Franklin Roosevelt, Harry Truman, and John F. Kennedy. He memorized speeches, including the changes in tone and points of emphasis. The hills became his audience, absorbing his verbatim reconstruction, which became the foundation for public speaking for which he became known.

Smelling the fresh air of a summer day more than sixty years later, Poshard remembers how his formative years shaped and influenced his thinking. He easily recalls three overriding influences: financial poverty, the closeness of family and friends, and the rigid black-and-white nature of the church. He was one of five children: Rose, the oldest, was grown when Glenn was young. Older sister Madeline became like a second mother. His brother Ed was a lifelong mentor. He shared most everything with Jolene, two years older and a best friend. On a daily basis, survival, meeting fundamental human needs, consumed much of the family's energy. In the hills, aunts, uncles, cousins, neighbors pitched in to ease the daily struggle.

Lib worked at odd jobs to generate income. He had lost his left arm at age thirteen when it came between a brother's shotgun and a rabbit. The doctor who sawed off the arm rode nine miles by horse and buggy from Norris City, completing the procedure without anesthesia, mitigating the pain by placing a towel in Lib's mouth. The limb was buried in 1913 in an unmarked grave at the rear of the neatly mowed Herald Cemetery, just a few hundred yards along a grassy lane behind the polling place. Despite his hard work and supportive neighbors, sometimes Lib needed help from the township supervisor, who oversaw a general assistance fund.

"There were times, hard times, when Dad just couldn't find work," said Poshard. "Occasionally, but not often, he would have to go to the township supervisor, Mr. Morris, and get an 'order' which would be redeemed for food. Dad would bring the food home and set it down on the kitchen table. It was almost always a large slab of bacon, some powdered milk, a five-pound bag of sugar, flour, several cans of pork and beans, and maybe a few perishables that we could keep in the 'ice box' in the smokehouse. We didn't have electricity, so the fifty-pound block of ice we got each week from the 'ice man' kept our milk, eggs, and meat cold for a week. This was one of those moments of childhood burned into my memory. Because, as Dad set the food on the table, his eyes looked away, shielding me from the pain, from the shame he felt at having to depend on government assistance. He may have had only one arm and a third-grade education but feeding his family was his responsibility, and in that moment he had failed. I left the kitchen quickly so that the chance meeting of our eyes would not take place, sparing both of us the pain."

The two-room house was constructed near a spring to accommodate a family of seven. When Glenn was a small lad, the family moved the house on sleds about a mile to the road. Before Glenn started first grade, Lib added two rooms onto the house, making a four-room bungalow. The kitchen was always cold in the winter. Heat from the big Warm Morning stove in the living room hardly reached the kitchen, so coats were always in order at study time. "Jolene and I studied every night at the kitchen table under the glow of a coal oil lamp. Its light was dim, stretching across the kitchen, leaving corners of the room still dark."

A bucket of cool water from the well sat on a small table near the doorway, the pitcher with attached glasses for each member of the family arranged in a neat row at the back of the table. Another table near the water bucket held a wash pan and drying towels. "If you left the house and came back into Mom's kitchen, you washed your hands automatically. Every night, the number-ten washtub in the smokehouse was filled with warm water heated on the gas stove in the kitchen, and baths were mandatory. Although there was no running water, no electricity, no refrigeration, and no indoor bathroom, Mom's house and her kids were scrubbed every day. Neighbors said you could eat off her floors."

Poshard and Jolene walked about two and a half miles a day along the gravel road to and from school. Cousins and neighbors joined along the way. On a cold winter morning, Glenn and Jolene might stop at a neighbor's for a few minutes to warm up.

"Those walks were sheer joy. Spring rains, the smell of wildflowers and clover, the whisper of fast-running creeks. Snowdrifts covering the fenceposts. Laughter across the valleys, between the hills, clinging to the clear, cold air of winter. Each day, at precisely eight fifteen, the thirty students or so would gather in front of the two-room school and raise the flag. Every student participated. If you weren't raising the flag, you were saluting the flag and reciting the Pledge of Allegiance, standing at attention with your hand over your heart. When we were dismissed, we returned to the classroom, where Bible reading and prayer took place before a single book was opened."

In the multicultural, pluralistic America of today, public schools do not start the day with a Christian prayer. "But we did, because our community was all Christian, and the difficult issues of the First Amendment were smoldering in the shadows of the peace and prosperity of the 1950s, awaiting the turbulence to come in less than a decade. In the meantime, our little school marched forward, one row of students for each grade, the older ones helping the younger ones, and by the time we got to high school, we were all pretty good students.

"Kindergarten didn't exist in 1951, and since I didn't turn six until the end of October, I started first grade when I was still five years old. In the two-room Herald Grade School, by the time I had graduated to the fifth grade, the other two students in my class had moved away. Mrs. Aud, the fifth- through eighth-grade teacher, felt I should join the three sixth-grade students, so I took the fifth and sixth grades together while I was still ten years old. I started high school when I was twelve."

Lib, who had grown up on the Wabash River, ensured there was plenty of time for fun.

"All through my grade school experience, from about the fourth grade on, I sat near the back of the room by the door because I was very young, small, and shy. There would be a light knocking on the door, and the teacher would walk back to answer it. I would hear my father's voice. 'I need the boy to help me in the field today.' My heart would start skipping beats. This was father's shadow side. An honest, forthright man, but fishing was in his blood and he was lying to the teacher. He didn't need me in the field with him. He needed me in the boat with him on the Wabash, fishing for catfish. I know, he wasn't setting a good example for a parent on those days, but they were some of the happiest days of my childhood. I can still hear our laughter drifting above the current, pulling us together, and making up for all of the days of silence when words could not be found to express our love for each other."

Poshard's mother, Cleatus Rose, shepherded the family participation at the Chapman Grove General Baptist Church with its simple altar, wooden benches, and fundamentalist teachings. In the summer, the church hosted what it termed a "meeting on the grounds," which meant that visiting preachers would participate in an all-day affair that included the best of home cooking, usually fried chicken dinners. Alcohol was strictly forbidden by the church. Sometimes "revivals" would go on for weeks with various preachers' sermons zeroing in on the unsaved. Glenn remembers those early experiences as fundamental to his upbringing.

"We were the most churched kids in White County," said Glenn. "Every Wednesday night, Saturday night, Sunday morning, and Sunday night we were in church. Mom made sure of it. With no indoor plumbing, a potbellied wood-burning stove in the winter, no air conditioning, screens in the windows during the sultry summer months, fans painted with a haloed Jesus in every hand, sweat pouring off the preacher, the unsaved seated on the back bench, and enough 'fire and brimstone' coming from the pulpit to literally scare 'the hell' out of every kid in that church, Chapman Grove General Baptist Church was the social and spiritual center of the hills.

"All of the great old hymns were sung right out of the Baptist hymnal, while someone was playing 'by ear' the old piano, which probably hadn't been tuned in years. Personal testimonies of one's faith were a part of every service, and my dear Aunt Bertha, the kindest, most gentle soul a person could ever meet, was prone to 'shout' at the end of her testimony. She would start in a very quiet, almost inaudible voice that would build to a roaring crescendo, ending with a booming shout. All of us kids would grab the back of the bench in front of us as soon as Aunt Bertha stood to give her testimony because we were never quite sure when the shout would come. If you weren't paying attention, it would scare the tar out of you. There were white knuckles all over that church. We were just holding on for dear life."

But church was fun. It was all family, neighbors, and friends who loved and cared deeply for each other, and it was amazingly free of racial, ethnic, and religious prejudice. In August 1960, a visiting preacher told the congregation that if John Fitzgerald Kennedy became president, the pope would rule America. "I was fourteen at the time. Although this was a common refrain from anti-Catholics in America, it was still shocking to a small group of parishioners, mostly farm families, to hear hatred preached from the pulpit. People sat in silence. They were torn between openly confronting evil and risking being thought of as unkind because they were a good, gentle people. On the other hand, to say nothing, they risked their conscience condemning them because they knew in their hearts what evil looked like and sounded like.

"At the end of the church service, my father, never wearing anything but his Big Smith overalls, the back of his neck burned red from the summer sun, approached the preacher on the front porch of our little church. I was standing only a few feet from my dad when he placed his hand on the man's shoulder. Dad told him how wrong his message was and that anyone who held his views would never be invited to preach in our church again. In my dad's judgment, he could not be a Christian and preach that kind of prejudice.

"My father had no material wealth to give his children, but that Sunday morning, he gave us a gift that I have had to unwrap many times in my life. I hope I have done my father justice, although at times my courage has failed me. Whatever I have been able to understand and practice in life about truth, love, forgiveness, kindness, caring, and understanding was laid as the foundation stone at Chapman Grove General Baptist Church."

Years later, in a Father's Day tribute to his dad, Poshard spoke of the "gift of giving" that he observed every day.

### *The Gift of Giving*

Before my father ever plowed an acre in his own fields, he first helped every neighbor get their crops planted. He did the same thing in the fall at harvest time. He said he had plenty of time to get his own crops in, so he felt good about helping his neighbors first.

Every year in the late fall, several families would gather at someone's farm and slaughter their own meat. It was easier when they helped each other. At the end of the day, Dad carried home only half a hog; the rest he gave to neighbors, because, he said, "they had more kids to feed."

There were some families in our farm community that didn't have a car. Dad and Mom picked them up every Saturday morning and took them into the little town of Norris City to "trade" their butter and eggs for a few groceries to get them through the week. Dad would laugh and say his '53 Ford was the only free taxi in the county.

Dad hardly ever had more than an extra dollar or two, but he had a soft heart for poor children. A soda pop or an ice cream bar was always in order for any kid he met in the little country store a few miles from our house.

Many times the generosity of my father would be met with rejection from our neighbors and friends, and Dad would always say, "Now don't deprive me of the gift of giving." He smiled, and they graciously accepted his gift.

But the greatest gift Dad gave me was the day he faced down the prejudiced preacher in our church. He may have lost an arm, but he never lost his voice. Thanks, Dad, for teaching your kids the "gift of giving."[1]

Government played a significant role. Two programs started by the Roosevelt administration forever changed rural life: the Works Progress Administration (WPA) and the Rural Electrification Act (REA).

A WPA initiative included rebuilding the nearby Shawnee National Forest and several road projects throughout southern Illinois. Lib worked as a water boy on the road construction crews. The WPA had also built a nursing home in Carmi where Cleatus scrubbed floors. Equally important to survival was Lib's trapping and hunting, enabling him to sell valuable mink, muskrat, and raccoon hides to the local fur buyer.

One day in fourth grade, Poshard remembers encountering men setting high line poles and stringing electric wire along the gravel road. REA had finally come to the hill country of White County.

"Our lives in the hills would never be the same. Jolene and I now studied under an electric lamp. Dad somehow managed to buy Mom an electric refrigerator. The 'ice man' never came to our house again. It would be another thirteen years before a rural water district would bring running water to our home, making it possible to seal up the well and to put a bathroom in the house. But for the moment, life was good."

Nonetheless, in Depression-era and post-Depression Herald, living with one arm was perhaps more of a hardship than lacking formal education. "My dad never made an excuse or complained," Glenn said.

Rather, Lib worked hard to overcome. "He could chop wood all day long with one arm," Glenn's brother Ed Poshard said of his father. "He could scoop a wagonload of corn as fast as almost anybody."[2] Lib rolled his own cigarettes, entertaining observant oil field workers in the process. In his overalls, one pocket was for the Prince Albert tobacco, the other pocket for the rolling paper. He placed the paper in a crease in his pants, carefully pulling the tobacco out of his pocket, filling the paper, then folding it between his fingers as he licked it closed.

For all Lib's efforts and the occasional township help, the family relied on older siblings for periodic help. "My brother Ed fudged on his age, went to work in the oil fields when he was fifteen, and eventually joined the Army, completed high school along with some college credits, and became the major breadwinner for our family. My sister Madeline, nine years older than I, was progressing through high school and being both a mentor and a caretaker to my sister and me. She oversaw our studies and would become the first member of our family to graduate from high school, a marvelous accomplishment that we celebrated with much happiness. My older sister, Rose, a great help to my mother, had married and moved away while I was very young. She was a compassionate, caring sister whom we all loved very much."

Lib and Cleatus shared most everything among their friends and neighbors, including food. That was both a social and economic reality. Economically, they had virtually nothing to spare. Socially, they knew everyone for miles. There was no crime. Everyone accepted some responsibility for the well-being of the community.

Sometimes the food came from the land or by barter. Fruit trees produced apples and peaches; blackberries were plentiful in the late summer. The pasture in the hills suited raising livestock that were butchered and then shared with neighbors, the meat heavily salted before being stored in cellars and smokehouses to keep it fresh through the winter.

Commerce was minimal, save for the sorghum mill of Glenn's Grandpa O'Neal. Horses powered the mill's grinder by walking in a circle while stalks of cane were fed into it, squeezing the sweet juice from the cane. Glenn's grandpa heated the product in a long metal vat, moving a paddle back and forth to produce the optimal consistency. Customers drove many miles, some from Missouri and Indiana and Kentucky, to buy the finished product in half-gallon buckets. "I was among the expert tasters," said Poshard.

Glenn's mother made her own bonnets from cracker boxes and cloth. "We got our flour in twenty-five-pound cloth bags. When the flour was gone, Mom would wash the bags, cut them down to the right size, and on her old, pedal-driven Singer sewing machine, she would make beautiful bonnets, sewing pockets along the front where she would insert cardboard strips from empty cracker boxes so that the bill protected her face completely from the hot sun. Nothing was ever wasted in our household." She hauled water, prepared food, cleaned the house daily, embroidered pillows, made quilts. She loved poetry, a love she passed on to Glenn. Her cursive-written notes in a pocket-sized family Bible are a special, enduring family treasure.

Cleatus also tended the garden, planting, weeding, and then harvesting fresh vegetables. Of all the siblings, Glenn was the only one who helped in the garden. Years later, he fondly remembers the experiences and his mother this way.

## *The Garden*

*Leaves from the pin oak falling softly across the lawn*
*The full moon coming up slowly over the pond*
*Memories of you even now in my seventies*
*At this time of the year planting the garden would have been first on our agenda*
*Long rows of tomatoes and green beans and onions and potatoes.*

*You, in your sun bonnet and long dress, bending over the garden hoe*
*Me, placing the potato slips in the mounds*
*Bareheaded and shirtless in the sun, hands and knees in the mud.*
*Day after day of hoeing and weeding and watering*
*Waiting patiently for our spring ritual to begin.*

*At six in the morning we would walk in the garden, the sun coming up*
*And pick two red-ripened tomatoes, still cool from the morning dew*
*We'd sit on the edge of the porch, salt shakers in hand*
*Enjoying the fruits of our garden, greeting the morning sun*
*Talking about the Sunday School lesson at the Chapman Grove*
*General Baptist Church*

*A few Christmases ago at the family gathering*
*Madeline, Ed, and I asked the same question*
*What did we remember most about you?*
*Rattling pans at 4:30 in the morning to get Dad off to work*
*And herding us all off to church on Sunday was easy.*

*But I was the only one who remembered the garden*
*Because it was just for me*
*Your own special gift to me.*
*Sitting here on the porch, listening to the chorus of crickets*
*in the woods along the pond*
*I miss you, and the moon and the pin oak miss you too.*[3]

Poshard also spent many hours alongside his father.

"Every day I was not in school, I was going to the fields with my dad. We had an old 'H' Farmall tractor, a two-bottom plow, an eight-foot disk, and a two-row planter. After helping the neighbors get their crops planted and before he could start his own planting, my dad would go to the First National Bank in Carmi and get a loan that enabled him to buy his seed corn and fertilizer, and we would start plowing the fields.

"I learned to drive the tractor at an early age so I could help dad with the plowing and disking. When we were ready to start planting, we would stack the fertilizer and seed corn sacks about every ten yards along the end of the field, and it was my job to empty them into the boxes on the planter when dad would reach the end of a row. I would then sit on the planter seat and lower the row marker which guided dad to plant the next row of corn.

"The happiness I felt in spending those days in the fields with my father are some of my best memories and served as valuable lessons for me in raising my own children. I learned that just giving kids things, which my mother and father were never able to do for us, doesn't give them the sense of belonging that children need. Providing opportunities for cooperation and contribution to the welfare of the whole family is what really matters, and as kids, whether it was doing chores or working in the fields or studying to make good grades, we all had to be responsible for holding up our own end, and we did."

In some ways, life was rich. People enjoyed each other's company. The kids played games. Life in the hills was physical and challenging, yet it included its joys, particularly when family was involved. Smiles often came at community gatherings, PTA cakewalks, and ballgames at the school, but especially on Saturday nights at Marlin Brothers General Merchandise.

"Marlin's store was the gathering place for people from miles around. Noel Marlin, the owner, and his wife Mabel, ran the store, located in the little village of Herald. The store was stacked with an array of canned goods, dairy products, meats, and dry goods. A counter for sitting and enjoying a soda or an ice cream rose up from the wooden floor, which was always covered with a liberal layer of sawdust.

"A post office with a postal box for everyone in the village was located in the back of the store where Noel also served as the postmaster. Outside were two gas pumps where one could easily 'fill er up' for about three dollars, gas seldom rising above twenty cents a gallon. Across the spacious parking lot in front of the store sat a large outdoor movie screen. On Saturday nights throughout the summer, Noel would run the latest cowboy movies on the big screen from a projector inside the store. The parking lot would be full of cars, with people sitting on their hoods or fenders under the summer night sky and cheering on Lash La Rue, Roy Rogers, Gene Autry, or Hopalong Cassidy. It was as good as any drive-in theater in the big towns of Carmi, Harrisburg, and Herrin, except it was free and the men in their bib overalls and blue work shirts and the women in their long, flowing dresses enjoyed a respite from the crushing poverty that surrounded them, if only for a night."

Of all his relationships, none were closer than the one Glenn had with Jolene. "We just knew everything about each other."

One Sunday in 1960, Poshard was among the neighborhood youth having a corn cob fight at his cousin's house, having fun, enjoying the fresh air. Jolene, her boyfriend, and four other friends drove across the Ohio River to Sturgis, Kentucky, to watch drag races at an abandoned airstrip. It was a favorite pastime for young people from the Illinois and Kentucky sides of the river. The youth included alcohol in their afternoon fun. When it was time to return home, Jolene sat in the backseat of a convertible with her boyfriend when one of the passengers lost his cowboy hat in the wind. The driver pulled onto a side road to go back and retrieve the hat but backed into the path of a tractor trailer going some sixty-five miles per hour. Five of the six teens were killed.

Glenn's cousin ran down to the barn lot to deliver the news that was spreading via word of mouth throughout the countryside. Jolene was among the deceased.

"She said, 'Glenn, you need to get home. Jolene's been killed in an accident.'

"I ran full speed all the way home. I could see dad sitting on the front porch while I was still a distance from our house. He was crying. It's the first time I had seen him cry. My brother came by a few minutes later. I got in the car with him and we drove to Sturgis. My brother asked the toll guy at the bridge if anyone had lived. The toll taker said one of them lived."

"Was it a boy or girl?"

"A girl."

"Was it Jolene Poshard?"

He said, "I think that was it."

"We got our hopes up, but found out it wasn't her."

His sister's tragic death and the deaths of four friends changed Poshard's life in every way. Years later, Poshard captured the essence in this poem.

### *The Walk*

*I have always loved May.*
*Walking home from the grade school*
*We attended a couple miles away,*
*We stopped to wade in Weasel Creek,*
*Flowing swiftly from*
*The fresh spring rains.*

*The wildflowers were thick*
*Along the gravel road to our house,*
*Their fragrance mingling with*
*That of the sassafras roots*
*And the sweet smell of clover.*

*On the last day of school,*
*We were allowed to stop in*
*The village general store and*
*Buy a treat to savor*
*On our walk home.*

*The store-bought candies*
*Were a poor second to*
*The bluebells*
*And the dogwoods*
*And the fields of clover.*

*Every day on that walk we shared poems.*
*We both loved*
*Edna St. Vincent Millay's*
*"God's World"*
*And would recite it to each other.*
*On those fleeting days of laughter*
*In May, we were kids,*
*Loving the woods and the flowers*
*And the sweet fragrance of life that was all around us.*

*Four years later*
*On a sunny May afternoon*
*I lost you to a speeding semi.*
*You were engaged to be married*
*After your high school graduation,*
*The last week of May.*

*Recently*
*I visited the old home place*
*After being away many years.*
*I walked the road again*
*From our house to the old schoolhouse*
*In the village.*

*I'm sure you know,*
*The meadow just past the bridge*
*Over Weasel Creek*
*Sports its exuberant*
*Yellow plumage,*
*And the bluebells*
*Are scattered liberally throughout the woods.*

*Along the road*
*Wisteria climbs some of the*
*Abandoned fence posts*
*Where barbed wire used to be.*

*I think of you often these days*
*And the pure novice love*
*We shared with each other*
*In those days of our youth.*

*I have kept it in my heart.*[4]

CHAPTER 2

# A Quiet Country Kid at the Front

Fifty-seven years after graduating from Carmi High School, Poshard parks his minivan in front of a multistory, white frame home, vintage about 1906. He is greeted at the front porch by a tall, slender man in his midnineties. Jim Endicott and his son welcome Poshard to the living room. Once everyone is comfortably seated, the conversation comes as easily as it has over many years, beginning when Endicott taught high school history to Poshard and thousands of others.

Poshard's healthy, enduring respect for Endicott remained consistent through their lifetimes. Initially as a young adult, Endicott entered Vanderbilt University's law school. Within two weeks, he realized he had made a mistake. His passion was working with students like Poshard.

"You talk about a teacher's influence never stopping," Poshard said. "I understand that. If I could write a book titled *The Teacher*, I would write his life story. He influenced generations. He gave me a great love for history and government, something I have tried to pass on to my own children."

Every summer, Endicott traveled across America with his family, visiting historic sites, battlefields, national parks, state capitols, Washington, D.C., and other landmarks like Fort Sumter in South Carolina, Williamsburg and Jamestown in Virginia, and Bunker Hill in Boston.[1]

When school started in the fall, every unit of history was backed up with slideshows and films and literature Endicott collected. "It gave us a rare insight into each important event in American history because he took us there," Poshard said. "It made history come alive for us."

In 1960, Endicott, a Marine veteran in his late thirties, engaged students including Poshard in the historic presidential election between Richard Nixon and John F. Kennedy. "To this day, I remember his Contemporary American History class in the fall of 1960. We debated every issue that Kennedy and Nixon debated in that campaign for the presidency. Whether it was civil rights, Quemoy and Matsu, Cuba, the Cold War, big government, or the nation's economy, we were expected to know both the pro and con arguments and debate them effectively, and we did. I loved Mr. Endicott, and had he not conveyed his love for American history to me as a young student, I am certain my life's career choices would have been very different."

The relationship with Poshard stood out, but Endicott's reach among young adults was broad. "At our fifty-fifth high school reunion, our class sat in absolute amazement at a fifteen-minute speech on patriotism delivered by Mr. Endicott, now ninety-six and as articulate and eloquent as ever. He drew liberally on important lessons from the Declaration of Independence, the Constitution, and our Bill of Rights and received a long, standing ovation from our entire class. An incredible teacher, still teaching at ninety-six."

Poshard's visit to Endicott's home included a stroll next door, where Endicott had converted a former church into a collection of memorabilia. The large, single-floor room features model trains, a hand-painted Gettysburg battlefield, and an assortment of political signs, including those promoting Poshard for Congress and the governorship. In a way, Endicott continued to deliver firsthand history to his guests.

"Aside from my father, no other individual has had more influence on my political career than Mr. James Endicott," Poshard said.

Red-brick Carmi High School, where Endicott taught, is one of the most imposing buildings in the community of about fifty-one hundred residents. It covers an entire block facing Illinois Route 1.

The grounds are neatly kept. A flagpole sits by the front doors, and a sidewalk leads to six concrete steps at the main entrance.

In a county seat like Carmi, schools and the courthouse are significant structures around which life revolves. "Coming from a rural two-room schoolhouse, I perceived Carmi Township High School to be enormous," Poshard said. "It was a sprawling, brand-new building with nearly six hundred students and, looking back, some of the finest teachers I have ever known."

Endicott was one of three Carmi High School teachers who had an oversized influence on Poshard. World history teacher John Evers delivered an important lesson that helped Poshard immediately after his sister's death.

"He was one of the most respected and well-liked coaches at our high school and was particularly looked up to as a role model by young men," Poshard said of Evers. "After my sister's death, I missed over a week of school helping my family get through this difficult time and missed a really important test in world history. When I returned to school, I asked Mr. Evers if I could take a couple more days to study for the test. I can remember his words to this day. He said, 'Forget the test, pal. I love you, buddy, and if you ever need to talk, come and see me.'"

Although Evers has passed on, his words are as clear and compassionate today as they were nearly sixty years ago. "He taught me to keep as a priority what is really important in life: compassion, mercy, and forgiveness. Much of what I have learned in the classroom over many years of study, I have forgotten, although all of my education has enriched my life. But those few words of Mr. Evers, spoken so long ago, were words of the heart, not the head, and I have let them influence me in hundreds of relationships in my life. A few years ago, I saw a bumper sticker on a car that read 'A Teacher Affects Eternity,' and so they do. Mr. Evers proved it."

A bright spot emerged one day in the most unexpected of ways. Glenn loved poetry. His mother wrote and sang poems, some of which the family retains. Jolene and Glenn shared poetry, including reciting favorite poems on their walks to school.

One day, Poshard sat quietly in the back of the room as Miss Emma Lou Dixon, a substitute teacher who spent several weeks in the class, discussed a unit on American literature and poetry. She asked for a volunteer to come to the front and read the poem "God's World."

Generally, Poshard was a shy, reserved student. He didn't seek attention or try to stand out. That day was different.

"By the time I knew her, Miss Emma Lou Dixon was semiretired but still teaching English at my high school. I was a sophomore, and we were studying a unit on poetry. I was very shy and sat in the back of the room, hoping to go unnoticed among the 'city kids' from Carmi. The poverty of my home life contributed to a sense of inferiority that both inhibited me and, at times, motivated me to overcome my fears. On this particular day, a war between those two emotions was going on inside me. Not only did I know this poem but it remains one of my favorites, and I could recite it from my heart. As a kid, walking along country roads on a sunny fall day, I felt the same exhilaration that Millay felt in observing the colors, the hills, and the clouds, and I would be overcome with spontaneous joy.

"I would not let fear win out in Miss Dixon's class that day. Suddenly, I was out of my seat and walking toward the front of the classroom. I had no book in my hands, and when I turned to face the class, I was completely calm. I recited the poem perfectly with all the emotion I would have felt if I were standing in the midst of nature's glorious fall display."

Poshard described the winds, the gray skies, the colors of the autumn woods, the passionate embrace of his heart to this beautiful world that God had created. "How many walks through the hills on sunny caramel days in October had my heart nearly burst out of my chest when I observed such beauty? I poured it all into that poem on that day in Miss Dixon's class. The room was deadly quiet when I finished, and as I walked back to my seat, I heard one of my classmates whisper to another student, 'Man, who is this hillbilly?' I was devastated. I had risked myself in a way I never thought possible, and I had failed. Boys didn't recite poetry nearly sixty years ago in class; it wasn't the manly thing to do. The teasing and ridicule were sure to come."

The fifth-hour bell rang, and students hurried from the class to lunch. Miss Dixon stood by the door and asked Poshard to wait. The classroom emptied and she closed the door.

"Glenn, I didn't know you liked poetry."

I replied that I did, that my mother loved poetry.

"Do you write poems?"

"Yes, I do."

"Would you share some of your poems with me?"

"Yes, I guess so."

"For the rest of the time Miss Dixon was there, she spent time with me. Lunch hours, study hall, whenever time would allow in her busy schedule, she took a special interest in me. She made me feel my love of poetry was okay and, more important, that I was okay. I didn't have to be embarrassed or feel intimidated for expressing my emotions when moved by a beautiful poem. She was caring. She was compassionate. She invested a part of her life in me. And since that day, in a career that has carried me all over the world, I have never feared public speaking or public debate. My love of poetry has grown even greater over the years, and the self-confidence she gave me that spring in 1960 has grown with it."

High school changed Poshard's life routine. No longer did he walk along gravel roads each morning. Rural students like Poshard rode to and from school in a forty-five-foot-long yellow bus that seated more than fifty students. Poshard's cousin, who lived just down the road from his parents, was the bus driver, which meant that Poshard was picked up first and dropped off last. The round trip of about ninety minutes each way traversed township and county roads, picking up students of all ages. Poshard stepped on the bus about 6:45 A.M. He arrived home about 5 P.M., just in time for evening chores.

School busing is thought of in terms of race and economics in urban life. In Poshard's rural world of 1960, the bus was a way to provide access to rural students. Glenn's brother Ed stressed the importance of a good education. Education and the military were vehicles many rural students used to open doors. Glenn recognized the opportunity. He loved his parents and the hills, but he yearned for a different future.

His parents blamed themselves for Jolene's death. They thought they had failed as parents and Christians. Their own grief at losing a child spilled into their daily life. As the remaining child at home, Glenn saw the conflict firsthand every day. He didn't fully understand the mental toll until a few years later. The immediate impact on his outlook was clearcut. Suddenly, school wasn't important. "It was like my life was coming apart at the seams."

Looking back, Poshard sees he was at a crossroads. A few key teachers and supportive older siblings helped push him forward.

"Mr. Endicott, Mr. Evers, and Miss Dixon were three of my greatest teachers, but I had many others at Carmi Township High School. At a time in my life when I was filled with loss, doubts, and uncertainty about my future, their inspiration and dedication to their students, especially me, planted seeds for my life to become a more caring and productive citizen. That's why being a teacher will always be the most honorable profession, because the potential to change the lives of our children for the better cannot be surpassed."

Poshard was an athletic teen. At about five-feet-ten and 170 pounds, he was strong and fast. The city kids recognized his physical conditioning. He had the fastest times in the 880 and mile runs of all the young men in the physical education classes and was an excellent baseball player, but he was needed at home after school and thus participated in no after-school activities.

Back in the hills, he continued to memorize and deliver political speeches on a stump in the woods behind his house. He hunted with his dad and his cousins, who were like brothers. He went to every political rally. But his first responsibility was always to help his parents with whatever job was needed.

In the Poshard home, the radio was a window to the wider world. "There were three entertainment musts in our home, and they were all on radio. First priority were the daily news broadcasts by Bill Baker on WROY radio in Carmi. Bill Baker was the 'news authority' for southeastern Illinois, and if he said it, it was true. My dad kept up on all the local, state, and national news and constantly quoted Mr. Baker as his source.

"Second, every Friday and Saturday nights, four hours of the Grand Ole Opry from WSM in Nashville, Tennessee, kept us glued to the radio. Chet Atkins, Ray Price, Faron Young, the Carter family, Minnie Pearl, Little Jimmy Dickens, Johnny Cash, and Patsy Cline were household names in the hill country.

"But the number one entertainment value in our home was listening to St. Louis Cardinals baseball games from early spring through the late fall. There were no Cubs stations that reached our home, but KMOX in St. Louis came on strong, and the Cardinals games were broadcast throughout the south on this powerful station. Dad and I would sit out on the porch in the dusk of early evening with the old battery-powered radio between us and hang on every word of Harry Caray as he described the play of my heroes, Stan 'the Man' Musial, Red Schoendienst, and Ken Boyer. Baseball was such an important part of my life, and games with my cousins took place throughout the summer when we weren't helping in the fields."

Unable to play school sports because he had to get home on the bus to milk the cows, Poshard enjoyed the adult games played on the ballfield. Every Sunday afternoon a local baseball team from Herald would play a team from another nearby community. Lib was the umpire. "I can still see him today as he called the balls and strikes. His one arm raised high in the air when the pitcher painted the outside corner with a third strike. Such memories. Baseball and politics were the ties that bound my father and me together, even in the toughest of times."

Poshard's brother-in-law, John Given, took eleven-year-old Glenn to his first Cardinals game. "The Cards were playing the Milwaukee Braves, and Musial hit a home run that night onto the right field pavilion and out onto Grand Avenue. Hank Aaron effortlessly tracked down a drive to the outfield wall and snuffed out a Cardinal rally in the ninth, ending the game with a win for the Braves. Not the ending I had hoped for, but like millions of other young fans who fell in love with major league baseball, I will never forget my first big league game and seeing the heroes of my boyhood."

His sister Madeline urged him to finish high school. His brother Ed coached him about life, including promoting the benefits of the GI Bill. Trips to Evansville and Indianapolis, Indiana, and to St. Louis, Missouri, expanded his horizons. Inch by inch, doors to the outside world cracked open.

"My last two years of high school were both exhilarating and extremely difficult. The death of my sister and four good friends combined with the turmoil in my parents' marriage had exacted an emotional toll. There had been alcohol at the scene of the accident, and alcohol was strictly forbidden in our home and our church. Mom and Dad blamed each other. In their hearts and, they believed, in the eyes of the church and community, they had failed as parents. I learned to suppress my feelings and fears, unable to share my sense of insecurity with anyone. As a young teenager, I was already struggling with issues of purpose and meaning. My days were filled with anxiety, trying to make sense of the instability that had changed my world in an instant on the day of Jolene's death. Had it not been for the encouragement of Ed and Madeline and the inspiration from my teachers, I would have joined the ranks of high school dropouts."

Years later, Ed and Madeline sat at a kitchen table to discuss this book, sharing their mother's Bible and stories that reinforced the strength of family bonds and the physical nature of farm labor. The meeting, complete with a delicious lunch, evoked the sense of belonging one feels during the growing-up years.

The relationships are rich. The love flows in abundance. The enduring memories are special.

At age sixteen, Poshard graduated from Carmi Township High School. "My dream," Poshard said, "was to go to college." A few short months later, when he turned seventeen, he took the next step.

## CHAPTER 3

# Military Life in Missouri, Korea, Indiana, and New York

Before sunrise on a December morning, Glenn and his parents were awake. They hadn't slept well. Stomachs churned. Over seventeen years, they sensed this day would come, a goodbye that meant life would be forever changed. Glenn's departure for the U.S. Army brought feelings of joy mixed with sadness.

Poshard captured that goodbye in a poem.

### *The Porch*

*Uncle Joe parked his 1954 yellow Chevrolet truck*
*on the gravel road leading past the barn lot*
*and came through the gate.*
*He asked you if you needed any help*
*and your reply was, No, the boy here helps me.*
*He's about the only help I've got. I was thirteen.*
*Four years later, I joined the Army on my 17th birthday.*
*I had to catch the train to St. Louis at four o'clock in the morning*
*I had never been away from home.*

*Mom cooked breakfast for me*
*and mostly kept her face toward the stove*
*crying quietly.*
*You sat on the front porch completely in the dark*
*except for one small sliver of light from the kitchen*
*falling across the far end of the porch.*
*I hugged Mom goodbye and stepped out onto the porch*
*I held my hand out into the darkness*
*and felt your one arm brush me shoulder high*
*It lingered for the briefest moment*
*like the beginning of a lover's touch.*
*You told me to take care of myself.*
*Years later, when I was in my early thirties*
*And you were about to die*
*The ingrate in me asked you if you had ever loved me*
*I think I broke your heart*
*The barn lot and the porch*
*Ought to have been enough.*[1]

Like many other young adults, Poshard welcomed the opportunity with the U.S. Army. Many family members distinguished themselves serving in battles across the globe.

"My brother Ed, whom I admired, had proudly served in the Army in the 1950s. I was equally proud to be a part of that calling. And besides, there was no money for college, my grades had slipped my last two years in high school, and I was now responsible for helping support my mom and dad. The Army provided a security blanket. I would have a job and an 'allotment' for my parents, would be trained for a job that would make me employable when my service was over, and would be able to go to college on the GI Bill."

He boarded the train in Carmi. In St. Louis, he walked to the induction station, hoping to qualify to become an electrician. "In a matter of a couple hours, my hopes were dashed. As I was going through my physical, I was presented a book filled with pages of colored dots. On each page, certain colored dots in the maze of dots formed either a letter or a number which I was to identify. I saw nothing. All of the dots looked essentially the same to me. I was told I was color-blind and therefore unqualified for electrical school. All of the electrical wiring was color-coded, and I was told 'there are no color-blind electricians in the Army.' That one test changed my three years of service in the Army and quite possibly my career choice for life. I was reevaluated and offered a slot in finance school, which I accepted and which greatly complemented my future administration and government service."

From St. Louis, the next stop was basic training. The Fort Leonard Wood United States Army base in the Missouri Ozarks had been created in 1940 to train infantry troops. In the summer, intense heat bakes everything around. Poshard arrived with milder temperatures in the middle of winter. In his world, the military represented a welcome opportunity.

Poshard was physically fit. He was skilled in the handling of firearms. Camping out and marching resembled life back home. "I was like a duck to water. I loved every minute of basic training.

"The most interesting part of basic training, however, was the people I met. My basic training sergeant felt the necessity of screaming at our platoon before each daily march to the rifle ranges, that he was going to 'bring smoke on our butts!' Believe me, marching at double-time speed for five miles did exactly that. At the end of the day, we would march back, completely exhausted, eat dinner in the mess hall, and fall in for mail call on the first floor of our old wooden barracks. The sergeant had collected our mail and would stand on top of a foot locker and scream the same threat every night before passing out the mail. 'Now gentlemen, you will wash your scurvy rear ends tonight, or I, personally, as an individual, will do it for you, only I will do it with a G.I. brush! Is that clear?' Since he stood about six feet five and weighed around 250 pounds, none of us were eager to challenge his admonition and feel the sting of steel wires on our rear ends, so we all answered in unison, 'Yes, Sergeant,' at the top of our lungs."

The eight weeks of basic training diverted Poshard's attention from White County. Then it was off to five months of finance school at Fort Benjamin Harrison in Indianapolis. "I studied hard for the time I was there and spent time on the weekends with my cousin Ida and her family, who lived not far from the post. At the end of five months, I had hoped for assignment overseas but I was sent back to Fort Leonard Wood in the late summer of 1963."

On November 22, 1963, Poshard was working in the finance office when the command was issued to return to his company. "Captain

Sullenger, a West Point graduate and our company commander, stood in front of us and told us President Kennedy had been assassinated in Dallas, Texas, and the entire military had been placed on the highest alert. Grown men, good soldiers, began weeping in the ranks. The whole situation was surreal to me. Had I not followed his whole campaign to be president? Did I not find excitement in studying and debating his positions on issues in Mr. Endicott's class? Had I not put up his signs and stayed up late that night at the polls with Dad to make sure he had carried our precinct? He was my president, my commander in chief, who had inspired my generation to 'ask not what your country can do for you, rather ask what you can do for your country.' And now he was gone. For someone who loved him as our president and respected the courage he had displayed in his life, it was almost more than I could bear.

"Standing there in the ranks, I remembered a conversation with Miss Emma Lou Dixon about the sadness I felt for my father, losing his arm as a young man, and the limitations that loss had imposed on his life. She referred me to a poem by Robert Frost titled "Out, Out—" in which a young man had lost his life in an accident while sawing wood. At first, no one could believe the accident had happened. It came so suddenly and at dinnertime, the most "looked-forward-to" time of the day. As they watched the life drain from his body, reality set in. Death ended the prospect of a bright future for the boy, but the affairs of their lives had to go on.

"Sometimes in life, loss is so unexplainable that complete detachment and indifference are the only way to cope. It doesn't mean that we give up the search for meaning or feel less sad about the loss, but life must go on, must be lived with determination to overcome. Standing there that day in the ranks, I clung to that conversation with Miss Dixon and to the words of my favorite poet."

Soldiers found time to hitchhike up Route 66 to catch a Cardinals game. In the last year of Musial's career, Poshard remembers seeing the Cardinals' slugger hitting home runs onto the right field pavilion in old Busch Stadium on Grand Avenue.

"Once I was hiking back to Leonard Wood from my home and got a ride on the outskirts of St. Louis. I was tired and fell asleep within ten minutes of getting in this total stranger's car. The next thing I knew the man had pulled off the road and was nudging me awake. We were adjacent to Leonard Wood, and I had slept the entire two-hour ride. I was embarrassed and apologized. The man just smiled and thanked me for my service. He told me he had been a soldier too, and he wished me well. This was an act of kindness I have never forgotten."

Shortly before Christmas in 1963, Poshard put in for a transfer to the Far East. He wanted to take advantage of his Army enlistment and see as much of the world as he could. In the spring of 1964, his orders came through. His new assignment would be with the First Cavalry Division in Korea, stationed near the demilitarized zone dividing North and South Korea.

For the first time he saw snow-capped mountains, on the train trip from St. Louis to San Francisco. The next leg of his journey, air travel, wasn't so pleasant. At Travis Air Force Base in Solano County, Poshard boarded a military plane headed for Hickam Air Force Base in Hawaii. He described the plane as a four-engine prop job that lost an engine two hours after takeoff. They returned to Travis to replace the engine, dumping fuel before landing, creating a wall of smoke around the wing.

That flight was relatively calm compared with what was ahead. From Hickam, about eighty people boarded a four-propeller plane headed for Wake Island, about halfway between Honolulu and Tokyo. The plane could not get above twenty thousand feet and thus flew through storms rather than over them. The rocky ride, some twenty-three hundred miles, created unease. The plane landed on Wake, refueled in about ninety minutes, and the soldiers were on their way to Japan.

Poshard describes the takeoff from Wake Island like this: "As we lifted off of Wake Island and the small island below us began to disappear, the same engine that had been repaired at Travis Air Force Base burst into flames. The pilot immediately turned back toward the air base, which was only a few miles away. He began dumping as much fuel as he could while making a wide circle to try to line up with the runway. The fuel, mixing with the oxygenated air combined with the engine fire made it look like the entire plane was engulfed in smoke. From where I was sitting, it looked like some sort of fire retardant was being sprayed on the burning engine, but I couldn't be sure. The fire was not going out! Across the aisle and a couple of seats in front of me, a young Navy officer and his wife were seated. He was on his way to Yokohama, Japan, to join up with his ship. His wife began to panic, and a male steward tried to calm her while instructing passengers to prepare for an emergency landing. It seemed like a long time, but I'm sure it was only a matter of minutes before the pilot's final approach to the runway. We were all in the emergency positions, and a lot of prayers could be heard as we touched down. The landing was smooth enough, and after a few seconds I raised my head to look out the window and saw a firetruck racing alongside the plane spraying foam all over the wing. As soon as we stopped, the emergency exits were opened, and everyone exited and raced away from the plane as quickly as possible. For a first-time flier like me, it was a little bit unnerving, but for the skilled pilots who flew those planes in World War II and Korea, I am sure they learned to handle many situations like this. I still feel the calmness and skill of the pilots that day saved a lot of lives."

Three days later, another engine arrived, was put on the same plane, and the soldiers headed for Japan once again. "We flew through a storm off the coast of Japan that was so frightening and the updrafts and downdrafts so severe, you could hardly keep your seatbelt on." Poshard tells the story now with a sense of humor. At the time, it felt like it could end his young life.

Once on base in Yokohama, Japan, Poshard spent a week learning, among other things, how much the Japanese loved baseball. Baseball was Poshard's first love in the hills, both playing with friends and listening to Cardinals games on the radio with his father. The Japanese played with the same passion, providing an unexpected cultural connection.

Poshard's next flight was extraordinary in a different way. As the men left Japan for Korea, "We flew around Mt. Fuji. I will never forget how beautiful that was."

Korea sometimes is described as a bowling alley. It features a wide valley that sits between mountain ranges. Fighting during the Korean War raged in that alley from June 1950 to July 1953. North Korea and South Korea then exchanged prisoners after ceasing hostilities, but signed no peace treaty. Rather, they created the demilitarized zone (DMZ), a buffer 160 miles long and about two and a half miles wide.

Poshard quickly tied into his work. A disbursement specialist, he made sure everyone got paid accurately and on time. He was thorough and efficient and soon became worthy of a promotion, from E-3 to E-5. At night he took college classes through the University of Maryland, taught by the colonel who was his company commander.

As much as he thrived on military life, inside, his mind silently churned. Like his father, Poshard didn't release his emotions. He struggled to come to grips with poverty and death. He worried about his parents and whether they would ever reconcile Jolene's death and feel the peace of forgiveness in their marriage again. The First Cavalry Division was stationed along the DMZ, and everyone, regardless of their work, had to stand guard duty around their base camp.

While he walked the camp's perimeter alone at night, his thoughts would return to the hill country and the sadness he felt for his parents. To counter the worry, he started committing to memory each one of President Kennedy's speeches and silently repeating them over and over as he walked guard duty. It was a distraction that served him well, and today, fifty-five years later, he recites those speeches word for word, even employing Kennedy's Massachusetts accent.

Soon, however, there emerged an outlet that consumed most all of his "free" time. Down the main supply route, several miles from his base, was the Song Jook orphanage, home to about eighty children, from small children to teens, Korean children who had been neglected and abandoned after the war. Korea was full of such children, outcasts in their own society with no families to care for them and no place to stay.

Song Jook consisted of concrete blocks on concrete slabs. One woman ran the place. The children slept on straw mats in several rooms with no blankets. Their diet was primarily rice cooked in large pots. A large yard provided room to play, but there was no equipment. Poshard knew poverty. This poverty gripped his heart. Seeing children treated as though they were invisible in their own country was something he couldn't accept.

Poshard and his buddies began to collect one dollar from each soldier in his company each payday, sometimes collecting as much as $150 a month. With the money they purchased food, clothes, and related items. They assigned each child an arbitrary birthday, and each month they celebrated with a cake. They had churches from home send blankets, quilts, and clothes. "The children loved to see the soldiers coming. Every weekend when we were off and sometimes through the week, we played with the kids. We went there every time we could get away."

As the end of his tour of duty in Korea approached, the questions of purpose and meaning flooded into his conscience. The orphanage impacted him on two levels. "I had started questioning Jolene's death. I was raised in a church with black-and-white thinking. I started questioning my faith in God. I had never done that before. I thought, how can a just God, how can He allow these children to be in this situation? How can this country be destroyed and families torn apart between the north and the south? This began weighing on me mentally."

Tough as his youth was, he always had clothes and food. The neglect was beyond his experiences. Never as a child did he wait for the neighbors' leavings in the trash to have something to eat, as children did around the Army base.

"Looking back I was struggling from Jolene's death. I was not mature enough in my faith to understand these inconsistencies. I thought 'I'll never see these kids again.' I was praying for understanding. I remember the day I got on the plane to come home, I was just distraught."

Years later, when he was president of Southern Illinois University, he regularly perused other university magazines in the hopes of picking up some "best practices" for his alma mater. He came across an article about Jini Roby, a professor at Brigham Young University. Professor Roby was an internationally acclaimed authority on child abuse, neglect, and abandonment. As he read the story of her life, a single paragraph caught his attention. She had been an orphan in the Song Jook orphanage during the time he had served in Korea. He immediately picked up the phone and called her at Brigham Young University.

"Yes, I remember the soldiers," she told Poshard, adding, "I'd like to do something to pay that back."

"Would you come spend a day at our university?" he replied.

In February 2014, she did, telling her story to Southern Illinois University students and faculty. She explained that she had been adopted by Mormon missionaries who had visited the orphanage and brought her to Utah where she grew up and followed her dream to help abandoned children around the world. Poshard gave her copies of photos. Roby said those were the only pictures her friends in the orphanage would have of that period in their lives.

For Poshard, it provided perspective. "It took God fifty years to reveal to me the good that came out of all that poverty and pain I witnessed in that orphanage. Now she is making a difference for hundreds of thousands of children all over the world." The life lesson to him is this: "You have to look at your contributions in the world as things you may never find out about. You're lucky if you see a small part of what you did come to fruition in the lives of others. We should never demand payoff for what we see and do now. To mature in faith, we have to understand it's enough just to give the gift."

He remembers the Korean people as emphasizing kindness and courtesy. He visited religious temples in the countryside, spent time walking through the villages and made friends with many Korean nationals. He learned to speak a little Korean and held many conversations with the villagers who farmed the rice paddies near his camp, trying to learn as much about the culture as he could.

One time, he made a mistake that could have threatened his service record. Every month his unit would bivouac along the DMZ. The trucks would be loaded in the middle of the night, and tents would be set up before the sun came up. Poshard was in charge of loading the truck with camouflage netting and stringing it in the trees to hide the tents beneath, not an easy task, especially in the dark. It was early winter, so gray netting had to be used to blend in with the trees. When the commanding general flew over the camp early the next morning, he saw nothing but green camouflage, exposing the tents. "He landed his helicopter," said Poshard, "and sought out the colonel who was over my company. Needless to say, I received a good chewing out because, had we been in battle, my mistake could have been fatal. My color blindness, not being able to distinguish between grays and greens, contributed to a critical mistake on my part."

While in Korea, Poshard had minimal contact with his family. He wasn't one to write letters, nor was he going to receive one from his parents. Soldiers were allotted a three-minute phone call at Christmas, which was about the only time he could call. Poshard's sister Madeline told him the family once went three and a half months without hearing from him.

On the train ride from San Francisco to St. Louis in July 1965, Poshard saw something else for the first time. There were no pats on the back nor words of thanks for returning soldiers. No one greeted them during their travel. It was but a small taste of what many who later served in Vietnam experienced.

His brother Ed picked up Poshard in St. Louis, and as they were crossing the river into Illinois, they stopped to watch some of the last sections of the Gateway Arch being put in place. The Arch is known as the Gateway to the West, a manmade steel marker commemorating westward expansion. Poshard's world was about to turn eastward. After a couple weeks in White County, visiting friends, hearing the hellfire and brimstone sermons at the Chapman Grove General Baptist Church, and eating Madeline's fried chicken, he was back on the train.

For the final six months of Poshard's military service, he was stationed at Fort Hamilton in Brooklyn, New York. He arrived at Grand Central Station with twenty-seven dollars in his pocket and a desire to learn the subway system on his own. He was told to just go down the steps and catch a certain train and he would be on his way to Brooklyn. He ended up catching the wrong train, going the wrong direction, and being miles from his destination with time running out before his midnight check-in. He retraced his route back to Grand Central Station, went upstairs and hailed a cab. He pleaded with the cab driver.

"I am going to be AWOL if I don't get to Fort Hamilton by midnight. All I've got to my name is twenty-seven dollars. If you'll get me there, I'll give you all I have."

"Get in soldier," replied the cab driver.

It was a long and harrowing ride through the streets of New York City, but he arrived at the gate shortly before midnight. The guard radioed his company and told the officer on duty he had a soldier who might be a few minutes late. Poshard ran through the grounds, being forgiven for being ten minutes late.

New York City was good to Poshard. He enjoyed going into the city, and the USO (or United Service Organizations), had plenty of tickets for servicemen to performances on Broadway and at Radio City Music Hall. Tickets to Yankee Stadium and Shea Stadium were always available. He and his buddies enjoyed Times Square, Chinatown, and Greenwich Village. He mastered the subway in a few weeks and, on his time off, traveled throughout the city, knowing his time there was short and wanting to take in everything he could before heading home.

Shortly before his enlistment was over, he was called into the office of his commanding officer. He was presented a commendation from the commanding general of the First Cavalry Division in Korea, which read, in part, "for outstanding service in Korea during the period 26 June 1964 to 8 July 1965. Specialist Poshard's personal character, devotion to duty, and professional competence won him the respect and admiration of his superiors and subordinates alike. His outstanding service reflects great credit upon himself, the 1st Cavalry Division, and the United States Army." That commendation still hangs on his wall nearly fifty-five years later. He calls it the greatest honor of his life.

## CHAPTER 4

# First in the Family

The bright, cool January morning in 1966 was well suited for a drive, a clear, brisk day that called for a modest jacket to neutralize the chill. Poshard and his father were about to experience something new, a trip together. They occupied the front seats of Lib's 1953 Ford, heading southwest. They passed through the familiar communities of Eldorado and Harrisburg, continuing on toward Marion and Carbondale. The seventy-one-mile trek to Southern Illinois University (SIU) ranked as one of the longest trips ever for Lib. More significantly, it marked the first time one of his children enrolled as a full-time student at a state university. Lib typically bottled emotions. On this day, he allowed a tear to roll down his cheek. Unlike the first time Poshard saw his father cry—upon the news of Jolene's death—this tear represented joy.

Lib dropped Glenn off for what was known as the "Woody Hall shuffle," a dash to register for classes for the upcoming term. Founded in 1869 as a school to prepare teachers, SIU was in a growth mode. A dynamic president, Delyte Morris, aided by influential lawmakers, saw opportunity to capitalize on the federal government moving much of its research to university campuses. The growing numbers of veterans qualifying for the GI Bill meant more prospective college students. Morris seized on the opportunity to develop SIU into a statewide force with diverse majors and additional, prominent faculty.

Morris, from nearby Xenia, was a visionary, adding buildings, programs, and students. "Doctor Morris was the icon," Poshard said. "He was the visionary with political clout behind him. He was not going to allow SIU to remain a regional university. The fifties, sixties, and seventies were part of the golden age of higher education in America when millions of dollars flowed from state and federal funds, and President Morris was the one guy who could bring the money home to SIU." By 1992 the SIU enrollment was nearly twenty-five thousand students, up from the four-thousand-student body it had been when Morris took over as president in the 1940s.

Days before, Poshard drove to a Carmi bank. During his three years in the military, before his discharge on December 27, 1965, he sent part of his pay home to help his parents, a stipend called an "allotment" by the Army. He also sent money for his parents to invest in savings bonds that would help make college financially viable. Between the GI Bill, which paid most of his tuition and fees, and the cash from those bonds, Poshard could afford to start at SIU.

"My enrolling at the university brought an incredible sense of pride to my father," Poshard said of the drive to Carbondale and then back home in the same day. "My parents never really had the time to push me educationally. They had no money at all. They were just busy trying to live, to survive. For a kid to go to college, that was a big deal, an emotional moment."

Years later, when Poshard was the SIU president, he was often reminded of the sense of pride in families who had a child graduate from a university for the first time. "You watch these families on graduation day; they are the ones cheering the loudest, just celebrating breaking that barrier. I was fortunate to witness that many times over. I've learned and witnessed how important that is for families in America."

The drive home was mostly quiet. Details about the upcoming SIU term didn't need to be shared. Rather, they quietly relished each other's company, recognizing the moment as another turning point. "My dad was glad he brought me and had a part in that day."

The next week, Poshard's sister Madeline and brother-in-law John drove him back to Carbondale. He had rented an upstairs room in a quiet neighborhood on West College Street, and they helped move him in with the sparse belongings he had acquired since leaving the Army.

Southern Illinois University is central to Carbondale and all of southern Illinois. It is critical to the region's economy and a gateway for students to encounter the wider world. The athletic teams are called the Salukis, named for an Egyptian hunting dog, derived from the region being referred to as "Little Egypt."

Student experiences at universities go well beyond the classroom, as Poshard quickly learned. In the late 1960s, the SIU experience was rated as among the most volatile in the country. Though he had experienced military life in both Korea and New York City, the world unfolding at SIU was unlike anything Poshard had experienced or envisioned.

He imagined that there was a strict dress code, that students "dressed up" for class. He asked John Marlin, an SIU student whose father owned the general store in Herald, how many suits he would need. "He said, 'What? Nobody wears suits.'" To the contrary, at a chemistry class in January, Poshard saw a female student in class wearing a raincoat and underneath, shorts and a halter top. The discipline of the military was nonexistent on the free-spirited campus of SIU in the 1960s.

This surprise was just the beginning. While Morris pursued and implemented his vision of expanding SIU, the university also became a hotbed of militant activism. The Vietnam War generated ongoing protests. National movements for civil and women's rights found roots on campuses. Labor unrest sometimes turned ugly. One day a professor in class promoted an upcoming protest at a nearby factory making munitions for the military. "I'm listening to this teacher, thinking, 'What's wrong with you people? I'm for the war in Vietnam.'"

As the unrest and protests unfolded at SIU, Poshard received news from home nearly as unsettling as his sister's death. His cousin Dennis, who was like a brother, became the first White County soldier killed in Vietnam. Dennis and Glenn spent nearly every day of their youth in the hill country hunting, fishing, playing baseball, sharing each other's secrets. The news was personally devastating, though Poshard bottled his emotions. As with his sister's death, Poshard allowed the toll of Dennis's passing to fester and build internally.

"Dennis and I were born only two months apart. My brother Ed was twelve years older than I was, so during much of my childhood and teenage years, he was already working away from home. Dennis was like a brother to me. All the joys of growing up in the hills with my cousins Carl, Dennis, Jerry, Harold, Rodney, and Gary offset the sadness of Jolene's and my other friends' deaths. And now Dennis was gone. The two most important friends of my childhood, my sister and Dennis, were tragically taken from me.

"Dennis was a gifted athlete and had died valiantly on the battlefield in Vietnam, being awarded the Bronze Star for bravery. How many times had we witnessed a winning hit or a great defensive play when he won a game for our school? How many mornings had we sat in the darkness under the hickory trees, waiting for the sun to come up and the chatter of the squirrels to begin? When we hunted for wild game to put on our table, he was always the best shot. Anything that required physical skill, he was the best among us, the fastest, the strongest. His loss was unbearable to me."

In high school, Poshard memorized A. E. Housman's beautiful memorial, "To an Athlete Dying Young," and it reminded him in a deep, sorrowful way of how fragile life really is, even in youth, where "fields of glory do not stay."

Housman describes a young athlete who wins his town the race but suffers an untimely death. Now he will never see his record broken by others; he will always be remembered for his heroic win as a young man. He will remain forever young in the minds of those who loved him, a fitting memorial for Dennis.

On the outside, Poshard observed a world of growing unrest. Spring of 1969 saw a campus full of tension with the administration being challenged on many issues. Students were convinced that programs such as the Vietnamese Studies Center and ROTC were unholy connections to a federal government intent on widening the war in Vietnam. Then on June 8, 1969, Old Main was burned to the ground. It was one of the most prominent buildings in the quadrangle, the older, more historic part of the campus, a landmark representing SIU's prodigious past. It came as a shock to the entire region but was only the beginning of a turbulent year on campus.

Throughout the fall of 1969 and into the spring of 1970, the demonstrations and riots grew in number and intensity, occurring almost daily during late April and early May of 1970. One day Poshard witnessed a large group of students move toward Wheeler Hall where the ROTC program was located. Their goal was to take over the building and throw out the ROTC. Seeing law enforcement officers wearing gas masks in preparation to protect Wheeler Hall, the student leader of the protest yelled, "Forget Wheeler, get Woody."

Woody Hall was across the street from Wheeler Hall and held administrative offices. The students took it over for days. The May 4 shootings at Kent State signaled a new level of combat on university campuses, SIU being no exception. The violence and unrest led to the unprecedented closure of the campus on May 12, 1970, for the remainder of the spring quarter. An indelible imprint of chaos and confusion would remain in the memory of SIU students for decades to come. "In the 1960s at SIU, Carbondale was the most chaotic and yet dynamic place you could imagine in higher education," Poshard said.

Poshard remembers learning in one class about the Guiding Fiction, a concept developed by Alfred Adler by which people evaluate their behavior against entrenched, constant principles. Those principles, the societal norms established over decades, were being challenged in every way.

"The civil rights movement meant African Americans were crossing the line separating them from mainstream America. The women's movement was breaking down barriers to women's progress that had been in place for centuries. The labor movement was challenging business and industry to provide more rights and better pay for their workers. The environmental movement was challenging industrial polluters to clean up their act and stop ravaging the air, water, and land resources of America.

"Southern Illinois was coal country, and professors on campus were insisting the university engage more heavily in clean coal research for a healthier environment. Other professors were demanding the mining of coal cease altogether, a proposal I felt was preposterous because thousands of jobs in our region depended on coal. No one had challenged the coal companies before to be more responsible. People were crossing the lines of the Guiding Fiction that had divided America, and the biggest illustration of that change was on college campuses."

While personally out of step with the university world on its view of the military, Poshard favored many other transformative issues such as labor support and racial equality, yet he didn't have the time or the energy to directly engage with protestors. He needed to work to pay his bills. He met his girlfriend Gayla at a community college basketball game in Harrisburg in the early spring of 1966. In their conversation, he learned her family operated a pizza restaurant in Eldorado. On one of his trips home to White County, he stopped at Gayla's father's restaurant. Poshard and Gayla began dating and were married in the summer of 1967.

He and Gayla lived in Marion, a sixteen-mile drive from SIU. While he appreciated the generosity of the GI Bill in covering tuition and fees, Poshard needed more income to financially support his family. Thus his time on campus was devoted to class attendance and working four hours a day in the physical plant, helping the university as it began to computerize its payroll.

To add income, he utilized one of his father's political connections. Paul Powell was an influential Illinois lawmaker who later became secretary of state. Poshard's dad met Powell at the White County Fair, and Powell understood Poshard's father was good for a couple hundred votes. Powell was a good friend of Tony Castellano, who also was connected with Dan Walker, who was running for Illinois governor. Castellano operated Tony's Steakhouse in Marion. After his father's talk with Paul Powell opened the door, "I went to see Tony, and he put me to work right away."

Poshard helped clean the bar and the restaurant, then stayed and bussed tables in the evening. Powell ate there every weekend he was in town, and after Dan Walker became governor, many southern Illinois Democratic meetings were held at Tony's Steakhouse. It's where Poshard began to meet and cultivate relationships with county chairmen and other officeholders, a practice that stood him in good stead years later when he decided to run for office. Tony took a special interest in Poshard and introduced him at every meeting as "a good young veteran trying to work his way through college." At Tony's Steakhouse, Poshard had a front-row seat to the ways of the political world.

While Tony's was mainly a weekend job, from three in the afternoon until eleven at night, Poshard also stocked shelves in his father-in-law's grocery store, Foodtown, in Marion. Thus, while he was working three jobs, and he and Gayla were both enrolled at SIU, they were looking forward to the birth of their son, Dennis, in the summer of 1968. A second child, Kristen, was born in the spring of 1973. The birth of a child is a great blessing to any parent, and both children were special to Glenn and Gayla.

Academically, Poshard found a home in the physical education department at SIU. Having started as an accounting major, Poshard discovered that working with spreadsheets wasn't what he wanted to do with his life. "I was sitting in Accounting 251A about midway through the term, and I said to myself, 'Wait a minute, what is it I really want that would make me happy?' I decided it was working with young people. I wanted to teach history and government, and I wanted to coach. Growing up, I had loved all manner of sports, so I switched my major to education, focusing on physical education."

The late 1960s were a golden era for SIU athletics, with future New York Knicks star Walt Frazier leading the Salukis to a National Invitation Tournament championship in basketball. SIU also had championship teams in track and field, gymnastics, wrestling, baseball, tennis, and swimming. Poshard had the opportunity to learn from some of the greatest coaches and professors in SIU history. Many times he felt overwhelmed with the studies and the three part-time jobs, but he developed an uncommon love for this blue-collar university that gave poor kids like him a hope for the future.

"Sometimes, even today, I walk the campus in the late afternoon, and my mind is flooded with memories of my favorite professors. I can still recount their lectures that inspired me to be a better person. I can still feel their challenge to 'do something' with my life, to make the world a more just place in which to live. They weren't only training us to get a job; they were training us to be citizens of a more democratic America. Yes, those were chaotic days, but they were filled with energy and excitement and I loved being here and being a part of it."

While he remained out of touch with other students about the war, in time those students earned his respect. "I became more impressed with young people who I thought in the beginning just didn't want to go to war. The more I saw, I realized that many in my generation opposed the war for ethical and moral reasons."

With the benefit of time, Poshard recalls his worldview this way: "I entered this intellectually stimulating atmosphere. I witnessed firsthand the beginning of the destruction of those artificial barriers of race, ethnicity, gender, religion, and economics that had divided America for so long, some of which are still dividing us. The assassinations of President Kennedy, Martin Luther King, and Bobby Kennedy broke the heart of our country. It was almost as though America were experiencing a massive nervous breakdown in the sixties. Earlier in my life, I saw unbelievable poverty and the abandonment of children in Korea. I had seen the breakdown of my parents' marriage after Jolene's death. The person closest to me outside my immediate family had been killed in Vietnam. Even though I was still in my early twenties, purpose and meaning for my life had become a huge challenge for me."

The sum of those life challenges led Poshard to what he calls a spiritual desert. He began to question things he was raised to accept as gospel. "Whatever I had been taught wasn't working for me."

Thus, as he graduated from SIU in 1970 and took his first teaching and coaching job at Galatia High School, he asked himself this question: "What do I really believe spiritually?" Around the country, sects of people were using transcendental meditation and other forms of religious experimentation. Poshard embarked on a one-person quest to explore his own spirituality. By himself, he studied Buddhism, Islam, Hinduism, and other world religions. "I began a monumental struggle in my conscience. The black-and-white things I had relied on were crumbling. I was having this battle inside me about purpose and meaning. It weighed on me in a way I can't begin to tell you."

In Poshard's upbringing, members of the congregation would go to the front of the church to kneel and pray for forgiveness of their sins and confess Christ as the Son of God, and they would be saved from their self-centeredness and accepted into the family of God. Poshard said he understood a person was supposed to feel something that brings about conversion. He just never thought he felt anything, so he didn't think he had been saved. In 1971, after more than a year of evaluating world religions, he settled on the Christian faith. "I finally understood the concept of being saved through faith by grace. My family were such workaholics. I thought we had to earn our salvation through works. I had completely missed the emphasis on God's grace as the essence of our salvation. I knew if I had to depend upon works to be good enough to merit God's favor, then I could never make it."

He soon encountered another life-and-death struggle.

CHAPTER 5

# Releasing the Demons

Galatia, Illinois, with a population of about one thousand, is one of four school districts in Saline County, which has about twenty-five thousand residents. It's rural, beautiful, and homey, a place with no strangers and few secrets, just like back in Herald. Galatia is a twenty-five-mile drive from Marion, where Poshard lived in his college years, and thirty-five miles from the hill country of his childhood. The surrounding coal mines were familiar, as was the beauty of the Shawnee Hills, the taste of freshly picked apples, and the smell of bluebells.

In 1970, Poshard joined the Galatia faculty as a high school teacher and coach. He loved his students, loved the families, loved the people of the community, and quickly found meaning in his career. It was everything he had hoped for, teaching subjects he loved and coaching young men in the sports he had grown up with. For a recent college graduate, life looked good. That was the view from the outside.

On the inside, the story was dramatically different. For years Poshard buried the emotion from the sudden loss of his sister and four friends and the ensuing deterioration of his parents' relationship. He bottled the emotion he felt from having his best friend die in Vietnam at a time when his fellow college students violently protested the war. Leaving young Korean orphans who deserved so much more remained embedded in his gut. His personal struggle with religion was in full force.

The unreleased turmoil in his mind increasingly dominated his internal war of words. The storm inside him refused to be contained. It demanded attention. Poshard describes this period of his life in the spring of 1972, his second year of teaching and coaching.

"I loved my job at Galatia High School. It was my dream job. I taught five subjects and coached three sports: basketball, baseball, and cross-country. The kids were great, no discipline problems at all. My fellow teachers really cared about their students. Gayla and I attended the local church, which was right next door to our home, and we had lots of friends in the community. Everything seemed good, but I knew something inside wasn't right."

Poshard worked on a master's degree at SIU by taking one evening class each term and a full load in the summer. "It was a way to stay busy, to never slow down, so I wouldn't have to confront the sadness and depression that had taken hold of my thoughts and was gradually exhausting my body. I was only twenty-five, and so far, I had remained strong and had beaten back the fear and the anxiety. I didn't know what was happening to me; I just knew that I was descending into a black hole, filled with despair and a complete lack of hope for the future. I kept telling myself, 'But you have overcome so much, you're on track with all of your goals, you'll be fine.' The self-talk gave me no comfort. Doctors' visits would end with some kind of medication being prescribed, usually Valium, which had no effect on me at all. My marriage was suffering. I became distant, noncommunicative, self-absorbed. I would lay awake at night, unable to sleep, my mind swirling, unable to untangle the chaotic thoughts of abandonment that I somehow felt over Jolene and Dennis being taken away and the emotional abandonment of Mom and Dad after Jolene's death. And in my warped way of thinking, I had somehow abandoned those desperate children in Korea.

"The sense of hopelessness and depression had been going on for over a year now, something I had hidden completely from everyone around me except Gayla. I was going to work completely exhausted every day and falling deeper and deeper into despair."

One day he collapsed on the living room floor.

"I had suffered enough. I had to get help. I resigned my job, knowing there was no way I could finish out the school year. The diagnosis was severe depression along with physical and mental exhaustion. My doctor admitted me to a hospital in Evansville, Indiana, where I received a form of mental health treatment that was devastating to me, electroshock therapy. The side effects were so severe that I temporarily lost my memory and part of my vision. After two and a half weeks, I checked myself out of the hospital, against the doctor's orders, in much worse condition than when I went in. That first night at home for me was a living hell; there is no other way for me to describe it. I had not eaten in nearly three days and had stopped the medication immediately; every part of my body was in intense pain. My mind was racing a hundred miles a minute. It was the most turbulent, emotional moment I ever spent. I just knew I was going to die.

"Out of a job and out of money, my only option was to seek help at the nearby Veterans Administration Hospital in Marion. The next morning after I checked in, I met Dr. Longwell, a psychologist for the VA. She was kind, and her words gave me hope."

For two weeks, they met every day. She readily agreed the diagnosis and treatment in Evansville wasn't the answer for Poshard's problems. Rather, Poshard needed to unravel and honestly deal with his past in a therapeutic technique that holds we are as sick as our secrets, and that secrets when exposed lose power. Longwell focused on talking with Poshard about his demons, the things he suppressed over many years and why they continued to trouble him. Gradually, over multiple counseling sessions that brought his personal issues to light, his load lightened. In three weeks, he was functioning at home.

"It was one of the most powerful experiences I have ever had. Dr. Longwell showed me how I had blamed myself for a lot of the adversities and traumas that happened in my life. She walked me through it. I'm absolutely convinced Dr. Longwell saved my life."

Poshard and Longwell continued to meet weekly for about six months. A predominant message from her was that as things occur, it's important to express and release them. Burying things inside is a recipe for trouble. Talking about and dealing with issues promotes positive mental health.

"When you grow up the way I did," Poshard said, "you don't outwardly discuss your feelings. Poor farmers don't go to psychologists, and neither do their kids. So all these things I just buried inside me."

Because mental health issues have a stigma among parts of the population, many people find it difficult to openly acknowledge such problems. As Poshard released demons from his past and opened the door to a brighter future, that issue followed him. Were he to seek elected office in the future, he felt details of his diagnosis and treatment would work against him, as it had against former U.S. senator Thomas Eagleton, when he was selected as George McGovern's vice presidential running mate in 1972. Thus, in personally releasing and learning to deal with negatives in his past, he also created an albatross that remained until 1998, when he ran for governor.

Later, in the Illinois Senate and the United States Congress, Poshard advocated strongly for mental health assistance, particularly for those areas of rural America where people were poorer and access was difficult. "I know there are people struggling with depression and anxiety. I want them to know they can overcome it. Having gone through this sort of thing myself, I want to assure them that they can have a good life."

Poshard returned to SIU to earn a master's degree in 1974 and his PhD in 1984. He emerged from his struggle with one major casualty. His first marriage ended in divorce in 1974. He and his ex-wife agreed to a custody arrangement in which he would see the children, Dennis and Kristen, every Wednesday and every weekend.

"I loved my children more than anything and tried to spend every moment with them I could, but I recognize that the divorce had consequences for them in ways I wish I could have prevented. With all the unresolved things I had in my life, I was not able to be the husband and father I wanted to be. By the time I started getting the help I needed and began the process of unraveling my own trauma, my marriage had greatly suffered and was nearly over. Thankfully, life has a way of helping us to become better people if we let it. Despite my initial stumbles, I have worked hard to be a good father to my children and grandchildren, and my love for them has grown every moment of every day."

In reestablishing himself, Poshard found opportunity at another small southern Illinois school. Thompsonville, a community of 530 people just eleven miles from Galatia, had an opening for a history teacher. Poshard drove over on the two-lane Illinois Route 34, stopping at Jim Elimon's barbershop to inquire about the job opening with the school district. He was directed to a school board member whose last name was Payne. "I remember walking out through the plowed field where Mr. Payne was working. He stopped the tractor and began talking with me. He went to bat for me, a measure of grace that I have never forgotten."

The superintendent, Allan Patton, offered Poshard a position on the faculty, beginning a friendship that continues today. "Allan encouraged me to really get involved with the students in the way I had at Galatia. He insisted I get my bus driver's license and then gave me access to an extra bus the district owned."

Poshard used the bus as a tool to help students unfold history and the world around them. His students explored and hiked in the Shawnee National Forest, learning the importance of conservation and environmental protection. They took multiple field trips to the capital city of Springfield and visited all the Lincoln sites. "I think I've read nearly everything that's ever been written about President Lincoln," said Poshard. "He was the greatest statesman in the history of the world, and for me to introduce him and his hometown to my students was a wonderful teaching experience for me." They took trips to Brown County, Indiana, camping out and learning about Westward Expansion, covered bridges, and other central Indiana history. Poshard's classroom was that old bus. "It seemed like we were gone every week somewhere," Poshard said.

Thompsonville entered competition against large schools in the St. Louis area in a model United Nations assembly at McKendree College in Lebanon, Illinois. His students, assigned Russia, researched for weeks at SIU's Morris Library to learn all they could about that country.

"We would leave right after school and drive the nearly hourlong trip to Carbondale. They learned to use a university library and were introduced to a higher education setting that was helpful in their future academic endeavors. Sometimes we wouldn't get home until nine or ten o'clock at night, but their hard work paid off. We won, hands down, as the best delegation, and next year we won it again. Our kids received a lot of media attention, even in the large Metro East papers, and they deserved it.

"Those four years I taught at Galatia and Thompsonville, I had the greatest kids in the world," Poshard said. "They had parents who cared about their education, who supported me as a teacher. Despite all the issues I had to deal with personally, including the strain and eventual breakup of my marriage, those were four of the greatest years of my professional life."

His success in being a creative teacher led to an opportunity in 1974 to join the staff of the Area Service Center for Educators of Gifted Children. The staff, composed of highly successful teachers, was charged with developing model programs to train teachers in identifying and working with students who displayed high intellectual and creative skills. In his role, Poshard worked with school districts across thirty-six southern Illinois counties.

"We have this egalitarian notion in American education that says we have to bring everyone to the middle," Poshard said. "In that notion, high performers receive no special initiative. Some consider programs for gifted students as elitist, arguing that the use of limited funds going to those who already excel is a misuse of public funding."

Poshard said the result is that many gifted students become stymied. That creates discipline problems and unfulfilled academic and intellectual goals. The better approach, he said, is to continue special programs for both low and high performers, providing opportunities for all to meet their potential, rather than squash their creativity and intellectual growth.

"I talked to one superintendent and suggested he needed to hire a couple of teachers for the gifted students in his school. He looked at me like I was crazy. He said the school district couldn't afford it. I told him he already had programs for the gifted; they're called athletics. We hire specially trained teachers called coaches to push student athletes to maximize their potential. We build expensive gymnasiums and athletic facilities where they can display their skills in competition with other schools. We spend a lot of transportation dollars transporting the athletes to other districts and even other states to compete. Our athletic programs are the best gifted programs we have. No one calls these programs elitist. But try to get a school to invest in developing programs to maximize academic, intellectual, and creative giftedness, and you're told that's just not democratic. We know how valuable the creative arts are to our communities. The arts are the glue that hold us together as a people and enable us to better understand our humanity. Art, music, dance, poetry, as important as they are, are usually the first things to be cut when finances become a problem. The fact that we want to stigmatize these kids with labels like *elitist* is not fair to them. We should take every child as high as they can go, not just the athletes."

As Poshard settled in the regional education role, he was emotionally stable. He learned from Dr. Longwell how to manage his thoughts and emotions. He was working with outstanding teachers and consultants, developing cutting-edge programs to stimulate great teaching in the classroom. During his teaching at Galatia and Thompsonville and during his time with the Area Service Center for Educators of Gifted Children, he carved out more and more time with Dennis and Kristen, wanting to make up for all the hours his work and illness had taken away from them. He felt he was becoming a better father, letting go of some of the workaholic nature that helped drive him to exhaustion. He knew it would take longer than a few months to peel back the layers of insecurity borne out of those early years, but he committed to the task.

The regional role suited Poshard in another important way. Traveling through his beloved southern Illinois, he met and interacted with people in communities of all sizes. He listened. He learned. He made friends. He saw firsthand the value of small school education and was reminded daily of the importance local schools hold in small communities.

Years later, when serving in the Illinois Senate, a proposal was put forth that the optimal enrollment for a high school was five hundred students. Some southern Illinois schools had as few as a hundred students and, under the legislative proposal, would be forced to consolidate. The state superintendent claimed research proved that a high school of five hundred students provided maximal learning opportunities for the students.

"I readily agreed," said Poshard, "and was prepared to support the consolidation effort. But when I insisted that this threshold should be applied to all schools, even those with two or three thousand students such as those that existed in the suburbs of Chicago, suburban and city legislators were unwilling to do that, of course. I then made the case that those students were being denied optimal learning environments. If a school can be too small, then it must be equally true that some schools can be too large. Eventually the proposal fell apart and did not pass."

Now, living in nearby Carterville, Poshard welcomed a life-changing turning point in his personal life. He began dating Betty "Jo" Roetzel. She was raised in Roberts, a village of five hundred people in central Illinois, the daughter of a Democratic leader in the Republican stronghold of Ford County. As she remembers it, her father helped make sure there were always contested races for local positions, realizing Republicans would win but believing it was important to "give Republicans an opponent and a run for their money." One of her most cherished possessions to this day is a sixty-year-old ruler with "Roetzel for Treasurer — Vote Democratic" on it.

Jo and her sisters, Sharon and Karen, were not strangers to politics. Their dad, Harold, was a Democratic precinct committeeman, and their mother, Rose, a faithful election judge. With her parents, Jo attended many political events, including county literature-drop caravans and fundraisers; she was accustomed to the rough-and-tumble world of politics. Yet in Roberts, friends and neighbors came first, with politics a distant second. "Glenn and I both grew up in politically active families, but we've never lost a friend over politics, and we hope we never do," states Jo.

She thought she would go into social work until her Roberts-Thawville High School English teacher, Mrs. Helen Otto, observed her teach a poetry lesson to a sophomore English class as part of her membership in the Future Teachers of America. "Mrs. Otto took me aside as I was leaving the classroom and said, 'Betty Jo, I think you're going into the wrong profession. You should be a teacher; you reached those students in a way that I haven't.' That's all it took. I had so much respect for Mrs. Otto that I changed my career path and have never regretted it for a moment. In 1967 I headed to Southern Illinois University, which my sister Sharon had attended ten years earlier. I thought it was both an exciting and beautiful campus, and my assessment at seventeen years old still stands today."

Glenn says this: "Mrs. Otto couldn't have been more correct. I trained teachers when I worked for the regional education office. Jo is one of the finest teachers I have ever observed in the classroom. Today when we are out in public, her former students come up to her with their children and tell her what a wonderful teacher she was."

Glenn and Jo had known each other as teachers in southern Illinois before Jo accepted a position offering greater opportunities and alignment with her teaching interests in the central part of the state, which she enjoyed for three years. When Glenn later joined the Area Service Center for Gifted Education, their paths would cross at trainings and education conferences. They enjoyed conversations about politics, teaching, and where life had taken them. After a year of spending more time together, they were married on June 12, 1976, at the Carterville First Baptist Church.

Poshard now returned to one of his early passions, which Jo also shared: local politics. He was elected Democratic precinct committeeman, carrying on in the tradition of his father. He became active in the Democratic Party, at the time a necessary component of laying the groundwork for anyone who one day might run for office. He became vice chairman of the Williamson County Democrats, a role that provided opportunities for him to meet and interact with local, regional, and sometimes statewide officials.

He was already using his organizing and speaking skills to support many Democratic candidates for office. Would the opportunity to see his name on the ballot be too far down the road?

# PART 2

# A PASSION FOR ELECTORAL POLITICS

CHAPTER 6

# Working for an Opponent

In August 1984 prominent labor leader and influential Democrat Eddie Smith was paying respects at the visitation for Gene Johns, an Illinois state senator who died from cancer. As he reached Johns's widow, Eve, at the casket, she mentioned that Smith could help her secure votes to succeed her husband. Smith walked to the back of the funeral home, where he encountered Bill Grindel, a contemporary of Smith's father, who told Smith that he would love to be the next state senator. When Smith arrived home in Cairo, Poshard called. "I'd love to talk to you about filling out the rest of Gene's term."

Smith's response was along these lines: "Glenn, you're going to be the guy. You've been loyal. Everybody likes you."

Two years earlier, Smith didn't return Poshard's phone calls. Poshard, while becoming more active in the local Democratic party, challenged Johns in a three-way Democratic primary that included Sesser mayor Ned Mitchell. Johns had cancer, had been indicted, and seemingly was ripe for a challenge. Knowing Smith's lead role in southern Illinois labor, Poshard unsuccessfully sought a meeting. When Smith hosted a fifty-dollar-a-person fundraiser for Johns at Smith's home, Poshard showed up with a fifty-dollar bill. Behind the scenes, Smith and his friends discussed how to respond, one possibility being to send Poshard away. "We finally said 'Take his money. It's a fundraiser, isn't it?'"

They left the house for a ten-dollar-a-person rally at the union hall. Poshard was there, too.

"Glenn said to me, I'd love to have your support," Smith recalls.

"I told him, 'Glenn, Gene may only get two votes, his and mine. He has a 95 percent voting record with labor. I'm going to stay with him.'"[1]

Johns won the primary. Poshard was a surprising second.

Poshard's next step opened the door to his political career. "Glenn did one of the most classy things I've ever seen anybody do," Smith said. "He went to work for Gene. Wherever Gene couldn't go, Glenn did." That opened eyes about Poshard in ways that led Smith and others to persuade county chairmen to appoint Poshard to the Illinois Senate in August 1984.

The pursuit of the state Senate seat produced other longtime friendships and supporters, like Ron House, who at the time was a township supervisor in Franklin County. "One day Glenn told me he was going to run against Gene Johns," House said. "He asked if I thought he would win."

I replied, "You don't have a snowball's chance."

Then Poshard asked, "Will you support me?"

I said, "Yes, I will be for you."

House echoed Smith's assessment that the primary campaign and the ensuing way Poshard worked for Johns created the "foregone conclusion" that Poshard would receive the appointment of county chairmen to replace Johns. "In the long run, he won," House said.[2]

His swearing in was an emotional time for his family and him. Busloads of supporters from southern Illinois converged on Springfield and filled the Senate chambers to witness his formal induction. Unfortunately, Lib Poshard had passed away in 1977, seven years before his son was sworn in. It was a day of celebration, but there was no time to waste before the next campaign. The general election was only two months away in November.

Poshard's Republican opponent was Bob Winchester, a fourteen-year veteran of the Illinois House who Poshard said had tremendous influence in who got state jobs, particularly jobs in the prisons that dot the southern Illinois landscape. Poshard remembers driving from

Harrisburg to Vienna along Illinois Route 45, seeing Winchester signs in almost every yard. I told my wife, Jo, "If those signs vote, we will lose."

Mrs. Johns ran as a third-party candidate, further complicating the race and potentially tilting the Democratic vote. "I don't think anyone gave us a chance to win that seat," Poshard said. "We all worked night and day. Jo, our kids, our entire family, and our friends just never stopped campaigning."

Among the supporters was House, who was the chief fundraiser. "Glenn's a worrier," House said. "He didn't have any money. The day of a fundraiser at the Travel Lodge, he asked, 'Ron, is anybody going to come?'

"I said, 'Glenn, I don't think there will be enough seats.' The place was running over. We raised about $40,000. In those times, it was a huge sum of money, given our circumstances. That race catapulted him to a political career and almost the governorship."[3]

Another key supporter was Larry Woolard, who Poshard sits next to each Sunday at church in Carterville. Woolard and Poshard helped each other on multiple campaigns in a friendship of more than forty years. "There were times in the early years neither one of us followed the political playbook," Woolard said. "We accidentally made things happen. I remember a mass of people at a fundraiser, including Republican precinct committeemen. We wanted everyone involved. We thought we should invite people from business. We were able to bring in large numbers of people who were not involved at all or maybe not involved in the Democratic Party. We had foot soldiers and had contacts with people working for us we didn't even have on our calling list. We were able to build coalitions between Republicans, Democrats, and independents, which is not necessarily how you are supposed to do it. The right way is not necessarily the best way."[4]

Poshard's work ethic played in his favor, too. He remembers meeting with mine workers as they got off second shift. On the way home, past the midnight hour, he saw a couple people in the Maid-Rite diner in Christopher, Illinois. He directed his staffer, Larry O'Brian, to pull into the parking lot so he could go in and ask the diners for their vote.

"We had been standing out in a sleet storm at the mine greeting the miners as they came off second shift. O'Brian was still frozen and coughing his head off; we had already been campaigning eighteen hours that day, and needless to say, this good Catholic boy directed some choice words at me under his breath. Despite OB's objections, I do believe I got those two people's votes."

As election day approached, Poshard organized a caravan with fifty-plus vehicles to drive through his district. From the back of a pickup truck, he delivered his stump speech in each county seat. Crowds came out in every community, and just as important, the local radio stations covered every stop. The caravan helped show support and build momentum for election day, capping an old-fashioned campaign full of long and exhausting days.

The stump speech was a staple of Poshard campaigns. He had delivered fiery speeches in the hills throughout his childhood. Now he connected on local issues. He wrote his own material, identifying three points to cover in no more than ten minutes. He practiced multiple times, identifying places for a strategic pause or change in voice inflection. In stump speeches, his passion shone. "Public speaking is an honor."

At one point, Poshard said he received a phone call from his good friend David Phelps, who was running for the state representative seat that Winchester was vacating. "David asked me to meet a guy in a pickup truck who would take me to meet a group of voters. David said they had to meet with us secretly for fear they would lose their jobs if certain people knew they had contacted us."

Poshard and Jo met the guy that night at the intersection of Route 1 and 13 in Gallatin County. Poshard parked his car, the couple got into the truck, and they headed south on Route 1 through the Shawnee National Forest. "It was a little unnerving at first," said Poshard. "I didn't know the driver, who kept his hat pulled down over his face, and I didn't know where we were going, but I knew the area like the back of my hand. I had grown up in those hills and knew every side road and where it led. Eventually we pulled off the highway onto a road I recognized as the road to Camp Cadiz, a CCC camp used during the Roosevelt administration to house workers building roads and providing conservation work to enhance the forest. We came to a gate, and a person stepped out of the darkness, opened the gate so we could pass through, closed the gate behind us, and jumped in the back of the truck as we lumbered up the hill.

"At the top of the hill about fifty people were waiting with David and his wife Leslie. Most of them I didn't recognize, but every one of them had a story to tell as we sat around that campfire. They had been coerced to display bumper stickers and yard signs for my opponent. Many were teachers or had other government jobs, which typically were the best jobs in the region. They wanted me to know that I had their support, but they could not be public. I told them you do what you have to do to keep your jobs. I told them not to do anything to risk their livelihoods. I expressed my appreciation for their willingness to meet with me. I also learned a good lesson on that hillside in the forest that night. I might make a call or a recommendation for someone in the future, but I told my staff, 'Never use a job as a sledgehammer to get someone to support me.'"

On election night, two of the first precincts to report were along the route where Poshard noted all the Winchester signs. "Those precincts were in the New Burnside and Tunnel Hill areas where my wife had been a teacher for a number of years, and I think the friendships she made helped us tremendously," said Poshard. He lost by just a few votes in those precincts, but knowing that he should outperform Winchester in his home part of the district, Poshard realized he was headed to the Illinois Senate.

The Senate Democratic leader was Phil Rock of suburban Oak Park, a man Poshard describes as one of the finest people he's known. "He was imminently fair and highly intellectual," Poshard said of Rock. "He was a straightforward leader who enjoyed a good working relationship with Republican governor James Thompson."

Democrats had a 31–28 Senate majority, so Rock walked the political line between advancing legislation that would impact the entire state yet leaving room for senators to remain electable in their own districts. Not being reelected would mean Democrats could lose their majority and their control over the legislative process. Rock told lawmakers like Poshard that their most important job was to get reelected. "Whatever it takes to get back here, that's what you have to do. If you have to get up on the floor and bash Chicago, do it. You're not going to hurt my feelings." As much as Poshard admired Rock, he tried never to take that advice. He never felt comfortable demagoguing the issues between Chicago and downstate.

As Rock introduced him to other senators, Poshard was awkwardly reminded of an experience in which he testified before a Senate committee. During his tenure with the Gifted Education Service Center, he sometimes presented to legislative committees. On one occasion, Poshard got home late the night before his testimony, changed into shorts and drove into Springfield about midnight with Jo so he would be ready to testify early the next day.

"When I took the white dress shirt off the hanger, I discovered to my amazement, there were no dress pants underneath, only a pair of women's brownish-yellow hip-huggers bell-bottom pants that Jo had purchased ten years earlier at a garage sale. The pants had an additional feature: there were six gold buttons, each the size of a nickel, which stretched from the navel all the way down the crotch in place of a zipper. There were no overnight stores in Springfield in the 1970s. These pants were all I had, and I couldn't skip the hearing. I was representing thousands of teachers, parents, and students all over the state. So I dressed quickly, wearing the form-fitting women's tight hippy pants, rushed down to the capitol while it was still deserted at 7:30 in the morning, found the hearing room, placed the twenty-five copies of my testimony on the witness desk for the page to pass out to each member of the committee, and sat down with my legs completely hidden under the desk. Since I knew I was first on the agenda to testify, I sat there, as the room filled up behind me and the senators filed into their seats. At least this way, I would only suffer the embarrassment I would feel walking out of the room after my testimony.

"The chairman finally was seated at his desk and began the hearing. He quickly pronounced that the committee was without a page today, and would Mr. Poshard please pass out a copy of his testimony to each member? Absolute panic. As I moved out into the open and through the committee, every eye in the room fell on those bellbottom pants with the gold buttons down the front. I made it back to the witness table, gave my testimony, took a few questions, and quickly exited the room for the long, silent ride home with Jo."

When introduced by Rock eight years later, Vince Demuzio remembered. "Yeah, I know you," said Demuzio.

Replied Poshard: "Senator, I don't believe we've personally met."

Demuzio reminded Poshard of his committee testimony years before. Demuzio with a smile said: "Your 'outfit for the day' convinced me to vote for the bill." Poshard laughed and said, "Those darn hip-hugger bell-bottom pants with the gold buttons down the front."

CHAPTER 7

# At Home in Lincoln Land

As much as Poshard reveres FDR and John F. Kennedy, as a student of history, he holds Abraham Lincoln in highest regard as the greatest president. Lincoln looms large throughout the region surrounding Springfield, Illinois' capital city. Visitors come to see his tomb, his home, the site of his law office, and since 2005, the Abraham Lincoln Presidential Library and Museum. About fifteen thousand books have been written about Lincoln, more than anyone except Jesus Christ. Springfield was Lincoln's base when he was a circuit-riding lawyer. Lincoln launched his 1858 campaign from the Old State Capitol, a Greek Revival–style structure also used as a backdrop for the 2007 presidential candidacy announcement of Barack Obama. At the state capitol, constructed from 1868 to 1888 in the French Renaissance and Italianate architectural styles, a bronze statue just east of the building depicts Lincoln as he left for Washington, D.C., in 1861.

Poshard visited Springfield many times prior to becoming a state senator. Sometimes he attended Democratic Party or other meetings. In his role as an educator, he testified before legislative committees.

He was called on often by his colleagues in education to represent their issues before the legislature, and he relished that role.

Thus, the capital city, about a two-hundred-mile drive from his Carterville home, was both familiar and comfortable. Poshard quickly found the legislative process to his liking and aggressively pursued a constituent-oriented agenda. As a candidate in both 1982 and 1984, he interacted with mayors, county and township officials, and civic, business, and union leaders. Those relationships gave Poshard a vivid picture of the top needs in his region.

A key piece of legislation in 1985 was the $2.3 billion Build Illinois program promoted by Thompson. The program led to construction projects ranging from convention centers to water and sewer projects in every part of the state. The rules were simple. Lawmakers who supported the tax increases to pay for the projects would get help throughout their districts. "If you're not willing to vote for the taxes, forget the projects," Poshard said lawmakers were told.

Poshard voted for the taxes and got multiple infrastructure improvements across his twelve-county district, working with many mayors and county boards to identify priorities. Among the funded projects were repair of the West Frankfort water tower, new waste disposal systems in Herrin and Carterville, expansion of a sewer line in Johnston City, and many other basic infrastructure needs of his district.

"These weren't exotic projects," Poshard said, "but they were the things that helped improve the quality of life for our people." The vote showed Poshard's support for a pay-as-you-go approach. He backed projects that would help communities and pay a living wage to construction workers. He opposed passing excessive debt along to future generations.

Both Governor Thompson and President Rock solicited Poshard's vote for the Build Illinois Plan. "I didn't hesitate for one second before I promised my vote," said Poshard. "My district needed a lot of help, and I ran for the Senate to deliver for my district. If people wanted to vote me out for the tax increases I supported, then so be it."

Build Illinois was a coordinated, statewide effort that generated headlines across the state. A couple months after the election, Poshard encountered a request that typified life of a lawmaker, an isolated request that highlighted a local need but was not tied to a broad legislative package. He was invited to the senior center in Golconda, a scenic community along the Ohio River with fewer than one thousand residents. "Their old bus was in terrible condition, and it wasn't going to make it through the hills much longer to pick up the seniors for lunch and activities," Poshard said. Poshard joined the seniors for lunch, then rode the rickety bus as it took people home. He was about to get honest feedback.

"We barely made it up the big hill in Golconda, the bus shaking and jerking violently. I thought it was going to fall apart. I was sitting about three rows back, and an elderly gentleman was seated directly across the aisle from me. As we drove through the hills, he proceeded to tell me that he'd just had his eighty-second birthday, and he sure hoped I could help them get a new bus. I noticed the driver glancing back through her rearview mirror and listening to our conversation. Eventually, she said to the little white-haired lady sitting in the first row right behind her. 'You just had a birthday too. Tell Senator Poshard how old you are and what you will do for him in the next election if he will help us get a new bus?'

"It seemed like the longest time but eventually the little white head turned to face me. In a most sincere fashion, she said, 'Mister Poshard, you can see this old bus is falling apart, and I hope you can help us get a new one. I enjoy the senior citizen center and visiting with my friends, and this is the only way I can get there. But I just turned eighty-five, and I've never voted for a Democrat in my life, and I'm not voting for you, either.' I laughed, but I thought of that lesson many times over the course of my career and came to appreciate folks like her who just told you the truth rather than tell you the words they think you want to hear. They got the new bus."

That same year Illinois was one of several states vying for a new Mitsubishi Motors auto assembly plant. By themselves, none of the southern Illinois communities could meet the bid requirements. That opened the door for Poshard to bring together competitive, independent-minded communities across the region to combine resources for the benefit of all. The region didn't get the auto plant, but a regional marketing effort based at SIU emerged, a concept that retains its importance many years later. The regional marketing effort is an example of another trademark of Poshard as a legislator in that he worked to bring together groups or entities that otherwise would work against one another.[1]

Poshard's style was a stark contrast to the other newly elected representative from southern Illinois, Republican Wayne Goforth of Tamaroa. The districts they represented were neighbors. Their approaches to governing were light-years apart. Goforth ran on a platform that too many bills are introduced into the General Assembly. He would address that problem by pledging not to introduce even a single bill.[2] Poshard estimates he put his name on as many as fifty bills in his first term. Now, nearly twenty-five years later, the five manila folders representing each year he served in the Senate bulge with yellowing newspaper clippings, some glued to brown construction paper, that mark his efforts.

The clippings represent a range of matters, from news articles to letters to the editor to editorial endorsements to copies of campaign literature to photographs with local community leaders. White sheets of notebook paper are interspersed in the material to introduce different legislative topics. The articles were published in daily and weekly newspapers. The smell and touch have a scrapbook feel. They cover the gamut of Illinois' politics of that era: a months-long effort involved in the rewrite of Illinois' unemployment insurance law, a massive educational reform bill, the regional economic development initiative, earthquake preparedness programs, and the founding of a regional Coats for Kids initiative that he and Jo started. Poshard was a major sponsor, along with Representative Bruce Richmond, of an agriculture revitalization bill called Rural Revival and worked on any legislation that impacted coal mining.

Going back and forth to Springfield, Poshard sometimes rode with Phelps, who was elected state representative to replace Winchester. The two first met each other at the Chapman Grove Baptist Church, where Phelps and his brothers sometimes sang gospel music for which they became known. Phelps later succeeded Poshard in Congress in 1998, serving two terms.

"We both had been schoolteachers, and we shared a humility about how fortunate we were to serve," Phelps said. "We honored each other when we got to speak. Glenn's a natural leader. He works to get people together from opposite sides. He was a peacemaker, a leader in every sense of the word."[3]

Along the way, Poshard learned from more senior lawmakers like Senator Demuzio. One legislative proposal that generated significant public interest was a repeal of a mandatory seat belt law. Poshard saw the benefits of wearing seat belts. When Demuzio, who was from Carlinville in central Illinois, asked him about his position, it initially was favorable. "You can't vote for this," Poshard said he remembers Demuzio responding. "There is a lot of opposition in my district in central Illinois; there has to be more opposition down where you are." Demuzio said, "The farther south, and the more independent-minded the voter, the more opposition to government-mandated laws."

Demuzio was right, and polls showed Poshard's district was heavily against mandated use. He remembered President Rock's admonition that the most important thing was to get reelected to preserve the Democratic majority. He capitulated and voted against the bill. It initially failed by that one vote but later passed by a comfortable margin. Poshard never felt comfortable with that vote but gave in to the political reality he faced in his first year in the Senate. It was the first of many decisions in his career when he would be torn between representing the public opinion and his desire to lead from his conscience and his best judgment based on the facts as he understood them.

Poshard and President Rock enjoyed a working relationship in which they typically partnered to find common ground. One time, however, Poshard dug in his heels to oppose legislation Rock thought fit the goal of mutual benefit. Poshard favored an effort for the state to purchase the Du Quoin State Fair, a southern Illinois tradition that would be stabilized under state ownership. As part of the state's purchase, Rock and Governor Thompson sought Poshard's support for expansion of Chicago's McCormick Place Convention Center. The Du Quoin fairgrounds purchase was $3 million; McCormick Place was $60 million.[4] "I just couldn't justify in my mind spending that kind of money," Poshard said of McCormick Place, but the bill eventually passed without his support.

Poshard continued to be active in another way that foreshadowed his career. Just as he had done with the regional marketing plan, he worked to bring sometimes competing interests together. An early example was development of a labor-management council that would address the image that labor unrest made southern Illinois an unwelcome place to do business. The sometimes violent, confrontational labor-management image dates back to at least as early as 1922, when twenty-three people died in what is known as the Herrin Massacre.

Strikebreakers, nonunion workers, were brought in by the owners to end a strike by the United Mine Workers, and violence ensued. It was a tragedy that southern Illinois still struggles with even today. The image has yet to be erased from the region's conscience. Poshard was solidly for organized labor but realized the region's image needed enhancement to compete for new business, and that it was in the common interest of both labor and management to be at the same table.

He promoted earthquake-preparedness legislation that recognized southern Illinois as having the second-biggest seismic fault in the country, the largest and most dangerous outside California. He wanted the schools to be prepared to protect children in the event of an earthquake. Poshard also promoted legislation that would help counties develop regional jails, addressing the issue that some counties with small inmate populations couldn't afford to pay for a local jail. He helped obtain funding for a feasibility study for a potential river-to-river road that would enhance tourism via a scenic highway connecting the Mississippi and Ohio rivers through a wooded, hilly area with multiple scenic overlooks.[5]

By 1986, Poshard said he found his footing as a state lawmaker. He was comfortable among his constituency, comfortable with his Senate colleagues, and establishing himself as a reliable partner with Rock. Party leaders noticed. Demuzio invited Poshard to be the keynote speaker at the state Democratic convention. "I want Poshard to make the major address at this function," Demuzio said. "He not only is a rising star, but he is one of the greatest speakers in the Midwest."[6]

In the primary, however, radical right-wing backers of Lyndon LaRouche won spots on the Democratic ticket. That conflict consumed headlines from the convention. Gubernatorial candidate Adlai Stevenson opted to run as an independent, as the party disavowed the LaRouche candidates. Poshard's speech focused on bringing together traditional Democratic constituencies, winning over the crowd with his passionate appeal for party unity. It was a theme he revisited often. He easily won reelection in 1986, garnering the most votes of any Illinois state senator and defeating his opponent, Richard Simmons, with more than 70 percent of the vote. Thompson handily won reelection as governor, though Democrats maintained control of the Senate.

Poshard maintained the aggressive pace of his first term. He promoted a teen pregnancy bill that addressed a problem common to both urban and rural Illinois. The highest rates for teenage pregnancy in Illinois were in poor rural counties in the south end of his district, and he wanted to give young people there a chance to succeed in overcoming the poverty of their childhood.

In Cairo, Poshard worked to keep open the emergency room at the bankrupt local hospital. Eventually, the ER, the last available health care within twenty miles, closed but only after the state helped multiple times to retain access for the impoverished community. He spent a great deal of time in Cairo, working with the schools and the health care agencies to help the citizens there in every way possible.[7]

During the 1986 session, he worked to support greater funding for gifted education, and he carried not only an LPN nursing bill to help overcome a shortage of nurses in his medically underserved area but also a school construction bill that brought much needed assistance to local communities trying to build new schools in the rural counties he represented.

As he started 1987, Poshard was appointed chairman of the Senate Labor and Commerce Committee. In making the appointment, Senator Rock was effusive in his praise, saying Poshard has been the author of major legislation, important to all of Illinois, not just his district. Rock wrote that Poshard's legislative accomplishments include Rural Revival, an economic development package for rural Illinois; the education reform bill of 1985, which saw major reform for Illinois' public schools; and the teen issues package, which addressed problems today's young people are facing as well as a merit recognition package to encourage teens to excel. According to Rock, Glenn Poshard had taken a leadership role in confronting problems that affected his district, such as infrastructure, by successfully sponsoring funds through the Build Illinois program. He had addressed a lag in the tourism industry by pushing legislation such as the River to River road and local tourism development. He had been a major leader in addressing problems such as health care and regional jails. And, Rock continued, Poshard had helped to work out complex issues of medical care in the southern part of his district, including keeping the emergency room open in Cairo and the ambulance running in Hardin County. It was a ringing endorsement of Poshard's abilities by the Senate president.

Rock had a bigger issue for Poshard to tackle. The unemployment compensation law in Illinois begged for rewriting. To do so required bringing together business and labor interests to find a formula that would fund the program in a way agreeable to both parties. The fund supporting the law was nearly broke and had to be fixed right away. Poshard's committee began the work, supporting the leaders from the governor's office, the Senate, and the House in a combined effort to resolve this long-standing problem. The months-long effort resulted in an acceptable compromise of competing interests.[8]

He also worked on rural health, rural home energy, alternative phone service bills, redistribution of the Illinois sales tax, and an override to restore education funding. His major accomplishments of the 1988 Illinois legislative session were passage of a bill to construct a nursing home for veterans in Anna, legislation creating economic incentives for poor communities along the Mississippi River, and sponsorship of a bill that improved the treatment of child abuse victims. Poshard believed that government could be a force for good in improving the lives of its citizens, and there was no issue beyond his reach or his energy. He took on perhaps too many issues, but the talks around the dinner table about how the Works Progress Administration had saved his family during the Depression were indelibly imprinted on his heart and in his head, and he had little time to waste.

Poshard enjoyed campaigning, the opportunity to speak and interact in familiar communities across the region. He also found campaigning has its hazards, and sometimes calls for a bit of humility and humor. Poshard remembers one such night in which the Community Center in Eldorado was alive, a full house for a Democratic fundraiser featuring several pots of the best chili in southeastern Illinois. Congressman Ken Gray and state representatives David Phelps and Jim Rea were at the head table with Poshard. While breaking crackers with a spoon, chili soiled Poshard's starched white shirt and neatly pressed dress slacks. "I was soaked with chili from my neck to my shoes."

In the men's room, he found no way to just wipe the chili off his shirt and pants. "I locked the door, took off all of my clothes and proceeded to wash them in the sink, hoping I could get enough chili off to put them under the hand dryer, re-dress, and join the gathering in time to give my speech. As I stood there totally naked, the door flew open and an eight-year-old boy appeared, completely frozen, while three elderly ladies walked by in full view. I yelled at the kid to close the door while attempting to pull my pants off the wooden divider, catching them on a splinter and ripping a large gash above the right knee. The kid went scurrying off; I relocked the door and, after twenty minutes, made my way back into the room looking like a real vagabond. The word had spread, and Congressman Gray, never one to pass up a juicy story, had already begun his speech.

"On this night," Poshard remembers Gray saying, "the real Senator Poshard has been revealed. Three ladies from this illustrious audience have seen the evidence and cast their opinions. Mrs. Brown says she will definitely be voting for Senator Poshard, Mrs. Hankins says she will definitely be voting against Senator Poshard, and Mrs. Johnson says she needs to think more about it before making up her mind."

The roar of laughter was deafening. Poshard was next at the podium. He knew that there were another twenty or so events with Gray prior to election day, and that Gray would retell the story each time. "I opened my speech with a warning: 'Don't trust the lock on that men's room door.'"

By late 1987, Gray said he wouldn't seek reelection to a seat long held by prominent Democrats. The district in the southernmost twenty counties in Illinois usually favored a Democrat though, with an open seat, was one that might interest more Republicans. Poshard filed papers to seek the Democratic nomination in late 1987.

In the spring of 1987, another opportunity had emerged. Poshard remembers being in a car with U.S. Senator Paul Simon as Simon discussed his plans to seek the Democratic nomination for the U.S. presidency. Poshard knew Simon well. He was enthusiastic about Simon's presidential run and eager to play a role in a national campaign. When Simon formally launched the campaign in March 1987 at a $100-a-plate dinner on the SIU campus, Poshard was among those who showed enthusiastic support.

Later, Poshard was among the volunteers who worked the state of Iowa on Simon's behalf. Beginning on the Minnesota border, they spent two weeks walking across the entire state. They walked through towns of all sizes, meeting with key Democrats, visiting with local media, telling people about Simon and why they considered him a great candidate for president. They were zealots, believing in their senator, extolling his virtues of authenticity and intelligence, his clean image. Poshard got a taste of politics at the national level. Simon competed in several states, finishing second in the Iowa caucuses and winning the Illinois primary. He dropped out of the race in April 1988 after a disappointing showing in Wisconsin. For Poshard, the experience was welcome. He loved politics, loved campaigning, and appreciated the opportunity to work on behalf of his friend Simon.

The 1988 Democratic National Convention that nominated Michael Dukakis was in Atlanta. Poshard and Jo left early to spend some time in Florida with their friends Ron and Diana House. House remembers that Glenn forgot a package and asked Ron, who was still in Illinois, if he would bring it. The package had a pair of old shoes that Glenn didn't want to go without for sentimental reasons. When Glenn's son Dennis delivered the package, Ron opened it. The shoes were an "old, old" pair of green canvas tennis shoes. "Just take them," Dennis told Ron. "If anything happens to those shoes, he'll go crazy."

From Florida, Glenn and Jo were traveling to Atlanta for the convention. Glenn needed a white shirt, so they went shopping. Ron went to the Manhattan-brand shirts. Glenn and Jo traveled to the ten-dollar rack. "These Manhattans look pretty good," Ron said.[9]

"These are good enough," Glenn said.

Before parting, Glenn asked Ron if he had any money. Glenn was out of cash. The Poshards still didn't own a personal credit card. Glenn wrote Ron a check for $100 and took the cash for the convention. When Glenn and Jo filled the gas tank in Tennessee on the way home, they spent the last of the money they had for the trip. That was Glenn and Jo. Humble. Frugal. Thoughtful. Good for their word.

"Credible leaders like Glenn," Ron said, "don't put themselves above others. Because of their principled ways, they attract other credible people. The decency around Glenn Poshard shines. He's the true image of a public servant. He's what we all expect public servants to be but only a few are."

CHAPTER 8

# On the Issues, a Race for Congress

On three Wednesday evenings in the fall of 1988, three different southern Illinois community college gymnasiums were filled with college students, miners, teachers, mechanics, retirees, and representatives of any number of other professions. Adults throughout the region voluntarily took an evening away from the living room to participate in American democracy. Many carried signs representing the congressional candidate of their choice. Most came prepared to exercise their lungs to voice their preference in old-fashioned political debates. The debates were central to an issues-focused congressional campaign in which the candidates made numerous joint appearances giving voters opportunities for side-by-side comparison.

State senator Poshard and his Republican opponent, Southern Illinois University law professor Patrick Kelley, stood at podiums, each prepped to probe the issues of the day. One would make a point that garnered cheers from one side, jeers from the other. The atmosphere resembled an athletic contest. Poshard recalls he might finish a point only to see supporters of his opponent stand, then rip in half one of his campaign signs. It was a good, old-fashioned hard-ball political fight, and both candidates took it on the chin from their opponents' followers. Back and forth the raucous crowd swayed with their candidate from question to question. "For someone who loves debate like I do, those debates were great," Poshard said.

A former Carbondale City Council member who was valedictorian of his undergraduate class at Notre Dame and his law school class at the University of Iowa, Kelley was well versed in the issues and a comfortable campaigner.[1] Poshard describes Kelley as well prepared. Kelley had a core of enthusiastic supporters, including many SIU students who boldly promoted his green placards that said "Kelley for Congress." Poshard supporters countered with "Poshard for Congress" signs with a donkey in the lower left corner.

The race generated intense interest in part because there was no incumbent. Congressman Ken Gray was retiring, ending his second stint of a career in Washington that began in 1954. In the five terms from 1974 to 1984, between Gray's first retirement and his return to Congress, the seat had been held by Paul Simon.

"I don't believe there has ever been a race like this in southern Illinois where the public was so involved in the campaign," Poshard said. "Those three debates were like soccer matches. There was tremendous energy in the gymnasiums. They were civil, but the crowd was definitely involved. It was what everybody who loved debate would dream of. This was real government in front of the people. They were all out by two guys who wanted the job and represented their positions well. I was honored to be a part of that."

SIU political scientist John Jackson said the debates typified a congressional race that focused on issues. "I think the debates were just one important indicator of what a high-quality race this one was," he said. "These were two very experienced and very well-qualified candidates. The race focused mostly on important issues of public policy. The candidates showed respect for each other and refrained from personal attacks. This was the kind of race we see only rarely in our highly polarized and mostly negative campaigns of today."[2]

The debates were held on September 14 at Shawnee Community College near Ullin, on September 28 at Rend Lake College in Ina, and on October 5 at Kaskaskia College in Centralia. In between the debates, Poshard and Kelley appeared at forums throughout the district on multiple occasions. About two hundred people attended a forum in Marion in which the minimum wage was a prominent issue, with Kelley questioning the impact an increase from $3.35 an hour would have on jobs, and Poshard saying people needed more income to pay their bills.

Family leave and aid for the homeless were top issues at a forum attended by about 150 people at the SIU Student Center. Poshard favored requiring employers to offer unpaid leave for a childbirth or long-term family illness. Sitting next to each other at an event in Mt. Vernon, Kelley and Poshard exchanged differences on the federal deficit, trade, foreign policy, and foreign ownership of U.S. businesses.[3] At a forum in Pinckneyville, Kelley contended big government was a hindrance to job creation. He backed reducing the capital gains tax and lowering government barriers for business.[4]

On some major issues, Poshard and Kelley had similarities that mirrored the mood in the district. Both opposed gun control, abortion, and same-sex marriage in a socially conservative district. Both supported the coal industry and a balanced federal budget. Differences emerged in budget details, in style, and in how the next congressman might be influenced by his party.

The congressional race was in the same election cycle in which Republican George H. W. Bush defeated Democrat Michael Dukakis in the presidential election. Kelley described himself as a Reagan Republican and attempted to tie Poshard to Democratic House Speaker Jim Wright. Wright, who was facing discipline from an Ethics Committee investigation into royalties he received from bulk sales of his speeches and writings, was viewed negatively by the press. Kelley hoped the negative publicity would rub off on Poshard. Kelley noted he would not vote for Wright as House Speaker. Kelley also tried to tie Poshard to all of the Democratic Party platform, even portions that Poshard consistently opposed.[5]

Poshard countered that he had a record of independence, of standing firm behind his convictions even when those positions opposed party leadership. Poshard cited economic development, infrastructure development, and upgrading the health care system as the three key issues. He backed those themes with examples from his voting record on how he supported the interests of the region. He reinforced the themes daily in visits to cafes, small socials, talks before service clubs, local party functions, and other spots where he could find potential voters.

Poshard cited numerous endorsements, including the Illinois Public Action Council, Illinois Agricultural Association, Illinois Right to Life, Illinois Education Association, National Council of Senior Citizens, Egyptian Board of Realtors, National Rifle Association, AFL-CIO, United Mine Workers, Laborers International, and several other labor entities.

Campaign literature that highlighted his state Senate accomplishments noted that Poshard, pronounced Pu-shard, will "push hard" for southern Illinois. One ad highlighted his endorsements, his background as an educator and a southern Illinois native, and a family photograph that included wife Jo, a teacher in Carterville, and his two children, Dennis and Kristen.[6]

Poshard received multiple newspaper endorsements, including one from the region's largest newspaper, the *Southern Illinoisan.* "Glenn Poshard is the most thoughtful, intelligent, energetic elected official to emerge from Southern Illinois in recent years," the *SI* stated. "There is no question but what the 22nd District should promote him from the Illinois Senate to the U.S. House of Representatives. . . . As a state legislator, Poshard has demonstrated the effectiveness required to push issues into focus and legislation into law. He earned the respect of fellow state legislators (he was named chairman of a key committee after just two years in office) and will do the same in Congress more quickly than most." Later, the editorial says of Poshard: "He knows how to listen to people and he's shown a willingness to tell them what they need to hear instead of what he thinks they want to hear."[7]

The *Daily Egyptian*, the student newspaper at SIU, praised both candidates without making an endorsement. "Both have stayed on the high road during appearances and press conferences. Their campaigns have stressed what they will do if elected. Their appearances have been long in explaining how the two differ on specific issues, but short on personal attacks that have undermined the campaigns at the top of the tickets."[8]

Poshard's praise for his opponent was effusive. "Pat Kelley was the most intelligent and articulate opponent I ever ran against. He had excelled in his career and had a tremendous command of the issues. I have thought many times what an outstanding congressman Pat would have made. I felt honored to have had such a capable person challenging me to be a better candidate myself."

Looking back at that first congressional campaign elicits many fond memories. Poshard relished spending time meeting people, listening to concerns, researching and understanding issues, and making the case for why he should be the next congressman from the "Deep South" Illinois district.

CHAPTER 9

# Not All about the Money

As thousands gathered on the National Mall in anticipation of the inaugural speech of President George H. W. Bush, members of the 101st Congress were gathering in the House chamber, awaiting their short walk to the "back porch" of the Capitol to be eyewitnesses to this historic event. Seated only a few yards behind the podium where President Reagan and congressional leaders were assembled, Poshard was astounded by the view down the mall past the Washington Monument and all the way to the Lincoln Memorial and the Vietnam Wall on this cold day of January 20, 1989. The day before, Poshard had gathered with some friends at the Vietnam Memorial to pay respects to his cousin Dennis, who had died fighting in that war. It was an emotional tribute.

As the newly sworn-in president began his speech, Poshard pulled a small notebook from his overcoat pocket and wrote the following poem.

### *The Wall*

*Sitting here*
*Seeing there*
*His name on the Wall*
*My name in the Hall*
*His words rang clear*
*Past the spire*
*Down the Mall*
*No more names*
*On the Wall*
*Lord make it so*
*And let Denny know*
*I see his wall from here*
*Hand on the Bible*
*Oaths so old*
*Frozen words*
*In the winters cold*
*Under Old Abe's gaze*
*The ghosts appear*
*Bending heads softly*
*The words to hear*
*Young soldiers all*
*Heard the nations call*
*Now hear his words*
*Shooting down the Mall*
*They nod consent*
*Toward the Hall*
*No more names*
*No more Walls*[1]

Inauguration day in Washington, D.C., is unrivaled in the career of a congressman for its political and historical significance. But Poshard knew there were serious issues waiting to be resolved in the twenty-second congressional district back in Illinois, and he was eager to get started.

In August 1942, a two-lane toll bridge across the Mississippi River opened to traffic, connecting Illinois Route 150 with Missouri

Highway 51 between Chester, Illinois, and Perryville, Missouri. The bridge is the lone place for vehicles to drive across the river in the 110-mile stretch from south St. Louis to Cape Girardeau, Missouri. The city of Chester, population eighty-five hundred, collected the tolls, kept a small percentage, and maintained the bridge. No tolls were assessed on the Missouri side.

As Poshard defeated Patrick Kelley handily in November 1988, the bridge emerged as a first major test in Congress. Chester, perhaps better known as the home to Illinois' largest state prison, was in his new congressional district. He knew the people and the bridge's regional importance. Chester's toll authority had expired in December, and the bridge required $1 million in repairs. Poshard was weeks out of the two-week orientation for newly elected congressmen at the Kennedy School of Government at Harvard when the issue hit his radar. The congressman who represented Missouri, Bill Emerson, wasn't interested in continuing with a toll bridge in which only the Illinois side collected money. A new solution was needed.[2]

Poshard organized meetings of state and local officials from Missouri and Illinois. Initially, the federal government appeared ready to financially support a compromise in which the states of Missouri and Illinois and the city of Chester would contribute the $1 million needed to paint and repair the bridge. The federal government would contribute a proportional share, but that share collapsed when disaster relief for Hurricane Hugo and California earthquakes more than consumed federal funding, meaning the two state governments needed to increase their shares.

The work was "textbook Poshard" in that he facilitated discussions with key officials on both sides of the river. He worked with local officials and federal agencies. The meetings included public sessions and behind-the-scenes discussions. "We finally worked our way through all the differences from people on both sides of the river and received the federal and state assistance we needed to repair the bridge and keep it viable for years to come," Poshard recalled. "It was so much work, and nerves were often frayed, but today, when I cross the Chester bridge, heading out to Kaskaskia Island or some part of Missouri, I feel a certain pride in knowing I led an effort in saving a vital transportation link between Illinois and Missouri. Congressman

Bill Emerson and I became good friends while working on this project, and later, I assisted him in the early stages of an architecturally beautiful bridge between my district and Cape Girardeau, Missouri, aptly named after the good congressman. In 1992, owing to the 1990 census, my district was split three ways, and I lost the counties on the Illinois side adjoining the new bridge, ending my participation in working with Bill on this impressive structure."

In the ensuing years, there emerged many more scenarios that called for the inclusive problem-solving approach. "You do it by having a command of the issue," Poshard said of the way he facilitated negotiations. "You have to know every side of the problem. Compromise is not possible if you are ignorant of the issue yourself, or if you can't see it from the other side's perspective. Once you know the issue, the key is to keep the parties talking, keeping the public informed along the way. In almost every circumstance, if you want to solve the problem, public input is an important element enabling you to identify potential compromises."

Behind the scenes, congressional staff set the table for success, compiling information, interacting with constituents, and having their own conversations with other congressional staffers. Poshard's first chief of staff, Beth Pierce Wright, is a southern Illinois native who first met Poshard when she was in high school and her father was pastor of the First Baptist Church in Carterville where Poshard attended services. During men's softball games, Wright often sat with Jo Poshard. A schoolteacher who grew up with Democratic politics, Jo played a lead role throughout Poshard's political career. "Jo is a delightful person," Wright said. "She's just steady. She has that sensibility of teaching. She also is a hilarious storyteller. We used to pull pranks on each other."

Early in her career, Wright worked for Illinois House Speaker Mike Madigan, then moved to Washington to work for Senator Alan Dixon. She joined Poshard's staff at age twenty- seven, which was young for the lead job on a congressional staff. Two things that worked in her favor were intimate knowledge of southern Illinois and a work ethic that mirrored Poshard's, typically extending her workday well into the evening. "I was the go-between between Glenn and everybody else," she said. "It was a different time in Congress, when people worked across the aisle a lot."

She remembers working with Emerson's staff as well as staffs of powerful congressional leaders like Dan Rostenkowski of Chicago. Wright said a typical approach was to be pleasant and approachable, even where there was disagreement. "If you're in a situation with two competing interests, that approach gives you an advantage." Of Poshard's approach with his team, she said, "Most of the time he would say this needs to be done, how are we going to do it? He was definitely a good listener. He had high standards, but not any higher than I had for myself."[3]

The Chester bridge was a first experience navigating a visible issue that would impact his district. Another introduction to Washington created a lifelong family memory and an enduring respect for President George H. W. and Barbara Bush.

During his first month in office, Poshard and his wife were invited to the White House to a reception for freshmen legislators with President and Mrs. Bush. Glenn and Jo faced a dilemma. Jo and Kristen were visiting in D.C. then, and they were scheduled for a 9:30 P.M. flight home from Washington National Airport. The White House reception was from 7 P.M. to 9 P.M., and protocol was such that guests were discouraged from leaving until the President and First Lady retired. Children were not invited.

There would not be enough time for the Poshards to leave the reception, drive back to their apartment to get Kristen, and get to the airport on time. So they took Kristen to the White House with them, and she was allowed to stay downstairs in a room and wait while they were upstairs at the reception.

In a conversation with Mrs. Bush, Poshard apologized that Kristen was downstairs, and said they may have to leave a little early to get to the airport on time. In a surprise to Glenn and Jo, the First Lady called a staff person over and directed him to go downstairs and bring Kristen up to the reception. Within a few minutes, Kristen was in the room. Mrs. Bush greeted her warmly and took her by the hand to meet the president. At fourteen years old, standing in the White House conversing with the president, she was in awe. She told him that he looked much younger in person than he did on TV.

He said most people tell him he looked much taller in person, since he stood nearly six feet, four inches. He asked her what year of school she was in. She said she was a sophomore. He said, "Oh, at the University of Illinois?"

"We all laughed," said Poshard. "That compliment meant she would always be a fan of President and Mrs. Bush."

A White House photographer snapped a photo of Kristen and the president that remains a prized possession. Poshard remembers it like this: "The kindness President and Mrs. Bush extended to our family in that first meeting will never be forgotten. First impressions matter, but we found over the next four years, President and Mrs. Bush were genuinely kind and thoughtful people."

Later, during one summer, Kristen got the opportunity to serve as a page in the U.S. Capitol, where she was assigned a job in the majority cloakroom, the nerve center of the Capitol. She met the legislative leaders of our government every day and gained unique insight into government, politics, and the spaces in between. She has spent a good deal of her career in grant writing and community, economic, and workforce development, in which she has excelled at job retraining and other efforts to help workers remain employable so they can support their families.

In April 1989, Poshard was tested in another way. The country mourned the deaths of forty-seven American sailors killed in an explosion on the USS *Iowa* as the ship sat in the Chesapeake Bay in Norfolk, Virginia. Poshard went on the House floor a couple weeks later to praise the response of Petty Officer Kendall Truitt, who helped extinguish and contain the fires, preventing more casualties. Truitt lived in Marion, one of the largest cities in Poshard's district, and Poshard knew the family. The opportunity to praise a local hero is a welcome congressional duty.

Weeks later, Poshard was on the phone with Truitt's father. Would the congressman speak with an attorney representing Kendall Truitt? The Marion sailor made national news from leaks to the media that the explosion may have been caused by a suicidal sailor, Clayton Hartwig. Reports were that Hartwig became distressed when his homosexual advances were turned away by shipmates. Truitt, one of Hartwig's friends, was the beneficiary of a $100,000 life insurance policy left to him by Hartwig. Investigators questioned Truitt as speculation grew.[4]

Poshard initiated an inquiry into the Navy's handling of the public affairs related to the tragedy and the impact on Truitt and Truitt's wife. A *Washington Post* headline said, "USS *Iowa* Sailor's Congressman Inquires into Source of Leaks." Poshard said he felt his duty was to ensure that the information released from a thorough Navy investigation was fair to Truitt and his family. He concluded in July that the inquiry was handled properly and that Truitt became caught in the middle of a difficult, high-profile process that, to some, gave the appearance of impropriety. The report showed clearly that Truitt had done nothing wrong.

The same month as the Navy incident, mine workers in Virginia and West Virginia, having worked fourteen months without a contract, went on strike against the Pittston Coal Company. The strike dragged on through the summer and fall, leading to wildcat sympathy strikes in eight states throughout coal country, including southern Illinois. Poshard was among the members who called for the company to negotiate. Throughout the fall he repeated calls to bring the parties together and end the strike, which was settled on December 23.[5]

"The constant pressure from congressmen representing the coal fields of America sent word to Pittston and other companies that a light would be shone on their unfair labor practices," Poshard said. "These were men and women who went down into the belly of the earth every day, risking their lives to help meet the energy needs of America. Their safety and financial security should always have been the top priority of the corporations that owned the mines, but in too many cases, it wasn't. The history of my congressional district was one of mine explosions taking the lives of hundreds of miners, and I was not going to turn a deaf ear to the concerns of those Pittston miners." The miners' strike and USS *Iowa* investigation are two high-profile examples of the role congresspersons play in the lives of constituents not directly related to the legislative process.

In that same first spring in Washington, Poshard was tipped off about potential irregularities at the Carbondale Post Office. A Postal Service administrator, related to the postmaster, had set up a fake construction company to which he would issue contracts for maintenance and repair of area post offices. Invoices for work that never happened would be sent to the U.S. Postal Service in Washington, D.C., and the payments would be forwarded to a post office box in Carbondale that served as the address for the fake company. Tens of thousands of dollars were swindled from the taxpayers in this fraudulent scheme.[6] Poshard called for an investigation by the Postal Service's inspector general and persisted when the investigation seemed to stall. In the fall, the Postal Service conceded wrongdoing without forwarding the case to the U.S. Attorney's Office for potential criminal charges. Once again, Poshard persisted. In early 1990 the case led to convictions, but the U.S. attorney decided he had too many larger cases and the only punishment meted out was the forced early retirement of the perpetrator. "In my judgment, it was justice denied, and the only ones punished were the taxpayers," Poshard said.

That same first spring, Poshard learned that the Arkansas governor, Bill Clinton, was coming to Washington to promote development of the Lower Mississippi Delta Development Commission. The governor was leading a newly formed coalition to promote investment in an economically challenged region along the southern Mississippi River to include parts of southeast Missouri, western Kentucky, Arkansas, Tennessee, Mississippi, and Louisiana.[7]

This was an economic recovery plan based on the regional model for Appalachia developed as part of the Great Society effort of Lyndon Johnson. Poshard understood his district well and knew that several of his counties shared the same cultural and economic needs as those of the Delta. He arranged to meet with Clinton and persuaded the governor to include eleven southern Illinois counties in the commission. He attended press conferences and other meetings with members of the commission, including the governors of Mississippi and Louisiana, and was later successful in adding an additional five counties in southern Illinois to the plan, which emphasized assistance in health care, education, housing, small business, and related issues.

While campaigning for Poshard in Chicago when he later ran for governor, Clinton emphasized his early work with Poshard on the development commission. "The result," Poshard said, "has been millions of dollars coming to southern Illinois as a result of this commission's work over the past nearly thirty years. When I look back over my career, getting southern Illinois included in the Lower Mississippi Delta Development Commission was one of the most important initiatives of my congressional service. It's brought a lot of help to our people. It was my earliest work with Bill Clinton, whom I admired greatly as an innovator and leader who saw a vision for one of the poorest parts of our country, a vision that I shared."

That same April, four months into his first term, Poshard testified before a House subcommittee for the $800 million Olmsted Lock and Dam project. Congressman Gray had proposed the legislation for the new lock and dam before he retired a year earlier. The testimony is a typical part of the congressional workload. It requires first identifying and understanding issues in and around your district, then making the case for those matters among fellow members of Congress, both formally through public testimony and informally through meetings and discussions in and around Washington. The Olmsted Lock and Dam was to become the largest inland waterways project in American history.[8] The project replaced two aging locks with a new structure to improve navigation along the Ohio River a few miles north of where it meets up with the Mississippi at the tip of Illinois.

The bid for the first phase of the project, a $300 million coffer dam, was won by a British company, Balfour Beatty.[9] Despite local officials, under the leadership of Ed Smith of the Laborers International Union, having prepared the local labor force for the hundreds of jobs the lock and dam would produce, Balfour Beatty refused to hire local people. Poshard caught a ride on a Secretary of State plane to London, England, and accompanied by a high-level official from the State Department, he paid a visit to the head of Balfour Beatty.

"The meeting started off civil enough," Poshard said. "After greeting several members of Balfour Beatty's leadership team who were in the room, I proceeded to give a brief historical as well as legislative history of the project. I emphasized how this was a long-anticipated project, and how we had methodically prepared the local workforce for the jobs the project required. This lock and dam would provide the highest-paid construction jobs in the region for the next twenty years, helping to stabilize the economy of the poorest area of the state. And afterward, the farming, coal, and manufacturing base throughout the entire Ohio Valley region would gain thousands of jobs from the improved river transportation network. The old locks and dams 53 and 54, built during the Roosevelt administration, were backing up barge traffic two and three days at a time, costing industry billions of dollars each year in lost time and productivity. The new Olmsted

Lock and Dam would be a moneymaker and a job producer, but our local people needed the construction jobs now, not twenty years down the road.

"All of this I made clear in my presentation, and it met with not a single sympathetic ear in the room. They were aloof, they were arrogant, and they let me know they were hiring their people through a defunct steelworkers' local somewhere out east, and they didn't need or want local help. At that point I let them know they were making a huge mistake, that their insensitivity to local needs would work against them in future contracts, and indeed it did. The coffer dam contract was the only one they received out of the entire $3 billion project.

"Another stormy meeting ensued when Ed Smith and I met in Senator Carol Moseley Braun's office in Washington with one of the same obnoxious officials. The result was the same that I had met with in London, which only strengthened our resolve to make sure Balfour Beatty would never get another contract.

"A third meeting took place at the St. Louis Airport with representatives of the Steelworker's International Union when they tried to justify the use of their defunct local as a real union, instead of the sham for which Balfour Beatty was using it. I was as angry as I have ever been, because I had never seen a union allow itself to be used in a sham operation against other union members who were deserving and needful of the jobs a major project like this deserved.

"By the time the next section of the project was put out to bid, we had contacted every major construction company in America, encouraging them to bid and providing vital information on everything necessary for their inclusion of the local workforce in their proposal. For the next twenty-seven years, local people from southern Illinois and western Kentucky were hired on the project. All of the struggle had been worth it. Senators Simon, Dixon, and Durbin and Representative Costello kept the project on track after I left Congress, but in those early years it was my major focus, and my good friend Ed Smith, with the International Laborers Union, was its chief lobbyist and advocate."

Poshard had lobbied for funding in each of his ten years in Congress, and in August 2018, he was present for the ribbon cutting of what had become a $3 billion project with over 45 million labor hours.

He attended the ceremony with his two good friends Senator Durbin and Ed Smith. Senator Durbin, in his remarks, referred to the work of Poshard and Smith and the extraordinary efforts they had undertaken to make the project a reality.[10] It was an emotional day for the three of them.

"I've worked with Glenn Poshard on a hundred projects or more," Smith said. "That was the biggest. It would not have been there without Glenn. Initially, we were not going to get one job [from Balfour Beatty] out of it. You're talking about some of the poorest counties in our state. These were jobs with union wages, health insurance, defined benefits, jobs where you didn't [have to] work all week and still be eligible for food stamps."[11]

Poshard regularly embraced opportunities to host meetings throughout his district both to educate people about issues and to solicit input. Early in his first term, he hosted a series of meetings in which he asked participants to show how they would spend federal revenue if they were elected officials.

Attendees at the meetings decided what they would leave in the budget and what they would cut. For example, a constituent who favored spending more on defense would then have to find other places to cut. "One of my responsibilities was to educate people about the process we went through in D.C., and since the budget deficit was the single greatest issue facing us, I wanted folks back home to understand it," he said. "People always said they wanted Congress to cut spending, but they never wanted the programs they supported to be cut. It was always the other guy's programs. Well, I wanted my constituents to grapple with the same challenges I faced in trying to balance the budget. I think they learned a lot because there were hundreds of people who showed up at the town halls and spent hours participating in this exercise.

"Teaching was one of the things I loved about my job in Congress. I wanted people to understand the complexity of the issues. I wanted them to see how you had to weigh pros and cons. I wanted them to see why I saw an issue a certain way. And I wanted to have a chance to bridge differences and promote understanding."

Just as a student might alter a teacher's thinking in the classroom, sometimes constituents caused Poshard to modify a position. "You have to listen," said Poshard. "If you're just going to follow your party on every issue, they could send a robot." Often people raised issues that opened doors to consideration of an important local project. "This happened more times than I could say."

Poshard voted for the base closure bill that impacted 145 domestic military installations. He voted to cut funding for the B-2 bomber by $400 million and opposed aid to Nicaraguan contras. He supported President Bush's initiative on space exploration. He also opposed the savings and loan bailout bill, which he said would cost more than the $90 billion estimate and put an unfair burden on taxpayers.

In Congress he lobbied for projects he knew would impact lives in his district. He learned that $1 million was needed to repair the Harrisonville levee in Monroe County that, left unrepaired, threatened thousands of acres of farmland and at least a thousand homes. The committee chairman who oversaw spending on such projects was not a fan of freshman lawmakers. Poshard made an appointment to see him and was told he had only a minute or so to make his case. He remembers almost to the word his pitch for the levee. As the chairman waved him out of his office without responding to his request, Poshard stopped at the door, turned, and thanked the elderly chairman for his service to the country. As the appropriations process proceeded, Poshard received a call. It was the chairman. "How much did you need for your project?"

"A million dollars," was the reply.

The appropriations bill included the Harrisonville levee. "To this day, I think the reason I got that money is because I took the time to thank him for his service."

In 1993 the Great Flood along the Mississippi River compromised many levees from Iowa all the way to Cairo, but the Harrisonville levee held, saving the homes and much of the farmland along that stretch of the river. A simple thank-you might have been the difference.

In May of 1989, Chinese troops with automatic rifles and tanks fired on and massacred many protestors in Beijing's Tiananmen Square. The incident resonated across the Poshard family. Poshard's daughter Kristen, a freshman in high school at the time, followed in the family's tradition of expression through poetry, writing this in remembrance.

### *Tiananmen*

*I saw him stand there*
*He was quite aware of the iron beasts*
*In front of him*
*Fear of their growling voices and hollow trunks*
*Never crossed his mind*
*Only the fear of never living his own life*
*He was like David battling a thousand Goliaths*
*But with no stone*
*But the beasts turned because of*
*Their fear of him*
*Maybe it was the interior of the iron*
*The machines inside had a slight*
*Sense of wrong*
*So the beasts turned*
*But the man challenged again*
*And the beasts turned again*
*The man so overwhelmed with hatred*
*For the beasts and passion for peace*
*Leapt upon the leader of the pack*
*Not to gain media coverage*
*But to gain life*[12]

"Kristen has always played such an important role in our lives and our political campaigns," Poshard said. "She is the true poet in our family, so creative in her writing and able to see the beauty in life even in the midst of trials. She hasn't always had it easy being the child of a politician, but she's strong and resilient. Sometimes when my critics seemed very harsh, I would call her, and the conversation often found its way into a poem or a verse of encouragement.

"There's not a political or social issue that my kids can't debate with the best of them. I don't know how many debates I have had in my career, but with the help of my son and daughter, I have never needed a debate coach or a consultant."

One perk Poshard welcomed was the annual congressional baseball game. In June 1989, Poshard donned a borrowed SIU Saluki baseball suit and started in left field for the Congressional Democrats.

"My two best friends on the team were Bill Richardson, who went on to be governor of New Mexico and United States ambassador to the United Nations, and Richard Neal, from Massachusetts, who is now chairman of the House Ways and Means Committee, the most powerful committee in the House. We were all three pretty good ballplayers, but on that day we faced a formidable task. The pitcher for the Republicans was Hall of Famer Jim Bunning, from Kentucky. In his fifties, this former major league all-star could still fire the ball. While the game was fun for the couple of thousand people who showed up, it was especially fun for me, loving baseball the way I did. But I had come to the game for another reason.

"Bart Giamatti, the commissioner of Major League Baseball, was the guest celebrity that night, and he was my favorite commissioner of all time. He was a real lover of the game, had studied its history, and had written books about its glorious past. He had been president of Yale University and left that job to become commissioner, something few people would have done if they weren't ultimate fans of baseball. Dave Stricklin, my communications director, had brought a brand-new Rawlings baseball to the office that day for me, so I could get Giamatti's autograph. After the game, when the crowd had cleared, Dave and I walked with the commissioner and his driver to his car. Just before he got in, he autographed the baseball for me."

A few months later, on September 1, the headline in the *Washington Post* read, "Giamatti Dead of Heart Attack." "It was a shock to me and the entire baseball world. I might have had one of the last baseballs he ever signed."

As commissioner, Giamatti had been prominent in banning Pete Rose from Major League Baseball and the Hall of Fame for gambling on games that he managed or in which he played. "I admired Rose as a great baseball player but never forgave him for the needless injury he caused Ray Fosse, a local Marion, Illinois, kid who had made it to the big leagues and was the starting catcher for the American League in the 1970 All-Star game." Rose separated Fosse's shoulder in a headfirst, violent collision at home plate, a play that later was instrumental in rules changes to protect catchers from runners. In July 1990, Rose ended up in the Marion Federal Penitentiary for income tax evasion.

"Now, if I could get Rose to sign the baseball that Giamatti had signed, then I could give it to a local charity to be auctioned off for a lot of money to help abused children, a passion of mine. I had visited the prison many times to meet with the federal employees there, so I knew the warden well. I called him and told him I had a baseball that I would like Mr. Rose to sign if he would do so. The warden said he would talk to Pete and get back to me later that day. He didn't think there would be a problem." When the warden later called Poshard, the warden said Rose made it clear he wouldn't cooperate. "Honestly," said Poshard, "it was worth the effort, but it was almost exactly what I expected Rose to say. I still have that baseball, but I'm certain Giamatti's name will be the only one on it."

In his first year in Congress, 1989, Poshard on multiple occasions brought key congressional leaders to his district to discuss issues. He maintained his tradition of a near-perfect voting record, including issues like these: support for the creation of the Agricultural Research Commercialization Corporation to expand domestic and foreign markets for American agricultural products; support for limited mailing privileges of members of Congress, known as franking, and using the $45 million in savings to help pregnant women addicted to drugs; opposition to congressional pay raises; sponsoring legislation that would allow local school districts flexibility in use of funds and regulatory relief in exchange for higher performance goals; asserting that President Bush's education proposals were disappointing and flawed (Poshard advocated increased education funding at both the K–12 and the college and university levels.); support for economic development efforts in part through grants to local airports and area-related defense spending such as a $4 million contract for the Marion-based Olin Corporation, which makes munitions; hosting seminars for small businesses interested in bidding on federal government contracts; hosting a hearing on regional tourism attended by the committee chairman, Ike Skelton, of Missouri; hosting the cochairman of the Rural Health Care Coalition, Congressman Mike Synar of Oklahoma, at roundtable discussions at various southern Illinois locations (issues addressed included reimbursement to rural hospitals, physician recruitment, and availability of emergency and related care.)

As his first year neared its end, Poshard played an important role in what he considered a legislative achievement that will be a long-lasting legacy. The House appropriated $2 million to purchase more than three thousand acres in what's known as the Cache River Wetlands and $1 million in the Shawnee National Forest for more than two thousand acres. The wetlands area includes thousand-year-old cypress trees that are part of swamps, ponds, and hardwood forests with thirty-six threatened species.[13]

"The Cache River Wetlands project is an excellent example of the government working with local landowners to protect areas that make southern Illinois so special. Without such measures, unintentional damage can result, and we can lose valuable resources for understanding our history and appreciating the beauty of our land," said Poshard. "Today, this area we helped preserve, working with Citizens to Save the Cache, the Nature Conservancy, the U.S. Fish and Wildlife Services, and other organizations, is recognized as a Ramsar Wetland of International Importance, a distinction carried by only a small percentage of wetlands around the world. The thirty-five thousand acres under management today act as the 'kidneys' for purification of waters moving through the southern Illinois basin and flowing to the Ohio and Mississippi Rivers."

On May 18, 1991, after years of work as a state senator and a congressman, Poshard joined others for the dedication of the Cypress Creek National Wildlife Refuge, the Frank Bellrose Waterfowl Reserve, the Cache River State Natural Area, and the Lower Cache River Preserve.[14] "It was one of the most significant undertakings of my career, to be a part of something that would inspire future generations to preserve the natural habitat which is home to so much of nature's diversity," Poshard said. "It remains one of Illinois' most treasured landscapes."

Also in that first year, Poshard sponsored the Illinois Wilderness Act, which he describes as the most contentious and also the most important bill for posterity for which he advocated in his years of public life. As was his longstanding practice, when Poshard worked for such legislation, he brought experts into his district and held public meetings. He embraced dissent, like the hostile, standing-room-only crowds that greeted him at the senior center in Golconda in October 1989. He told the crowd that wilderness designation would preserve environmentally unique areas while allowing landowners' to use their property. Poshard said southern Illinois residents should agree and promote wilderness designation or face having more onerous restrictions imposed on them. Wilderness designation was seen by local people as a "takeover of public lands that belong to us. It was a feeling I understood, having grown up near the Shawnee and my father working on a road crew when scrub land was being converted to a national forest by the Roosevelt administration. It was a very personal thing, the love of this forest."

Poshard's friends were among the opposition in this debate over wilderness, and many supporters broke with him on this issue. "You can't hold your finger up to the wind on every issue," he said. "I went to Congress, I had this privileged position. I got to see information not everyone had. The job was not just to go along with public opinion. I never worried about whether people voted for me or not. My job was to tell people what I honestly saw. I tried to help them understand why I took the position I did and why I thought my decision was best for my district and my country. I never took the attitude I had to change their mind. I wanted them to see all sides of the issue, help them broaden their perspective, and if they disagreed with me, that was all right too. They could then decide whether to believe me and trust my judgment, and if they didn't, then every two years they had the opportunity to remove me from office. That way, both the officeholder and the public fulfilled their responsibilities: mine, to educate and inform and listen to their concerns and criticism and make adjustments, if appropriate; theirs, to give input and to vote.

"As difficult and explosive as these meetings were, I could see some people beginning to understand the need for wilderness protection, and today, nearly thirty years later, these beautiful but fragile areas—Bald Knob, Bay Creek, Burden Falls, Clear Springs, Garden of the Gods, Lusk Creek, and Panther Den—are some of the most visited areas in the Shawnee Forest."

Today, the Shawnee wilderness areas bring thousands of tourists to southern Illinois each year. The protection of these wild and rugged areas for the enjoyment of future generations was part of Poshard's opening remarks to participants in the Arkansas, Missouri, and Illinois Wilderness Conference several years ago.

"I accept all the values of wilderness, but there is one thing in my life I will carry with me always. Those were the cold December nights when my dad and I sat near Camel Rock at Garden of the Gods in total silence and looked up at all of the stars filling the night sky. When I became a teenager and began to study world history, I could only imagine a night, like those I shared with my dad, when Peking man, or Cro-Magnon, or Homo habilis—I don't know when it began—walked out of his cave and looked up at the expanse of the universe, and reflective thought came into being. Who am I? Why am I here? What's my purpose in life? Where am I going? Whether it's Lusk Creek Canyon or Burden Falls or Bald Knob in the early morning when the sun gradually spreads across the wilderness below, the wilderness areas provide a touchstone for us to feel the presence of God in a way that our hurried lives seldom permit. We don't ask questions of purpose and meaning in the middle of a busy workday or in a traffic jam on the way home from work or at a weekend filled with sports. The wilderness areas of the Shawnee take me back to my roots. There is a connection between the creation and humans as caretakers, as stewards of the resources God has given us. If my grandson can sit on the boulders at Garden of the Gods with his son and take in the sky and the lakes and the woods like I did with Dad, then I'll be satisfied with whatever small effort I've made to preserve that experience."

The battle to pass the Illinois Wilderness Act carried over through much of the following year until President Bush signed it into law on November 28, 1990. Signings like those were among the most satisfying moments in Congress for Poshard.

As busy and interesting as Poshard's workload was in that first year, he became frustrated with the fundraising demands of the job A meeting in his first month at the Democratic Congressional Campaign Committee headquarters, during which freshman legislators were encouraged to raise a minimum of $5,000 a week, fifty-two weeks a year, didn't sit well with Poshard.

He had just spent an inordinate amount of time the previous year meeting with individual donors, political action committees (PACs), and other organizations to raise money for his campaign, and it was exhausting. But the most difficult thing for him was that to get the PAC's support, you had to commit to a position on particular issues before you ever had the time to gain a national perspective by listening to debate or researching an issue.

"A person just entering Congress views most things from a very parochial or district perspective," Poshard said. "Now, you are sitting in committees and listening to debate on the floor from people of different professions or different geographic areas, and their views on a particular issue may be very different from yours. You are being introduced to a national perspective, and you come to a point where you really begin to grapple with what the role of being a congressperson is. How do you balance what is in the best interest of your district and what is in the best interest of the country? They are not always the same. I can generally vote the interests of my district every time and greatly maximize my chances for reelection. Where then is the tipping point, when you feel the tug of conscience and fact finding that requires the courage needed to go against the majority opinion of your district? Where then is the tipping point, when you have to tell the special interest groups that have supported you, you can't support their agenda any longer?

"As a freshman, I voted for some bills that I didn't feel any longer were in the best interest of the country, but I had given my word. Finally, one day I became so upset with myself after going against my conscience, I walked straight out the door and down the steps of the Capitol. I felt a sense of shame. I walked to my office, gathered my staff, and told them that things were going to change."

Poshard described the meeting this way. "The tipping point may come on any number of issues, but the one factor that hugely complicated the decision-making for me was the 'money chase.' You don't get the money or the endorsement if you are 'against' the donor's position or if you tell them you want to 'think about it.' You get the money if you support their position, and the money puts you in a box, especially as a freshman legislator. You are the most vulnerable you will ever be and that's why you're told, even thirty years ago when I went to Congress, you have to raise $5,000 a week just to survive. It has to be astronomical now when even state representatives are spending over a million dollars to get elected. You don't want to vote against legislation that you promised someone a year ago you would support, and they gave you their money and endorsement. You don't want to be called a 'liar' and lose the support of the PAC's constituents in your district even when you know in your gut your vote is not in the best interest of the country. So you 'go along' to 'get along.' At a minimum, the money bought access to the legislator, and no one will ever convince me that more access doesn't relate to more support for the donor."

Beth Pierce Wright remembers walking to the Library of Congress, where retired Wisconsin senator William Proxmire had an office. Proxmire made the decision years earlier to forgo PAC money, and thus was a good sounding board for Poshard. Proxmire supported the decision, but said fundraising would be difficult.

Wright said Poshard also received support from a Democratic National Committee official who advised that campaigns should fit with the beliefs of the member. "Doug [Fosdick] had worked with [Governor] Jim Hunt in North Carolina," Wright said. "He [Fosdick] felt candidates need to be who they are." The support was welcome, but the decision to decline PAC funds remained a minority view of incumbents.[15]

In his first year in Congress, Poshard made the decision that he would no longer accept PAC funds. Similarly, Poshard declined to use what was known as the congressional franking privilege, in which most members sent out free "newsletters" to their district highlighting their accomplishments in Washington, a practice Poshard called "an incumbent protection device."

In an August 1989 news release, Poshard said the campaign finance reforms under consideration fell short of what was needed. He said he would abide by a mandatory $100,000 limit for campaign spending; accept no PAC contributions; limit individual contributions to $250 dollars per election cycle and $500 in total; forbid the use of the franking privilege for unsolicited mailings; disclose all individual office mail accounts; accept no gifts; reject all subsidized out-of-state travel [trips paid for by PACs] other than committee business; and hold no Washington fundraisers and accept no assistance from the national Democratic Party.[16]

"More recently," said Poshard, "the 'Citizens United' decision of the Supreme Court has dealt another blow to representative democracy in America. It has doubled or tripled the influence of money on polluting the election process in our country, while providing anonymity to those who have the money to influence public policy behind closed doors. Given the makeup of the present Supreme Court, it is unlikely that this decision will ever be overturned in my lifetime. Access and influence by those who control great positions of wealth in this country have now been solidified by the highest court in the land. The scales of justice have tipped heavily against those who are most in need of equal representation under the law."

Throughout his ten years in Congress and during his run for governor of Illinois in 1998, Poshard continued these practices. He received criticism from many in the Democratic Party leadership for his position on refusing the PAC funds and limiting individual donor contributions, believing he "was tying one arm behind his back," but he felt his practice should be consistent with his beliefs. "If I could have won the governorship without taking the big money, then maybe I could have set an example for the rest of the country to follow, and we could have eliminated much of the influence of money on our present process. I didn't win, so I will always have critics, but I did what my conscience dictated, and I did what I thought was right."

Glenn and his sister Jolene pictured with their parents, Lib and Cleatus Poshard. Jolene and Glenn enjoyed a special sibling relationship until she was tragically killed in an automobile accident. Photo from Glenn Poshard personal file.

Poshard attended the Chapman Grove Baptist Church in rural White County multiple times a week throughout his childhood. Photo from Glenn Poshard personal file.

Poshard attended this two-room schoolhouse through eighth grade. The flag was raised by students before the start of daily academic work. Photo from Glenn Poshard personal file.

Poshard and a fellow soldier on guard duty in Korea. Photo from Glenn Poshard personal file.

Poshard held the only boy at the Song Jook orphanage during his deployment in Korea. Soldiers regularly visited the orphanage, bringing items to improve life for the children. Photo from Glenn Poshard personal file.

Poshard stood aside a car he used in his state Senate campaign. Photo from Glenn Poshard personal file.

The Poshards stood in the bed of a pickup truck Glenn used to make stump speeches in his state Senate campaign. Photo from Glenn Poshard personal file.

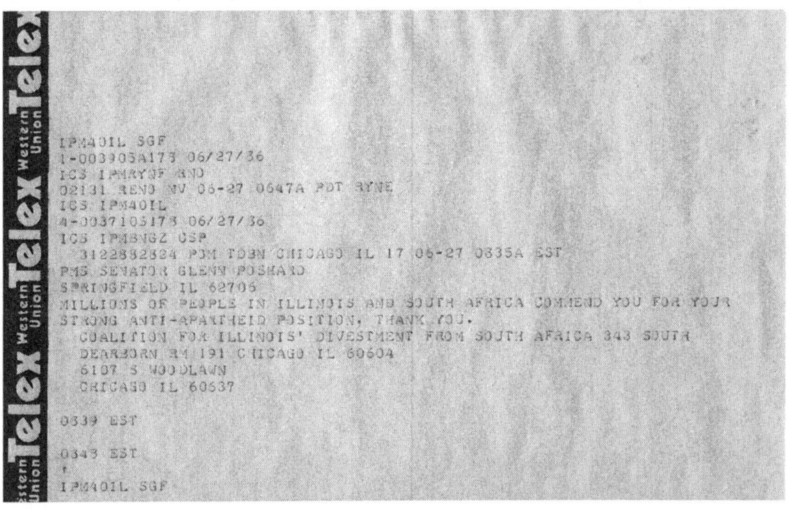


IPM4OIL SGF
1-003905A178 06/27/86
ICS IPMRYSF RNO
02131 RENO NV 06-27 0647A PDT RYNE
ICS IPM4OIL
4-0037105178 06/27/86
ICS IPMBNGZ CSP
3122882824 POM TDBN CHICAGO IL 17 06-27 0835A EST
PMS SENATOR GLENN POSHARD
SPRINGFIELD IL 62706
MILLIONS OF PEOPLE IN ILLINOIS AND SOUTH AFRICA COMMEND YOU FOR YOUR
STRONG ANTI-APARTHEID POSITION, THANK YOU.
COALITION FOR ILLINOIS' DIVESTMENT FROM SOUTH AFRICA 343 SOUTH
DEARBORN RM 191 CHICAGO IL 60604
6107 S WOODLAWN
CHICAGO IL 60637

0839 EST

0843 EST

IPM4OIL SGF

This picture of a telegram thanked Poshard for his anti-apartheid vote in the Illinois Senate. The original telegram is framed in Poshard's home office. The vote stood as a highlight in his career. Photo from Glenn Poshard personal file.

State Senator Poshard with Governor James Thompson at the signing of the rural revival bill at a farm outside of Springfield. Photo from Glenn Poshard personal file.

This van was used by supporters in one of Poshard's early congressional campaigns. Photo from Glenn Poshard personal file.

A family portrait of Dennis, Glenn, Kristen, and Jo. Photo from Glenn Poshard personal file.

Poshard shook hands with baseball Commissioner A. Bartlett Giamatti at a congressional baseball game in Washington, D.C. Photo from Glenn Poshard personal file.

Jo, Kristen, President George H.W. Bush, and Poshard at a White House reception. Photo from the George H.W. Bush Presidential Library and Museum.

CHAPTER 10

# A Change of Heart

Beginning his second year in Congress, Poshard received letters daily. Picket lines formed. Protesters howled. Phone calls came from across southern Illinois and beyond. The issue wasn't about the congressman himself or any of his policy positions. Rather, people felt left out as the Environmental Protection Agency announced what was perceived as a sudden, aggressive timetable to remediate polluted soil in a piece of land familiar to most everyone in southern Illinois.

At issue was the cleanup of the Crab Orchard National Wildlife Refuge, which encompasses about 43,890 acres almost evenly divided between a protected wildlife area and a recreational outlet that attracts locals and tourists. It rests off Illinois Route 13 between Marion and Carbondale, a prominent location just a few miles from Poshard's Carterville home at that time.

Beginning in the 1940s, industrial wastes from manufactured electrical components, ordnance production, and related activities contaminated the soil. As early as the 1970s, the Environmental Protection Agency took notice. In the mid-1980s, Crab Orchard made the EPA's Superfund list of high-priority sites for cleanup. The cleanup issue, more than five years in the making, took center stage in late 1989 and early 1990. The EPA announced a $25 million plan to incinerate soil contaminated with PCBs (polychlorinated biphenyls) to rid the area of its contaminants. Protests developed immediately. The opposition questioned the EPA's plan and the speed at which it was being implemented.[1]

First, Poshard successfully persuaded the EPA to extend the public comment period by thirty days. That was less time than opponents wanted but more than the EPA had intended to give.

He hosted public meetings, engaged both regional and national EPA leaders, and set a course to learn about the implications of incineration. While the decision rested with the EPA, people wanted to know the position of their congressman. "This was a very difficult decision," said Poshard. "The situation had existed for over forty years, and there were several different approaches to cleaning it up. All had their positives and negatives. My staff and I spent a large amount of time researching and trying to learn about the best possible approaches."

In August, Poshard expressed support for the EPA's approach in using a new technology of in situ vitrification, the use of heat and fusion to convert contaminants into a glass or a glassy substance, to remove the PCB contamination, but that process would take years to develop. This was a problem that needed to be resolved more quickly. "I was afraid if we didn't act as soon as possible we would be removed from the Superfund list and lose the federal support for cleanup. I felt the incineration process was safe, and the EPA should proceed. The cleanup worked, but more important, most people felt their voice was heard."

As the Crab Orchard debate unfolded, Poshard dealt with a national environmental policy issue that threatened the regional economic core. The Clean Air Act of 1990 was a top priority of the Bush administration and had substantial support in Congress. For southern Illinois, however, it was disaster.

High-sulfur coal was an economic cornerstone across the region. Generations were raised to recognize coal as a key ingredient to the regional well-being. One estimate showed more than four thousand jobs in the coal industry alone could be lost with passage of the Clean Air Act.

Poshard met with Henry Waxman, the chairman of the Energy and Commerce Subcommittee on Health and the Environment, and John

Dingell, chairman of the Energy and Commerce Committee, among many others. He realized he couldn't stop the entire act but sought to mitigate its negative impact. "I went straight to the mines and explained the issue; I didn't pull any punches with anybody," Poshard said. "This was legislation that would devastate the coal economy we had relied on for years and years." The region of southern Illinois, southern Indiana, and western Kentucky had enough coal to power the country for three hundred years, but it was high-sulfur coal for the most part, and coal had become a dirty word for many lawmakers who resided in urban areas.

Poshard's efforts centered on trying to nationalize the solution. From his standpoint, the country came together to share the impact of issues like the savings and loan bailout and natural disasters like Hurricane Hugo. He reasoned that the same approach to building projects like the Hoover Dam and the Tennessee Valley Authority, which solved energy supply problems for important parts of this country but required national support to be built, should be applied to this problem. Developing clean coal technology should receive national support to save large parts of the economy in many states stretching from Missouri to Virginia. When legislation like the Clean Air Act imperils a regional economy, Poshard believed the cost of the solution should be shared from coast to coast. As the legislative process moved forward, however, Poshard realized his efforts to derail the bill didn't have the votes.

"Southern Illinois should prepare for the worst and hope for the best," he said at one point. "It was hard to see the Clean Air Act pass knowing the damage it was going to do to our area. Some issues are so overwhelming you literally lose sleep. You walk around with a knot in your gut. You see the tsunami coming and know there is no way to stop it."

Pass it did, despite objections from Poshard and Illinois' two Democratic senators, Paul Simon and Alan Dixon. "There were many legislators working to defeat this bill or at least modify its devastating effects, but when it passed it felt like such a personal failure. I knew I had done everything I could do, but the fact remained it passed on my watch. I had let down my district and all the hard-working families who were going to lose their jobs and try to find other work that just wasn't there. I became depressed, and it took some time before

I determined to redouble my efforts to help my district in every way possible and to forgive myself for failing my people.

"It's one of the great ironies of politics that sometimes the people with whom you battle most ferociously are the people you most admire. I had great admiration and respect for President George H. W. Bush. He was one of the finest people I ever met in the political world. Even after losing this battle on the Clean Air Act, I never felt resentment or disrespect toward him. He was doing what he felt was right for the country. I was doing what I felt was right for my district. We remained friends and found common ground on many other issues. A few years ago, Jo and I drove up to Kennebunkport, Maine, with our good friends Jean and Rick McNeill. The president was too ill at the time to see us, and I never would have imposed on the family to do so. As I stood across the bay from his home, I was overcome with emotion. I had only been a small player on the stage of American history during one of my country's most important legislative debates, but I knew I had shared a tiny portion of that stage with one of America's finest presidents. Jo and I loved President and Mrs. Bush." President Bush considered the Clean Air Act his biggest legislative accomplishment. Communities across southern Illinois and several neighboring states would challenge that assessment. For better or worse, coal no longer held the king status it once enjoyed.

While the Crab Orchard cleanup and the Clean Air Act dominated the news, Poshard started the year renewing efforts to educate constituents about important issues that don't always make headlines. He met J. Richard Munro, the cochair and co-CEO of Time Warner, when Munro testified before the Education and Labor Committee. They had a good conversation, and Munro accepted Poshard's invitation to visit the Twenty-Second District.

On February 5, 1990, Munro participated in a series of meetings to highlight the importance of improving America's literacy rate.[2] "I want us to become more aware of the impact illiteracy has on our human resources and on the competitiveness of business," Poshard said of Munro's visit.

During a week off in February from duties in Washington, Poshard scheduled town hall meetings throughout his district, visiting Pittsburg, Metropolis, Mounds, Vienna, De Soto, Ava, Cobden, Cairo, Carrier Mills, Eldorado, Ridgeway, Elizabethtown, Golconda, Ziegler,

Thompsonville, and Johnston City. In April, he hosted town meetings in Waltonville, Bluford, Okawville, Beckemeyer, Buckner, Farina, St. Elmo, Vandalia, Salem, Dupo, and Columbia.

His visits to small towns provided important feedback and helped him both forge and strengthen relationships. Of the role town meetings played, SIU political scientist John Jackson said this:

"For anyone interested in the life and work of a member of Congress, this list is instructive. It is a routine set of meetings, events, and policy commitments that are typical for any member, but especially for members from rural areas. The subjects and particular policies involved might be somewhat different for members from the urban areas or the suburbs, but generically the work and the objectives are the same. To be a true representative in our mass democracy, the member of Congress must be willing to do the nitty-gritty work for the folks back home no matter what the demographics of the district look like. Poshard's activities during this period [are] the essence of public service for any legislator."

Staff member Jim Kirkpatrick was among those who accompanied the congressman around the district. He remembers stopping for fuel during one long day on the road. Poshard had discovered there was no fat in Skittles, so they became a go-to snack. "We were in Mt. Carmel, we had been on the road, and Glenn said I'll go in and get us something to eat. He came out with two bags of Skittles."[3]

The town halls covered a variety of areas, including some of these legislative issues: support for a school reform bill designed to allow school districts flexibility in spending federal money provided they meet performance goals ("The concept is what works in Brooklyn probably doesn't work in Brookport," Poshard said. "Schools in different parts of the country and under different demands often have different needs for their federal funds"); continued efforts on behalf of rural health care in supporting a $1.1 million grant to the Shawnee Health Services group to increase availability of primary care and obstetrics to Medicaid, Medicare, and uninsured patients; receiving input regarding the U.S. Army Corps of Engineers studying recreational policy changes that would impact Rend Lake and Carlyle Lake in southern Illinois; securing release of $2.6 million for the Williamson County National Guard Armory; supporting legislation that would require universities to make campus crime information public; receiving input from veterans in a series of town hall meetings with Congressman Lane Evans, chairman of the Veterans Affairs Subcommittee on Oversight and Investigations, into issues relating to the Veterans Hospital in Marion, Illinois.

As the year progressed, another front-burner national issue emerged, one in which Democrat Poshard sided against the liberal wing of his party. Poshard consistently supported a pay-as-you-go approach to government. He was willing to levy taxes for things he considered important. But he opposed spending beyond the country's ability to pay.

A proposed Balanced Budget Amendment to the Constitution received considerable attention nationally. Poshard supported the amendment, which had broad support but fell short of the needed two-thirds majority. "Until we have this amendment, we can summit, shadow box, read lips, or read tea leaves for that matter, but we will still not have our fiscal house in order," Poshard said. "This is not a pleasant choice for many people in Congress, but it appears to be the best way to make real progress on our debt, which is now over $3 trillion."

On weekends in the district, summer and fall often included participating in some of the numerous community festivals. "My family were my best campaigners, and they proved it on a beautiful fall day in 1990 in Ridgway, Illinois. Southern Illinois is famous for its town festivals throughout the summer and the fall, and it would not have been unusual for us to have made two or even three parades on a Saturday. We would pile into our old Dodge and head out for the circuit bright and early."

On this Saturday, the 10 A.M. parade in a neighboring town got a late start, making it unlikely to make the Popcorn Day Parade in Ridgway which started at 1 P.M. An hour from Ridgway and an hour from the start of the parade there, the family pushed the speed limit along two-lane highways. "We took a back road into town, knowing the main parade route would be closed and wound our way to the parade starting point near the old high school. To our amazement, we had made it."

Horses were always the last group in the parade, and for good reason, which the Poshards experienced firsthand. "The four of us trailed Trigger and about fifty of his friends . . . Jo and I walking in the middle of the street, throwing candy out of full buckets, Dennis and Kristen walking alongside holding up our signs. To say that this parade was uneventful would be the understatement of a lifetime. It was like playing hopscotch for a half mile, jumping on one leg to avoid the horses' 'gifts' and trying to land the other foot on a clear spot. One eye on the crowd, one eye on the crap. People laughing and yelling about politicians finally being put in their rightful place, politicians being horses rear ends, and politicians getting what they deserved for always being late. For most people, it was good-natured ribbing, but for some folks in the crowd wearing my opponent's hats and shirts, it was all the evidence they needed to believe I was a pile of manure. We weren't bothered at all with folks having a little fun at our expense, but the absolute fear of stepping into a pile of horse manure in front of two or three thousand people was totally paralyzing. We didn't. We felt lucky. I thought it was my finest hour as an aging athlete."

As the summer heat turned to fall, still another emotion-filled, multifaceted environmental issue emerged involving the management plan for the Shawnee National Forest. "It's doubtful that in the history of Southern Illinois there has ever been more environmental activism than during the years this forest management plan was being developed," said Poshard.

Multiple groups contested every part of the plan. Logging, ATV trails, hiking trails, wilderness protection, horseback riding, endangered species protection, research, water conservation, and a myriad of other issues were hotly debated over a period of years. Poshard was sought after by every group to advocate for their position.

"The Shawnee was the smallest national forest in the country, consisting of about 265,000 acres, and yet it had more written responses on its forest management plan during the public comment period than any other national forest in America. It was a great exercise in democracy. Messy, chaotic, constant protests, pro bono lawyers lining up right and left. We were trying to work with the Forest Service, Fish and Wildlife, and other federal agencies and be respectful of their research and professional judgments and yet be sensitive to the needs and concerns of our constituents."

In August, Poshard repeated his support for a balanced forest management plan. "My position, as it always had been, was that the Shawnee should be managed to provide recreation, conservation, and economic activity, each within reason and where appropriate. That was exactly what the Shawnee Forest management plan advocated: a multiple-use approach balanced between these different goals." In making the statement, Poshard said he opposed clear-cutting timber but supported harvesting small tracts of trees that provided jobs and affordable wood. He opposed unprofitable timber sales. At the same time, Poshard said some recreational uses and timber sales made sense. He noted in a three-page analysis that the plan was developed over ten years with substantial input from all involved. His good friend federal judge Phil Gilbert, walked the forest, as Poshard had many times, with competing interest groups, and was instrumental in mediating a final solution to the plan.

"I don't know any federal judge who would ever take a hands-on position like Judge Gilbert did in helping resolve one of the most important issues for the future of our region," Poshard said. "He deserves great credit.

"The Shawnee is an asset that should be preserved for generations. Having grown up on the eastern edge of this beautiful forest, I know that no amount of hours or energy to save it for the enjoyment of our children could ever be enough. I am grateful to have had the opportunity to work with so many people who love the Shawnee for all the reasons I have loved it my whole life."

As he moved through his second year in Congress, Poshard was in a great position politically. He proved adept at handling difficult issues. He had strong support from his party and community leaders, and he was having success finding support for key issues like the Olmsted Lock and Dam. He had no announced opposition for the 1990 election until after his midsummer vote opposing a constitutional amendment on flag burning.

The vote represented a switched position for Poshard, who a year earlier cosponsored a constitutional amendment that would have criminalized flag desecration. As a military veteran in a socially conservative district, Poshard knew what the reaction would be. Years later, he describes in an op-ed essay published in the *Southern Illinoisan* the struggle he went through in making the decision to vote against the bill.

"In 1962, I joined the United States Army on my seventeenth birthday. I had just graduated from high school and was following in the tradition of my family's military service. They had served in the Civil

War and fought their way across Europe and the Pacific in two World Wars. Some were POWs, and one, my first cousin and closest friend, Dennis, awarded the Purple Heart and the Bronze Star for bravery in Vietnam, was the first young man from our county to be killed in that war.

"During my three years of enlistment, I served a tour of duty with the First Cavalry Division in Korea. When my active duty was finished in December 1965, I immediately entered SIU on the GI Bill. Protests against the Vietnam War were already gripping the campus. They were abhorrent to me, particularly when the American flag was used to symbolize anger toward the government. But I was busy, carrying a full load of classes, working three part-time jobs, and trying to support a new family. By the time Old Main burned and the campus closed in the spring of 1970, I was beyond anger at the thousands of protesters desecrating our flag and destroying my beloved university."

Referring to experiences as a youth, he said, "I made no attempt to understand the difference between the symbolism of the flag and the substance of the Bill of Rights as it pertained to freedom to speak against perceived wrongs of our government. Years later, as a member of Congress, I was forced to grapple with this volatile issue again. In my first term, a bill was submitted to amend the Constitution prohibiting the desecration of the American flag as a means of protest against our government. Now, I had to understand this issue in its deepest, broadest context. My family and I went to Philadelphia, where I sat in Independence Hall, contemplating those early debates of our forefathers on issues of equality, justice, and freedom. Moved to tears, I was about to cast a vote the historical significance of which reached back to arguments that formed the founding documents of our country, the Declaration of Independence and the Constitution.

"We drove to Gettysburg and I stood where our greatest president, Lincoln, delivered his address, taking us back to our Declaration of Independence, which stated 'that all men are created equal, that they are endowed by their Creator with certain unalienable Rights, that among these are Life, Liberty, and the pursuit of Happiness.'

"When our forefathers thought they had been denied these rights long enough by the King of England, they fought a revolutionary war to gain them. And they fought a civil war to extend those rights to slaves. Over the next one hundred years, they fought all over the world to secure these rights for other people. President Kennedy spoke of this in his inaugural address. He said, 'And yet the same revolutionary beliefs for which our forefathers fought are still at issue around the globe—the belief that the rights of man come not from the generosity of the state but from the hand of God. We dare not forget today that we are the heirs of that first revolution.' The Declaration goes on to say that when any form of government becomes destructive of these rights, then it is the right of the people to protest and alter that form of government so that those rights are secured to the people. And in the 1960s and 1970s, people protested against what they believed was an unjust war that imperiled their lives, their freedoms, and their pursuit of happiness. They believed that nearly sixty thousand deaths were enough in a war our government either could not or would not win.

"When hundreds of thousands of mostly white young men in the sixties and thousands of mostly black young men today protest against their government, it is because they feel their God-given rights are threatened. But why involve the flag? In a Supreme Court decision, *Board of Education v. Barnette*, in 1943, Justice Jackson wrote words especially relevant to this issue. He said, 'But freedom to differ is not limited to things that do not matter much. That would be a mere shadow of freedom. The test of its [freedom's] substance is the right to differ as to things that touch the heart of the existing order' ( i.e., our flag ). For many, it is not enough to send a letter to their congressman, attend a meeting, or participate in a march. They must take the most important thing symbolizing our freedom, the flag, and cast it at the feet of their government to show how emphatically they disagree with government allowing the infringement of their rights. Millions of people of color in our country today feel threatened. They just want to enjoy the same security and freedom we all enjoy, and the flag has become central to their protest precisely because it matters, as it did in the sixties to an earlier generation.

"When I protested as a young man in my church that it was not necessary for God to send His only Son to be sacrificed for my freedom, that He could have provided another way, the pastor said, 'Oh yes it was, because He could not win your freedom from sin by sacrificing that which didn't matter much. He had to sacrifice the most important thing He loved, His Son.'

"The Supreme Court has said that the use of the flag in dissent against the government does not diminish it or the contribution of the men and women who fought for our freedom, but instead stands as a powerful symbol to illustrate the substance of our Constitution's Bill of Rights.

"I listened carefully to the debate in 1990 on the flag desecration amendment, which for the first time in two hundred years would have amended our Bill of Rights. These words from President Reagan's solicitor general, Charles Fried, express my beliefs entirely. 'The flag, as all in this debate agree, symbolizes our nation, its history, its values. We love the flag because it symbolizes the United States; but we must love the Constitution even more, because the Constitution is not a symbol. It is the thing itself.'"

In his speech during the debate in Congress, Poshard said, "We will remain secure, not by suppressing the free will of the people, regardless of what national or political purpose we believe that serves, but by allowing the free will of every single citizen to love or not to love." He concluded that neither America nor the flag is in any danger as long as the precious Bill of Rights, which gives them both meaning and purpose, stays as it has for the past two hundred years, unamended. Poshard said, "Listen to the words of the First Amendment one more time: 'Congress shall make no law abridging the freedom of speech.'"

Thinking back on it now, Poshard says this: "I didn't go to Washington to just sit and play it safe. I was involved in highly contentious issues, and I feel I learned to be a better citizen and legislator from every one of them."

With the flag-burning vote came an opponent, Jim Wham of Centralia, who ran on a third-party ticket. Public opinion on the flag-burning issue favored Poshard's opponent. When voters considered the entire picture, however, it was no contest. Poshard prevailed in the November election by a four-to-one margin.

CHAPTER 11

# Worth the Fight

As a veteran who served in Korea and received a meritorious service commendation, Poshard was a sought-after speaker at Memorial Day, Veterans Day, and Fourth of July celebrations. During his second term in congress, he was invited to be the keynote speaker at the POW-MIA ceremony at the Marion Veterans Hospital. As part of his remarks, he penned the following poem to honor America's veterans.

### *American Warriors*

*When the enemy was strong, you*
*Who protected freedom were stronger.*
*When evil government stood for so long, you*
*Who loved America stood longer.*
*When it seemed the madness of men would close the door on*
*Freedom's flickering light,*
*It was your courage which kept the candle aglow*
*Through liberty's darkness night.*

*You taught us faith, you taught us hope, you taught us to believe*
*That greatness lies in giving up ourselves*
*For the freedom we all receive.*
*You paid the price, you stood the test*
*In a hundred battles or more.*
*It is you to whom we owe the debt*
*For defending freedom's open door.*
*You are the patriots who stood with America's warriors of old,*
*To defend the right, to defeat the might of dictators brazen and bold.*
*You could have had the glory, you could have had the fame,*
*But you rejected it all.*
*You returned to your homes, you returned to your families*
*You had answered your nation's call.*
*"A job well done was enough, you said.*
*Besides, there were others,*
*Your comrades left for dead.*
*And you'd never rest easy until you could say*
*They're here now, where they belong, in the USA.*
*Welcome home is the final refrain*
*From a nation still grateful and free.*
*Warriors you were, and warriors you are*
*And warriors you will always be.*[1]

* * *

In a congressional committee hearing in the spring of 1992, Poshard learned about proposed legislation called "Small Business Technology Transfer (SBTT)." He immediately became interested. The proposed program partnered small companies with universities to deliver emerging technology to the marketplace. That's something that could be beneficial in a rural area like Southern Illinois with a research university like SIU. Jon Baron, counsel to the House committee, remembers that staff were looking for a House member to express passion about the idea. "He wanted to champion the bill," Baron said, remembering his working relationship with Poshard. "It needed a champion. You need someone who will take it on as their cause and move it forward."

Baron said the bill was the first major legislative initiative on which he worked. He learned from Poshard and his colleagues on the committee staff how to work through the process. In this case, that included Poshard and Baron walking to the Senate for meetings to deal with questions from key senators like Carl Levin and Warren Rudman. "The meetings were very successful," Baron said. "He [Poshard] did what it took."

Afterward, Poshard shared the credit, including acknowledging Baron by name in public remarks. "He was very generous in giving people credit," Baron said. The program has been reauthorized three times and in 2020 is a $450 million initiative reviewed favorably by entities such as the National Academies of Sciences. Baron said that as of November 2020, Illinois had received $146 million in grants.

"He was remarkably interested in substance of legislation and getting something done," Baron said of Poshard. "He focused on the details and the end results. . . . It was an important accomplishment at the time, and has become even more significant as the years have passed."[2]

Because of the favorable experience on the SBTT legislation, Baron followed Poshard's career from a distance, including his 1998 run for governor. "I admired his principled approach to politics, including refusing special interest and corporate money when he ran for governor. I learned so much working with Mr. Poshard, especially at such an early time in my career."

Delving into policy suited Poshard. He was as much at home in a debate as he is now looking out on the rolling hills at his farm that abuts the Shawnee National Forest. At each end of the workweek in Washington, however, he felt discomfort that fits with his unease in airplanes. On Mondays of congressional sessions, he drove to St. Louis or sometimes to Evansville, Indiana, for a flight that left about 8 A.M. A staff member picked him up at Reagan National Airport, so he would arrive at the Capitol by noon and make the first votes of the week. Sessions usually ended late on Thursday, when he repeated the process, traveling from Reagan National to St. Louis, often making a stop or two in his district before pulling in his driveway for a late dinner.

Poshard's insistence on making almost every vote and committee meeting added demands to an already tight schedule. He was determined to continue the near perfect voting record he established in the Illinois Senate, where he had cast the highest number of votes of anyone in his four and a half years there. Twice in his five terms in Congress, he was rewarded by *Roll Call*, the newspaper that covers the work of Congress, as one of six "workhorses not showhorses," who do their job, don't miss votes or committee meetings, and don't seek the limelight.[3] "There were times when it might have made more sense for me to have missed a vote to attend an important meeting in southern Illinois," he said. "But I believed my first responsibility was to make my views public and put my vote on the record."

Through Poshard's years shuttling back and forth to first Springfield and later Washington, D.C., his wife Jo was an elementary school teacher. Jo spent many evenings and weekends at political events in southern Illinois and worked numerous hours supporting their family and his career.

One of Jo's teaching jobs was at New Simpson Hill grade school in the unincorporated community of Tunnel Hill, known for its namesake railroad tunnel. In that role she became troubled by students who lacked appropriate coats and shoes in the winter. She and Glenn discussed the issue. Kids should have appropriate clothing, they agreed. Their solution was to direct the proceeds from Poshard's annual fundraising golf outing to establish a Coats for Kids fund.

Glenn and Jo worked with regional school superintendents, who notified teachers about the program. Teachers selected the students and took them shopping. At the checkout register, the teacher collected a bill that was forwarded to the regional superintendent, who arranged the payment. By empowering the teachers, the program was designed to elude politics. The shopping experience created a student-teacher bond. The coats helped students through the winter and sometimes generated self-esteem. One little boy, for example, fell for a pair of red cowboy boots that became an important part of his identity. "That was a program that started in Jo's classroom," Poshard said. "I'm very proud of her for that. We're grateful that labor unions picked up leadership of the program when I left office and continue it still today, nearly thirty-five years later. Thousands of poor children have received new coats and shoes as a result of that effort starting in her class."

Poshard's own classroom roots emerged, too. Community halls became his classroom. He regularly hosted town meetings throughout his district. On multiple issues, he arranged a series of meetings. In March and April of 1991, such meetings were in Mt. Vernon, Mound City, Centralia, Nashville, Vandalia, Carlyle, Du Quoin, Murphysboro, Shawneetown, Harrisburg, Metropolis, Vienna, Johnston City, Benton, Cairo, Anna, Elizabethtown, Golconda, Waterloo, and Sparta. "Getting ready for these town hall meetings meant I had to review a whole host of issues, both nationally and regionally. I never wanted to show up at a meeting and be unaware of local issues. Showing the people that you have a grasp of their concerns gives them a greater confidence in representative democracy, and I took that responsibility seriously."

Open meetings often attracted those with views different than Poshard's. Emotion-charged matters generally were considered opportunities by the congressman. On two issues, wilderness and gun control, Poshard said he felt meetings could have led to violence.

While explosive meetings on the Crime Bill would come later in 1994, the first series of meetings where emotions ran high were on the issue of wilderness designation of thousands of acres in the Shawnee National Forest. Here again, the benefits of public meetings far outweighed any concerns Poshard had about his personal safety. "I looked at every town hall as a classroom," Poshard said. "I never took the attitude I had to change their minds. I wanted people to understand the issue, to see all sides, help them broaden their perspective, and if they disagreed with me, that was all right, too."

Divisive issues naturally are a part of the landscape for members of Congress. Rarely does a member choose to insert himself in emotional community controversy outside the federal government. Poshard, however, made a habit of it.

In 1991, schoolteachers in Harrisburg, a community of about 10,500 people, went on strike, a key issue being a hiring policy in which current teachers were guaranteed to fill any vacancies, provided they were legally certified for the position. As the strike progressed for weeks and then more than a month, the community became increasingly divided. Friends and neighbors took contrary sides. Emotions ran high. Poshard offered to arbitrate a settlement. The school board initially declined. Under pressure, the board relented, inviting Poshard and regional school superintendent John Wilson to mediate.

The mediators kept negotiators at the table overnight on a weekend, helping to piece together a compromise that ended a twenty-seven-day strike.[4] "It wasn't a perfect compromise—no plan ever is—but it was better than going into a second month of the schools being closed," said Poshard. For his part, Poshard said he considers one of his strengths being able to help solve conflict and find common ground that bridges differences. "Why wouldn't I use that and try to be helpful? I saw it as part of my job."

Nationally, a dominant issue in 1991 was America's role in Iraq and Kuwait. Poshard hosted a roundtable discussion at John A Logan College in early January specific to the Persian Gulf crisis.[5] He said a threat to national security may have existed, but he favored giving sanctions against Iraq more time before considering offensive military action. "It seemed there was a rush to find evidence that Iraq had weapons of mass destruction, and while I had the greatest respect for Colin Powell, the briefings we received in Congress left me and many of my colleagues unconvinced."

Poshard opposed a resolution authorizing President Bush to use military force, but the resolution passed. "While I admired President George H. W. Bush, that's one of the things I broke with him on," Poshard said. "I became convinced that sanctions would work."

On the domestic front, Speaker Thomas Foley appointed Poshard to the Public Works and Transportation Committee, an assignment he welcomed. A voice on that committee helped Poshard promote public works projects and have a hand in crafting the six-year national transportation plan. Southern Illinois received millions as a result of Poshard's work, including money to complete making Illinois Route 13 four lanes from Marion to Harrisburg.[6] The other biggest regional pieces were an upgrade of Illinois Route 1, a railroad overpass in Du Quoin, an interstate interchange in Metro East, and an upgrade of Feather Trail Road near Olmsted. Poshard recalled that he had a scheduling conflict and missed the ribbon cutting for the Route 13 project but that Governor Jim Edgar made a point of recognizing the congressman and the federal role in the improvement. "Edgar was good that way in giving credit whether or not the receiver was a Republican or a Democrat."

The federal budget also included $23 million that Poshard promoted for a new outpatient clinic at the VA Medical Center in Marion.[7]

"We have a growing number of veterans who need a wide range of medical services," Poshard said at the time. "I see this as an important step forward in providing health care for the men and women who have answered the call of duty and served us so well in our time of need."

Among the highlights of Poshard's second term was a meeting with Jim Brady, the former press secretary to President Reagan who was shot in a 1981 assassination attempt on the president. Brady, whose hometown of Centralia was in Poshard's district, became an advocate for handgun control. "I liked Jim Brady and had a good meeting with him," Poshard said. "As time went on, I had become more and more uncomfortable with the NRA's all-or-nothing position on every Second Amendment issue, but for the moment I couldn't support his bill."

Politically, 1991 was the year that former Arkansas governor Bill Clinton emerged as the Democratic nominee for president. Clinton attended a fundraiser in Carbondale shortly before formally announcing his candidacy, which Poshard supported. "I was for him from the beginning and had worked closely with him on the Lower Mississippi Delta Development Commission. He had a brilliant mind for problem-solving, and I liked that in a presidential candidate."

In Illinois, Senator Alan Dixon faced a challenge from Cook County recorder of deeds Carol Moseley-Braun, whose bid was to become the first African American woman in the upper chamber. Poshard met and liked Braun, but he favored Dixon with whom he had worked well over many years.

"Alan Dixon was someone I admired tremendously. He would delve into things you were trying to get done for your district. He wasn't afraid to get his hands dirty supporting your efforts for sewer or water or transportation projects. His door was always open. He was focused on Illinois, and being a downstater, he focused on central and southern Illinois." But Dixon's vote to confirm Clarence Thomas as a Supreme Court justice put him at odds with enough Democratic primary voters to propel Braun's upset victory. Poshard would miss Dixon, but as he concluded his third year in Congress in 1991, all seemed well. Too well, really. In politics, quiet isn't necessarily good. Often it means an unexpected challenge awaits.

The 1990 Census meant Illinois would lose two of its twenty-two congressional seats. Since Illinois became a state in 1818, the far southern region had always had a district. The early proposals Poshard saw retained that tradition. He should do well in any southern Illinois configuration.

In an instant, however, things changed. Via a roll of dice, Republicans won the decisive slot on the commission that would draw the new congressional district boundaries.[8] They put forth a plan that created a new minority majority district in the Chicago area but divided southern Illinois into pieces of three districts. Much of Poshard's district and his home would become part of a district also represented by Jerry Costello of Belleville. Another slice of Poshard territory became incorporated into a district represented by Dick Durbin of Springfield. The remaining counties were folded into a geographic monster that stretched nearly two hundred miles north. The incumbent in that district was Terry Bruce of Olney.

Poshard was, essentially, without a district, and no good option. Southern Illinois residents fought the initiative through a petition drive, the court system, and a public relations campaign. But a federal judge approved the Republican plan. Quietly, Poshard was encouraged to seek the vacant chancellor position at Southern Illinois University and to allow the other three incumbents to retain their seats. Not a bad idea, but not what he wanted.

"Senator Dixon called me twice and told me he would be supportive if I wanted to pursue the chancellor's job at SIU and encouraged me to do so." Poshard's wife Jo remembers the call from Senator Simon encouraging Poshard to do the same. Poshard recalls, "No one wanted a primary. Durbin, Costello, and Bruce were all excellent congressmen, and the party didn't want to lose any of its members, including me, but I was the least senior member and was more expendable. That's just politics."

He talked with friends in the Metro East area, a part of which he had represented in the past three years. They expressed their appreciation for his service, they liked him, but they could not support him against Costello. The district designed for Durbin wasn't viable, either. That left the only option as the new Nineteenth. The northern part of the district, the most populous, had no incumbent but was closer to Bruce's southeastern Illinois home in Olney. Poshard would have to start from scratch, introduce himself to central Illinois party and community leaders, and sell the argument he could represent their interests while living three hours away.

Poshard took his time. This was a career-altering decision. He said he would announce his decision at a press conference on November 23. The night before his announcement, he still hadn't finalized his decision. He didn't want to leave Congress. In his analysis, the only window to victory rested in the new Nineteenth District, but it was an uphill battle. The question became, is it worth the fight? With Jo upstairs, Poshard, alone in his basement, turned to a familiar method to sort through his thoughts. Quietly, he read to himself the Robert Frost poem, "Reluctance."

This beautiful poem describes a life of exploration and risk-taking, leaving the safety of home, and climbing the hills of view to look at the world. But time and circumstances take their toll on life, and while the heart aches to go on, to finish its course, the question becomes whether it's time for reason to prevail and end the quest. In the end, the heart prevails, reckoning that no matter what reason says, it would be treasonous to "go with the drift of things" and just "accept the end of a love or a season." Everyone said to me, "Be reasonable; there are other opportunities." But it wasn't where my heart was. I had to finish the race.

CHAPTER 12

# Redistricting and a New Constituency

"You are entering a war zone." The big, bold letters on a billboard were Poshard's introduction to Decatur, Illinois, as he arrived at the intersection of Illinois Route 121 and US Route 36 in late 1991. Decatur was the biggest city in the nineteenth congressional district and the farthest north, with a population at that time of 85,424. This trip marked the congressman's first impression of a community vital to his political future.

Decatur is about 180 miles north of Poshard's former Carterville home with no direct highway route. It sits amid a collection of five central Illinois communities with distinct identities. To the east is Champaign-Urbana and the University of Illinois, a Big Ten, research-based land grant university. To the west is Springfield, the seat of state government. To the north is Bloomington-Normal, corporate home of State Farm and Country Financial insurance companies. To the north and west is Peoria, at that time the corporate home of Fortune 100 heavy-equipment manufacturer Caterpillar.

Decatur blends corporate America, manufacturing, organized labor, race relations, and agriculture production into a mix that once led to the slogan "Pride of the Prairie." In 1991 it was the headquarters of Archer Daniels Midland Company (ADM), a global, agribusiness giant that called itself the "supermarket to the world." ADM housed a fleet of jets at the Decatur airport to shuttle executives around the country and across the globe. Its chairman at the time, the late Dwayne Andreas, had a Rolodex that included presidents, prime ministers, and numerous celebrities.

Down the street from ADM headquarters was a massive production facility where Caterpillar made heavy mining equipment. Around the corner was a block-long red brick production facility that produced Firestone Tires. Decatur was the home of the A. E. Staley corn processing plant, owned by British multinational corporation Tate and Lyle.

The billboards referred to labor unrest that rocked the Decatur economy and its psyche. In 1991, Caterpillar workers represented by the United Auto Workers were on strike. The company used management employees to continue production and threatened to replace the entire unionized workforce. There was labor unrest at Firestone that was the precursor to a strike in which the company immediately began hiring replacement workers. In time, the Decatur Firestone plant became history. Tate and Lyle locked out more than seven hundred workers in 1993 in a bitter labor dispute.[1] Estimates were that a quarter of Decatur's blue-collar workforce was on strike or locked out in the early to mid-1990s.

Poshard remembers another issue from his initial visits to Decatur. Leaders were looking for ways to address excessive high school dropout rates, particularly among African Americans, who represented more than 20 percent of the city's population. "I met with Mayor Terry Howley. I asked him what he considered to be the most important problems facing the city. I expected him to dwell on the strike and lockout situation affecting the plants, but his greatest concern was the dropout rate of the city's high school population, especially young black men. He said the labor situation would resolve itself in time, but recovering those young lives would be a much more difficult task and weigh more heavily on the city's future. I was impressed with his compassion for his city's youth."

To Poshard, the names and faces were new. The issues were not. He had experienced volatile labor issues between coal companies and mine workers. He had flown to London to face a British corporation in the early stages of the Olmsted Lock and Dam project. He experienced violent, emotional, community-changing race relations in Cairo. The difference now was he entered as an outsider who must quickly show he could be effective helping to forge solutions to community-changing issues.

His first and perhaps most important move involved his staff. Poshard's son Dennis was working in Springfield for state Senate president Phil Rock. The combination of Dennis's experience in Springfield, his knowledge of southern Illinois, and his father made him a fit for campaign chairman. Dennis lived in Springfield but spent sixteen-hour days in Decatur and began working to establish relationships with party and community leaders in the north end of the district, knocking on doors, attending meetings, and working to understand the community.

Dennis started with the fundamentals. He and his father met every precinct committeeman. They met with elected Democrats. They met city officials, economic developers, and industrial leaders. They eyed potential opportunities like Republicans who might cross over in the primary. "There were so many nights when the snow was deep on the ground, that we would be walking streets in Decatur with our flashlights trying to find a committeeman's house," Poshard said. "We worked as late as we could, knocking on doors, and would then go back to the headquarters and work until midnight. The streets were deserted when we would finally walk a few blocks to the parking garage, and I'd stand there and watch my son drive off into the night, my heart filled with love and gratitude for this unique experience God had given us together."

Dennis set and arranged the schedule for his father's trips to the area. He helped devise and then update the campaign message. His intimate knowledge of his father's career was helpful. Poshard's education background served him well, too. It fostered an attitude of learning about the new district. Yes, time was short, just a few months of primary campaigning. But Poshard balanced the temptation to be pushy with caution to focus on showing that he cared and would listen. He sought to cultivate a kinship that showed values consistent with the issues most important in Macon County. He remembers at a joint appearance with Terry Bruce at a union meeting, his son advised at an important moment that Poshard show overall restraint and respect for those leading the meeting. His political savvy paid off, and Poshard left the meeting with many new supporters.

Politically, the Decatur area was new territory for Bruce, too, as were neighboring communities like Mattoon, Charleston, and Shelbyville. Overall the Nineteenth District strongly favored a Democrat winning in November, so most people considered the March primary between Poshard and Bruce equal to the election. But many of the new areas near Decatur in central Illinois were Republican. A question arose, would many or any Republicans choose a Democratic primary ballot to have a voice in the congressional race?

As incumbents, Poshard and Bruce quickly entered campaign mode with developed themes. Poshard emphasized fiscal responsibility, his pay-as-you-go approach, support for universal health care and fair wages, and his opposition to use of the congressional frank to mail newsletters. Poshard's socially conservative views resonated with many of the region's Republicans, but some questioned how it would play in a Democratic primary.

Poshard criticized Bruce for "not voting with us," on Clean Air Act amendments in 1990 and for taking a campaign contribution from the Pittston Coal Company, which had locked out their workers. Bruce said he worked to soften the act's impact on coal mining jobs and to preserve as many jobs as possible, since he had known the Clean Air Act would pass.[2]

Bruce criticized Poshard for voting for the 1990 budget compromise that included a gasoline tax increase. Bruce said Poshard's vote contributed to a national recession. Poshard countered that the budget agreement included significant transportation and other projects that Bruce took credit for but was unwilling to pass the revenues to pay for them. "You can't have it both ways," Poshard said.

One debate, with no live audience, was made available on public television stations. The candidates made a few joint appearances such as a forum in Carmi and a union meeting in Decatur, but mostly they led separate schedules. Bruce had more than $700,000 in his campaign fund, while Poshard, who refused to take PAC monies, had less than $50,000.[3] Despite Bruce's enormous financial advantage, Poshard raised enough for some advertising along with political staples like flyers and yard signs. He carried with him considerable support from his southern Illinois base.

"When there was a parade somewhere in the northern end of the district, hundreds of people would drive the nearly two hundred miles to be there and carry signs and spend the day knocking on doors," Poshard said. "Our volunteers were completely motivated, and my son had every day organized to take full advantage of their energy. We were never at a loss for volunteers."

Poshard received key endorsements along the way, including from George Shipley, a former congressman who had represented much of the area. But he didn't get the support of the Illinois Education Association, an organization in which Bruce's brother Ken played a lead role.

As the campaign ended, several Macon County Democratic leaders drove to Benton in southern Illinois and formally endorsed Poshard. The group included auditor Dave Sapp, county clerk Steve Bean, sheriff Lee Holsapple, coroner Chris Vallas, and township supervisor Clara Mann, along with several county and township board members. Sapp told the cheering crowd, "You take care of Glenn down here, and we'll take care of him up there."[4]

Poshard later recalled, "That meeting in Benton was the moment our campaign caught fire. The atmosphere was electric. We knew our base in southern Illinois would turn out, but the district was so huge that the people down south didn't know if we could get support from central Illinois, where the greatest population lived. Those endorsements proved we had strength across the district, and our base redoubled its efforts to turn out the vote."

Poshard's path to victory was to win at least 65 percent of the votes in the far southern counties. He needed nearly 40 percent of the votes in the counties where Bruce was the incumbent and 42 percent in the northern counties, which were new to both candidates.

As returns came in, Poshard exceeded his plan in every area. In the southern portion of the district, he received more than 90 percent of the vote in some counties. He held his own in the counties that had been represented by Bruce, getting nearly 45 percent in Bruce's home county of Richland. In the northern counties, Poshard got almost exactly the number of votes his plan called for.

It was an impressive victory, with Poshard getting 62 percent of the vote overall. "My base turned out so much more heavily than Terry's," Poshard said. "For the most part, Macon County endorsed me. We didn't win that county, but because of my son, the way he worked and got to know people, we got a whole lot more votes there than we thought we could get."

Poshard faced Doug Lee, a thirty-year-old Decatur lawyer and political newcomer, in the general election. This time Poshard entered as a heavy favorite. Lee anticipated struggling in the southern part of the district. The counties Bruce had represented trended Democratic. And even in his home area of Macon County, Lee was little known.

Poshard cruised to victory with two-thirds of the vote.[5] Just a few months before, he had received the call from his friends Senators Dixon and Simon. He had been tempted to take their advice about the job at SIU, but his gut told him he could win the primary. People in southern Illinois deserved a congressman who knew their issues, he thought. He was confident he could fairly represent central Illinois, too.

There was much work ahead. It wouldn't be easy. But for a moment, just a moment, he could say to himself, "It was a hard fight, but it was worth it."

Typically, the final days of a campaign are a time to make last appeals to voters while ensuring a strong "get out the vote" effort within his organization. Yet as the campaign concluded, Poshard turned his attention elsewhere. As a youth he learned to support neighbors in need. He understood the importance of physical presence to support grieving friends and neighbors. As important as the election was, there was a more important calling. On the Saturday before the election, a big story regionally and nationally was the October slayings by rebels in Liberia of five Catholic nuns from southern Illinois.[6]

One of the five, Kathleen McGuire, was from Ridgeway, a community of about nine hundred people near Poshard's home area. That the Poshards had known the McGuire family for years personalized for Poshard the violent death of the nuns who were senselessly ambushed and shot. Poshard's focus turned to support the grief of his friends and neighbors. He remembered, "They were in Liberia because they felt called to care for the poor and neglected in that country. They were doing what God calls every person of faith to do: to serve and not to be served. Their convent in Ruma served many people from my district."

On election night, Poshard, a Baptist, attended a memorial service for McGuire at her home Catholic parish. "I was so shocked and saddened by their deaths, the campaign became secondary to me. I attended a memorial service for Sister Kathleen at a country parish outside Ridgeway. It was more important to me to be there in memory of her than to be at the campaign headquarters to await the early returns. Her death put a lot of things in perspective for me. Winning the election was important, but it wasn't everything."

CHAPTER 13

# Welcoming Central Illinois

It's 6 A.M. on a weekday. Glenn Poshard walks into a rural Macon County diner, planning to meet some of his new constituents as their newly elected congressman. He's casually dressed, fit, and neat in his five-foot-ten-inch frame. Some eight to ten farmers gather at a circular wooden table, enjoying their eggs, toast, and coffee. Poshard sits alone and orders his breakfast, opening his ears to the farmers' conversation.

From what he hears, Poshard easily knows he's in the new, northernmost part of his district. The numbers he hears tell that story. The farmers are negative about their crops, because corn yields are only about two hundred bushels an acre this year. The congressman bites hard on his tongue as he considers their conversation.

"Listening to those farmers, my memory went back to my teenage years in the late fifties when dad and I were farming 120 acres of red clay along the Wabash River. It took us all spring to get the crop out, and then we prayed for fifty bushels an acre come fall." These farmers enjoy better equipment, better seed, and rich, black dirt, among the most fertile in the world. Soil like that found in Macon County results in yields that led to 2017 exports valued by the Department of Agriculture at $21.6 billion for soybeans and $9.1 billion in corn.[1]

As he learns more details about issues in central Illinois, Poshard is at home talking with city and economic development leaders, labor unions, teachers, and others. Central Illinois and the problems there would become as familiar to Poshard as those in southern Illinois.

In the heart of the corn belt, ethanol is an oversized ag issue. Ethanol is a blended fuel that increases the domestic market for corn and thus helps drive the price and farm income. Midwesterners contend that it's better for the environment to be able to rely on renewable United States agriculture for fuel rather than Middle Eastern oil. In the congressional session of 1993, Midwest lawmakers, including Poshard, pushed for additional markets in nine major cities that would add market share and value to ethanol. "Congressman Durbin led the fight for federal support for increased production of ethanol. I joined him. It was a win-win situation in our eyes: a new market for agriculture, a cleaner-burning fuel, less dependence on foreign energy sources. The Nineteenth was a large agricultural district, and the farm community needed this support. Today, ethanol is less heralded as the savior of agriculture and has more environmental and economic critics, but it's still an important part of our agriculture economy."

In most of southern Illinois, Poshard needs no introduction. In Macon County, he's the new guy out to show that he won't allow distance from his home to prevent him from providing personal service throughout the district. He knows he has a lot to prove. In central Illinois, a majority of his new constituents in rural areas are Republicans. They know southern Illinois as a great place to hunt and fish, to visit for its beauty, but not necessarily for political representation. Poshard feels his views on budget discipline, infrastructure development, and social conservatism will work well. He hopes, too, that his constituent service will earn people's trust and support.

In the new Nineteenth District, Poshard often deplanes in St. Louis on a Thursday evening and has a staffer drive him to Decatur or Mattoon or Effingham, hubs of the territory he hasn't previously represented. He hosts meetings in the area on Friday and Saturday, staying in a hotel. By Saturday night, he heads home in a two- to three-hour drive to Marion, where he had to move to reside in the new district, only a few miles from his former Carterville home. He will spend a night at home and have Sunday for activities in the southern part of the district.

He signed up for the job, but sometimes the district's scope seems overwhelming. Once, while in Washington, he bemoaned the challenge of effectively covering so much territory. Across from him at the lunch table was his friend Pat Williams, the only congressman in Montana, who explained that his district covers 147,164 square miles, the equivalent of putting one corner in Chicago and the other in Washington, D.C. "I didn't complain anymore after that," Poshard now says.

In many ways, the formula Poshard deployed in the larger Nineteenth District mirrored the one used in his first four years in Congress. He set out an aggressive schedule of town meetings. In February the schedule included Fairfield, Mt. Carmel, Lawrenceville, Sullivan, Decatur, Shelbyville, Mattoon, Toledo, Marshall, Robinson, Effingham, Newton, Olney, Flora, Albion, and McLeansboro; in May he was in Westfield, Neoga, West Salem, Allendale, Cisne, Mt. Zion, Pana, Moweaqua, Bethany, Lawrenceville, Flat Rock, Noble, Louisville, and Teutopolis. In July he held meetings in Vienna, Herrin, Junction, Harrisburg, Elizabethtown, Golconda, Metropolis, Mound City, West Frankfort, Grayville, and Dahlgren. Those meetings were in addition to NAFTA town hall meetings in Fairfield, Carmi, Johnston City, Harrisburg, Ullin, Martinsville, Effingham, and Decatur and highway announcements in Decatur, Olney, Lawrenceville, Robinson, and Harrisburg. He also hosted budget meetings in Robinson, Mattoon, Decatur, Mt. Carmel, Olney, and Harrisburg. Poshard said getting out to see constituents is an opportunity to learn from them and to educate them on issues and his perspectives.

To effectively and efficiently work with and help constituents, Poshard relied on staff led by Judy Hampton. "I remember the first piece of advice I received after my appointment to the state Senate in August 1984. It came from Senator Vince Demuzio, who would become one of my closest friends over the next many years. He said, 'Nothing you do up here will be as important as what you do back home to take care of your people. Hire the best person you can find to get that job done.' I found Vince's words to be true, not only for the state Senate but for the U.S. Congress.

"The person I hired for that 'most important job' was Judy Hampton. Judy had been the former assessor for Williamson County and was working as an assistant to Senator Gene Johns before his passing. She had excellent administrative skills, knew the Senate district well, and was completely trustworthy. Judy was district manager from my first day in the Senate until my last day in Congress. We hired staff who were competent, lived throughout the thirty-nine counties I represented, and well-trained in excellent constituent service. The staff worked hard to help every person who walked into our offices. Every piece of correspondence required a response within three days. There was only one iron-clad rule—we never asked anyone their politics. Judy enforced that rule religiously. We were there to serve all the people whether they voted for us or against us. Politics ended at the office door.

"I followed Senator Demuzio's advice from the Senate to Congress and to SIU. You're only as good as your staff, and I will always feel I had the best."

Hampton was among a group of former staffers who gathered in a conference room at John A. Logan College to discuss this book. Joining her were Betty Davis, Jim Kirkpatrick, Pat Dawson, and Regina Dunbar Hendrickson. They remember seeing Poshard agonize over issues ranging from flag burning to a local water problem. Often, they quickly rearranged the schedule so he could address an emerging concern. They remember that relaxation for Poshard might be enjoying some popcorn and a baseball game.[2]

Staff members also saw firsthand Jo Poshard's commitment. One visible example came each summer, when Jo spent time in Washington. Congressional offices were allotted a number of White House visits. With Jo taking time to have a daily presence, she escorted guests from the Nineteenth District on tours through the White House and the Capitol with the added benefit of their getting to spend time one on one with Jo.

Back in Washington, the nation and its lawmakers watched the transition in power to a new president, former Arkansas governor Bill Clinton. Poshard had worked closely with Clinton on the Lower Mississippi Delta Development Commission. Clinton had helped him add about twenty southern Illinois counties to the commission, all of which had been in Poshard's former congressional district. Both Clinton and Poshard considered themselves centrists seeking practical solutions to sometimes complex issues.

Poshard responded in part to President Clinton's first State of the Union address with these words: "He talked about real action on this deficit problem, and we've all known for a number of years that we've got to put this government on a pay-as-you-go basis. We've got to cut programs and spending, but we also must have the courage to pay for things when they're needed. I'm glad he took that approach—that's realistic—and if our children are going to have any future, then I think we have to go that direction."

Poshard was helped by reports such as one by *Congressional Quarterly* that ranked him fifteenth best among 263 House Democrats on the issues of cutting spending and reducing the deficit. In August 1993, Poshard supported controls on entitlement and discretionary spending along with cuts that he said included "truly tough choices." Citizens Against Government Waste ranked Poshard the top Illinois Democrat in support of spending cuts. The Concord Coalition, an organization founded by former Senators Paul Tsongas and Warren Rudman to educate Americans about the budget deficit's impact on future generations, cited Poshard on its House Honor Roll with a score of 83 percent on a report it titled "Tough Choices—Who Made Them . . . And Who Didn't."

In his years in Springfield and Washington, Poshard stayed close to his philosophy of a balanced budget and a pay-as-you-go government. "We shouldn't be afraid to support tax increases that cover the real needs of our people: health care, education, transportation, food security, military preparedness, et cetera, and I have certainly voted for my share of tax increases," he said. "On the other hand, we shouldn't be afraid to make the tough choices to control spending where it isn't needed. The Concord Coalition and other reports in the *Congressional Quarterly* consistently ranked me as one of those congressmen who fought for a balanced budget based on those principles. And when we finally achieved a balanced budget in the latter years of the Clinton administration and were no longer deficit spending and actually started paying down the nation's debt, I was grateful that I had played some small role in helping my country get there. It makes me sick today to see our government borrowing trillions of dollars to fund massive tax cuts for the wealthiest people in this country and putting the burden on future generations who will have to pay off those debts. It's a shameful practice."

In his second month representing the Nineteenth District, Poshard received calls about the labor tension at A. E. Staley in Decatur. Staley, a hundred-year-old American corporation, was now owned by the British conglomerate Tate and Lyle, which, in answer to stalled labor negotiations, had locked out union employees. Poshard's response was a three-page letter to the *Herald and Review* newspaper suggesting that a committee of four unbiased local leaders be formed to mediate a compromise settlement.[3] The union was favorable to the congressman's approach; the company rejected the offer, saying mediation had been unsuccessfully attempted. Poshard reflected on that time.

"Mayor Brechnitz and I tried in every way to bring the two sides together, but the company refused our overtures. I had twice now attempted to deal with British corporations, at Olmsted and Decatur, that came into my congressional district and tried to deal local unions a death blow. They literally tore up the contract of the union workers at Staley's and demanded concessions, and when the union wouldn't agree, they locked them out. In my judgment, it was ruthless and uncalled for."

A major national issue in 1993 was the North American Free Trade Agreement (NAFTA). Decatur-based ADM was a major supporter. Poshard was among a group of congressmen in opposition.

"About thirty of our House members who had real concerns about NAFTA kept trying to get a meeting with the Mexican trade representative who was responsible for negotiating the agreement for Mexico. We tried several times to meet with him in Washington, D.C., but he wouldn't meet with us. The way we viewed the treaty, raw materials would be extracted from America and sent to large auto parts plants built by American manufacturers on the Mexican side of the border, where they would be fashioned into automobiles and other products. Those products would be sent right back into this country to undercut the manufacturers who tried to stay here and pay American workers a decent wage to support their families while abiding by the environmental laws to protect our environment. We simply wanted the agreement to reflect as much of a level playing field as possible. Just pay the Mexican workers a living wage and don't fill the environment with manufacturing waste to poison the water and land.

"We couldn't get a meeting in D.C. with the trade representative, and those of us viewed as anti-NAFTA were kept out of important negotiating sessions. I represented Decatur, Illinois, home to the world's largest agribusiness, ADM. I got a call from a member of the Andreas family asking me to meet with their corporate leaders at their headquarters in Decatur on a Friday morning when I was in the district. I went there and, to my surprise, was greeted by the Mexican trade representative who would not meet with a whole group of U.S. congressmen in Washington but who happily was at the beck and call of ADM. The raw power of American corporate interests in shaping government policy was on full display."

Poshard voted against NAFTA, which was approved by the Congress and signed by President Clinton. In November 1994, Poshard backed the General Agreement on Tariffs and Trade (GATT), citing key differences between GATT and NAFTA. He said GATT was more diversified than NAFTA, which he considered a one-sided agreement detrimental to American labor. By contrast, Poshard said GATT spread the potential risks and rewards while lowering tariffs and reducing trade barriers around the world, not just in North America. Both agriculture and the coal industry supported GATT, including ADM and other major farm exporters.

Perhaps the most contentious, partisan battle of the early Clinton administration years involved health care reform. Poshard long supported a single-payer health system. He advocated over many years for health reforms that retained access to quality care with cost controls. Health care reform, Poshard said, was among the most partisan issues, to the detriment of consumers. He said countries around the world have proven the single-payer system delivers better health care results for substantially less money. But, he said, such a plan would never pass in the United States while lobbyists for insurance companies and pharmaceutical companies flex their considerable financial muscle. "If you have the economic wherewithal, you can get the best health care in the world in America. If you do not, you take what you can get. We have a completely bifurcated system of health care, and when you propose to change anything, you are accused of being socialist."

Poshard said every county in his district was cited as medically underserved by the federal government. Financial issues closed some rural hospitals, including one in Poshard's hometown of Carmi. In response, the Rural Health Care Caucus, which Poshard cochaired, helped pass legislation that attempted to encourage more providers to locate in rural areas and also promoted teleconferencing technology that allowed a specialist in a larger facility to consult with a rural provider on unique cases. One reform bill Poshard supported offered technical assistance grants for rural providers to coordinate services; incentives for providers to practice in rural areas; aid for community and migrant centers along with emergency room expansion; and relaxation of hospital antitrust laws and changes to medical school graduate programs to encourage primary care and rural-based education.

The most important legislation Poshard and the Rural Health Care Caucus sponsored was intended to designate rural hospitals as critical care providers, thus increasing their Medicare reimbursement rates and enabling more of them to survive. "Most hospitals in my district had a 75 percent or better Medicare and Medicaid patient load, and they were losing money on each patient," said Poshard. "The critical care designation upped the reimbursement for each of these patients and helped bring financial stability to many rural and inner-city hospitals." The system, however, retained many challenges, including transportation for pregnant women, many of whom had to be rushed to appropriate facilities by emergency helicopters.

In May 1994, Poshard received a personal note from President Clinton that said in part, "I appreciate your support for the single payer option included in the Health Security Act. As you know, I believe strongly that each state should have flexibility in implementing health care reform to meet the specific needs of its citizens. That is the reason why we included the single payer option for states in the Health Security Act. I look forward to working with you more closely to assure universal coverage for all citizens and flexibility for all states, as we move health reform through the legislative process."[4]

Throughout his district, Poshard hosted town meetings focused on health care. He tied the issue to quality of life, viability of small business, and overall economic health. He succeeded in helping obtain grants, such as $672,664 for the Christopher Rural Health Planning Corporation (Rea Clinic).[5] Larger national health care issues promoted by Clinton, however, would wait for another day.

In September 1993, President Clinton invited Poshard to a ceremony on the south lawn of the White House for the signing of the Israeli-Palestinian agreement. Clinton watched as PLO chairman Yassir Arafat and Israeli prime minister Yitzhak Rabin placed their names on the latest effort toward Middle East peace. The invitation to Poshard includes this excerpt from the Declaration of Principles on Interim Self-Government Arrangement: "it is time to put an end to decades of confrontation and conflict, recognize their mutual legitimate and political rights, and strive to live in peaceful co-existence and mutual dignity and security and achieve a just, lasting and comprehensive peace settlement and historic reconciliation through the agreed political process."[6] A front-row seat to history is welcome, and Poshard enjoyed working on foreign affairs. He knew, however, the folks back home would cast their ballot for a congressman whose focus was on everyday matters. (For more on community initiatives, see appendix A.)

The transition to the new district was going smoothly. He was working hard to meet the needs of his new constituents as well as those he had been serving for a number of years. He was maintaining a nearly perfect voting record in Congress and a perfect attendance record in his committees. *Roll Call* had again named him one of the workhorses of Congress.

As the 1994 Crime Bill developed, the Democrats in the House caucused to discuss the bill. Poshard remembers the meeting. "We met in a large basement meeting room in the Capitol. There were so many good things in the bill, including funding for a hundred thousand new policemen, a strong prevention program for violence against women, money to build prisons, and other crime-fighting measures. But, for those of us in very conservative areas, the assault weapons ban was an absolute poison pill. Tom Foley, the House Speaker, asked for a show of hands on who could support the bill with the assault weapons ban intact. I raised my hand. I knew my vote would be highly controversial in my district, but I had won reelection by a wide margin in 1992, and I had a strong record of supporting Second Amendment rights. I believed in my ability to explain my reasons and help my constituents understand the offsetting strengths of the bill, even though they may disagree with me. I was opposed to the federal assault weapons ban, but I didn't want the bill to fail because, on balance, I believed it was good for the country. In any case, we were told that President Clinton would agree to a separate vote on the crime bill with the assault weapons portion left out. The next day, a *Washington Post* article said that option was ruled out by the White House."

Poshard knew a core group of constituents would be furious. He returned home to a firestorm of criticism and a schedule of seventeen town hall meetings in which he defended the vote as the best possible legislation to address a serious problem. Some constituents placed a large picture of Poshard in the back of a pickup truck. Also in the truck bed was a spool of telephone wire. At each meeting, a crank was used to roll the wire around the spool, unveiling a moustache on Poshard that made him out to be infamous traitor Benedict Arnold.

Some of the meetings were so volatile that it was one of the few times in his career Poshard feared for his safety. Trucks lined parking lots of his capacity town halls. Many felt betrayed. "I voted for the bill and came home to town hall meetings with hundreds of people overflowing every meeting hall. I was always prepared for meetings because most people who show up are 'anti,' opposed to about any position you've taken, and you want to at least explain your vote and the reasoning behind it. But these meetings were emotionally charged. Before I could even begin, yells of 'Liar, Traitor, Benedict Arnold,' and other accusations and obscenities filled the rooms. I had to listen to stories of trainloads of Russian soldiers heading to Chicago to take over the city, of black helicopters flying over homes and harassing people. Charges that I had taken weapons away from regular citizens who would now not be able to defend themselves against such enemies, especially their own government, were made during the entire length of the meetings.

"After nearly two weeks of these town halls each night, I was exhausted. But more disappointing to me was the sense that I had failed to convince anyone of the bigger picture I was compelled to see as their congressman. I had to be satisfied that I had done my best to teach, to educate, and then leave my future in their hands."

A letter to the *Southern Illinoisan* newspaper published August 31, 1994, summed up the depth of anger Poshard faced on this issue. "There are certain things that I will tolerate. Communism is not one of them. Allow me, if you would, to take this opportunity to bid farewell to a longtime Southern Illinois political figure who has fallen into the clutches of the old red dragon of communism."[7] The letter, by Scott Clem, described how the writer had happily volunteered in Poshard's last campaign and celebrated his victory. The crime bill vote changed everything. The letter ended with these words: "Goodbye, Congressman Poshard."

CHAPTER 14

# Trusting Only America

Late in 1995, Poshard was asked to join a fifteen-member congressional delegation proposed by President Clinton to ascertain what role America should play in the horrific civil war in Bosnia. The ensuing story is one he told often over many years. The delegation met December 1–4, 1995, with diplomatic and military leaders, including the presidents of Bosnia, Croatia, and Serbia The group flew seventeen hours from Washington to Belgrade to begin their mission. Poshard described how the group first met with Serbian president Slobodan Milosevic, whose army had systematically murdered tens of thousands of civilians because they were a different religion, a different ethnicity, or a different race.

"We sat in his government palace, surrounded by his armed guards, and to a person, all of us looked him in the eye and offered the same advice. 'Stop the ethnic cleansing in Bosnia and Croatia, or America will come after you.' I was very proud of our bipartisan delegation because we did, in that moment, what America is supposed to do when people are threatened with no just cause by bullies and dictators. President Reagan referred to America as the 'shining city on a hill.' This is not only who we are to the oppressed people of the world but who we must continue to be. When we cozy up to bullies, the rest of the world loses faith in us and loses hope for their own freedom. There is no compromise with the evil practices of the Milosevics, Putins, and Kim Jong-un's of the world. There is no gain great enough in our relationship with these kinds of dictators that is worth sacrificing the sacred position that America occupies in the international community."

The second stop was in Zagreb, Croatia, to meet with leader Franjo Tudman. A dinner meeting with the president and his staff involved discussion about Croatia's possible alignment with Bosnia against the Milosevic government and the extent of America's involvement in helping to bring peace to the region. After the breakup of Yugoslavia under Tito, Tudman had been a leader in forming an independent government in Croatia and very much opposed any Serbian interference in his country.

The third stop took the delegation to Sarajevo to meet Bosnian leader Alija Izetbegovic. "We flew in on an armored C-130," Poshard recalls, describing how he took the opportunity to ride in the jump seat behind the two young pilots and observed their defensive maneuvers to stay out of the range of gunfire on the plane's descent into the Sarajevo airport. "When we landed on the only runway still open, a gigantic earth-moving Caterpillar pulled up to the plane, and we walked behind its blade to our security detail. We were still wearing our flak jackets as we boarded the bus that would take us through the city. The Muslim security detail then took our delegation through what once was one of the most beautiful cities in the world, now with few standing buildings. We noticed people running out from burned-out basements and overturned railcars, people clapping. They knew some American congresspersons were in their city, and we were going to have something to say about their future. We kept imploring the guards to let us stop and talk to the people. Their reply was, 'The people won't talk to you; they're too scared.'

"At some point, the guards gave in, and the bus pulled into a square where the beautiful city library had recently burned. Hundreds were coming from side streets and alleys into the square as we got off the bus. In the crush of that crowd—I'll never forget it as long as I live—this one elderly gentleman with only a couple of teeth left in his head, grabbed me by the arm. He told me his last remaining brother had been killed in this square a month ago. 'My wife is gone. My children are gone.' He grabbed me and said, 'Do you not understand, we only trust America. We only trust America.'

"We went on and met with President Izetbegovic and his staff. We could hear mortar shells fired from the surrounding mountainsides going off in the city while we talked. Finally, we retraced our route to the airport, staying behind as many of the standing buildings as we could. We had to leave during daylight since there were no lights left on the runway.

"We stopped in Naples, Italy, and spent part of the next day with the commanding general of NATO forces in that region and then headed to Germany to meet with our troops who might be asked to intervene and stop the bloodshed. On the way to Germany, I finally understood the old man's words. He wasn't saying, 'We only trust America's military or economic strength to save us.' He was saying, 'We trust the experience of America.' He knew the story of our country, that people came from all over the world with different ethnic, religious, racial, and social backgrounds to form America, and for nearly 250 years, they had chosen to live with each other despite all of their differences. Not perfectly, and we still have a long way to go, but he knew the story of America, and he believed that if America could make it despite our differences, then maybe his country could make it, too."

That was the message Poshard brought home and shared with the president in the White House debriefing. He told the president, "The world relies on America, its diversity and its principles, to defeat our own worst impulses and those of autocratic leaders like Milosevic."

Upon his return home, Poshard hosted town meetings on Bosnia in Decatur, Mattoon, Effingham, and Herrin to help constituents understand a faraway war that otherwise was a few lines in the daily newspaper and a clip on the evening news. He described his two key questions: are the countries involved committed to peace, and will American troops be safe in enforcing a peace pact known as the Dayton agreement? In the summer of 1995, Poshard had opposed sending American troops, saying outside forces weren't the answer, but after his trip, he was quoted in a news release as saying, "I believe we are militarily prepared to accomplish this mission, and that the people of Serbia, Bosnia, and Croatia are ready for peace. America is in a position to lead in securing that peace, and I believe the troops being sent to attain that goal deserve our full support." A fact-finding trip to that war-torn part of the world had changed his mind about America's role there, and he publicly advocated for his country's involvement.

A staff member who helped put together the presentation on the Bosnian conflict was David Gillies, who was in his first week working with Poshard. Gillies, who led Poshard's legislative staff during his last four years in Congress, said he quickly learned of the typical Poshard approach. "He's learning, and he's always wanting to educate his constituency," said Gillies.[1]

The trip came near the end of Poshard's fourth term in Congress. He defeated challenger Brent Winters for a second time by a wide margin in the November 1996 election, securing a fifth and final term.

During his fourth term, Poshard joined the Republicans and their House majority on a few of their priorities, supporting term limits for the House Speaker, a one-third reduction in House staff, a limit on committees, and term limits for committee chairmanships. The support for reducing staff size was a way for Poshard to continue promoting spending cuts and a balanced budget amendment. "We owe it to our children and grandchildren to stop deficit spending and begin the process of paying off our debt," he said. "If we can't control our own spending in-house, how can we ever expect the agencies to reduce their staffs or enact efficiencies to control their spending?"

He called for applying $12 billion in budget cuts to deficit reduction rather than support tax breaks or have it transferred to other programs. "I've had twenty town meetings the last five Saturdays and not one person has shown up pleading for a tax break. Many have shown up to voice their opinion in favor of the balanced budget amendment and reducing the deficit."

A *Washington Post* editorial cited the ideas of the Blue Dog Democrats as the way for the Republican Congress and President Clinton to reconcile their differences. While not a member of the Blue Dog Democrat caucus, Poshard supported many of their fiscally conservative positions. But too many of the members held socially conservative views with which Poshard disagreed. For instance, he advocated for a much smaller tax cut than the Republicans and many of the Blue Dogs favored. He wanted to preserve more of the social safety net important to Democrats like himself who believed that Republican tax cuts were weighed much more favorably to the wealthy at the expense of helping the poor with basic necessities of food, health care, and education.

The Concord Coalition again recognized Poshard for votes to cut government spending and reduce the deficit. He was the only Illinois congressman and one of thirty overall to make the group's honor roll.[2]

In April 1995, Poshard was one of the primary sources for a *Los Angeles Times* report related to politics and the Christian Coalition.[3] In a floor speech, Poshard questioned whether the organization owned the "Christian" position on issues like welfare reform and family tax credits. He noted the Christian Coalition publishes scorecards that "almost always" align with Republican positions. "One could conclude, then, that Democrats are less Christian. What troubles me," he was quoted as saying in the April 10, 1995, article, "is when I see a particular position being portrayed as the Christian position and yet in my heart I feel, as someone who has shared this basic Christian culture all my life, that the position doesn't match up to my understanding of the Bible."

The article cites Poshard's floor speech as saying that God's response to the poor isn't a wild-eyed liberalism with a guilty conscience. "But neither do I believe that God's response to the poor is to treat them as though they are the least priority."

Poshard said he received multiple letters from the Christian Coalition regarding the related issues. Frequently he was at odds with Ralph Reed, the organization's leader. Poshard contended that while the country needed a balanced budget, it also needed investments that open doors of opportunity, especially to the lower economic classes in our country.

Gillies remembers a one-hour speech on the floor showing where tax dollars are spent. Another speech on welfare reform incorporated Poshard's reading of the Bible, with emphasis on welfare recipients. "He had great faith in government and what it can do for people," Gillies said. That was consistent with Poshard's emphasis on balancing the budget. "We were not going to consider tax cuts until we balanced the budget."[4]

On September 10, Poshard was among the Democrats to accompany President Clinton to Southern Illinois University for a speech on student financial aid in which the president proposed a $2,600 annual voucher for displaced workers to attend college, the very kind of educational opportunity Poshard supported wholeheartedly. A crowd estimated at more than fifteen thousand attended the president's speech.

"It was an important speech, and it was my honor to join Senator Simon and Congressmen Durbin and Costello in welcoming the president to Southern Illinois. It was a special occasion because arrangements were made for my entire family and staff to meet briefly with President Clinton before the rally began. They all checked through security, and while they were talking and taking pictures with the president, I noticed a woman in the room who was not part of our family. I assumed she was part of the security detail, and no longer paid attention to her during our visit.

"Later, as I was sitting on the stage with other speakers, I received an urgent request from the agent in charge of security to come immediately to the holding room where we had met with the president. I left the stage and was escorted to the area where security was detaining the woman I had observed earlier in the room with the president and my family. I was asked if she was a member of my family. I replied no, that I had never met her. They told me she had checked through the security line immediately behind the last member of my family and passed herself off as a member of our group. I was shocked because I had assumed she was a member of the security detail, and they had assumed she was a member of my family. Had this woman been there for nefarious reasons, this could have been a tragedy. I never learned what happened to her or if any consequence evolved from the situation.

"Before we returned to Washington on Air Force One, the 17th Street Bar and Grill in Murphysboro, Illinois, which had won many championship trophies in national competition for their incredible barbecue, delivered a large platter of their famous ribs to the plane. Senator Durbin, Congressman Costello, and I joined the president in eating every one of those ribs all the way back to D.C. It was the only time I had ever seen a president with barbecue sauce on his fingers and lips. If we had only had cell phone cameras back then."

Through the budget process, Poshard renewed his support for campaign finance reform. "What should matter most is a person's stand on the issues and their willingness to put in the time and effort to serve the people," he said.

The year 1995 included several recurring themes. At the start of the year, labor issues in Decatur made headlines. Bridgestone/Firestone hired permanent replacement workers in its labor dispute with the United Rubber Workers. Poshard helped arrange a meeting with union leaders and Department of Labor secretary Robert Reich who discussed the Decatur situation with local officials during a visit to Galesburg, Illinois.[5] The efforts to bring the parties together ultimately were unsuccessful, and the plant closed in 2001.

Poshard became cochairman, with Republican Steve Gunderson of Wisconsin, of the Rural Health Care Coalition, a group focused on access, quality, and affordability issues in rural areas. "Our Rural Health Care Coalition brought a lot of needed help to rural America," Poshard said. "Critical care access designation for our rural hospitals, mental health care services, and telemedicine were just a few of the improvements our bipartisan group got passed in the Congress. I was very proud of our efforts to work together across party lines. We made a difference and helped a lot of people."

Poshard's predecessor, Congressman Kenneth Gray, was known for making a difference as the "prince of pork" in deep southern Illinois. He served the area during the Great Society days of Lyndon Johnson, and the federal funds were flowing to build America's infrastructure anew. Interstates, roads, bridges, lakes, prisons, airports, locks and dams, post offices, courthouses, the golden age of higher education funding, and many other developments to make America the world economic leader were in progress during this time, and Gray knew how to bring federal dollars home to southern Illinois. He held an important leadership post on the Public Works and Infrastructure Committee in the House, and southern Illinois benefited greatly from his ability to help his district.

"Following Ken Gray, I always held in the back of my mind the need to bring important federal dollars back home to my district," Poshard said. "By the time I got to Congress in the late 1980s, the federal funds were drying up. The country was piling up a huge debt, and fiscal policies under Republican presidents Reagan and Bush were more constrained. And going into my third term, my congressional district stretched from Cairo to Decatur, with few of the traditional southern Illinois counties remaining in my district. But I was determined to bring home every available dollar I could find. I was haunted by the ghost of Ken Gray."

Gray also was known for a colorful wardrobe. He loved wearing suits in pastel colors. The difference between Gray's attire and Poshard's more conservative approach led to a memorable line Poshard used frequently and which often drew laughter. When Poshard started his term, he was in a reception line being introduced to House Speaker Jim Wright of Texas. As Poshard put out his hand saying he represented the Twenty-Second District in Illinois, Wright quipped, "Well, I'll be damned. I didn't know you could buy a black suit in southern Illinois."

While the money didn't flow as freely as it once did in the Great Society days of Johnson, the respect of his colleagues for his work ethic and his ability to articulate the needs of his district helped Poshard bring home more than his fair share of federal assistance. (For more details on district projects, see appendix B.) In doing so, he worked with many local and regional officials who advocated for the work. "It has been my honor to work with some of the greatest labor leaders of our time in southern and central Illinois," Poshard said. "Doc Allen, Dale Choate, Wes Cook, and Dee Stahlhut of the operating engineers; Gary Roan, Harvey Frey, Steve Hugart, and Paul Noble of the electrical workers; Bill Gouch of the bricklayers; Max Aud of the teamsters; Andy Prebell of the ironworkers; Ed Smith and John Penn of the laborers; Mimi Gentile, Skip Dempsey, Tommy Caliper, and Phil Koclane of the plumbers and pipefitters; and Dave Perko of the carpenters."

At the end of 1995, a budget impasse caused a temporary government shutdown. Republicans sought a $246 billion tax cut that was part of the Contract with America. Democrats favored a smaller tax cut to preserve funding for government functions. At a town hall meeting in Marion, Poshard faced nearly two hundred people, many of whose paychecks were delayed because of the impasse. Poshard quietly donated three months of his pay, what he could afford at the time, to provide interest-free loans to some of the impacted federal employees. "That was all I could do," he said of his frustration with the shutdown. "These were government workers who took care of our veterans at the Marion VA Hospital. I just wanted to show some solidarity with them. They didn't deserve a government shutdown."

From the time he first ran for Congress, Poshard established a personal term limit of five terms. He said he believed people who wanted to seek a congressional office should train themselves and engage in a career, leave that career for a time to serve in the national legislature, then return home and allow others with fresh ideas and experience to take their places. He felt the ability to raise money and the accoutrements of office, both of which come with more seniority, lead to a Congress whose members are compelled to hold onto power for as long as they can, whether they continue to be productive members or not. He is one of only a few people who set a personal limit on his service in Congress and kept it.

"The whole system is set up for incumbency protection, from the ability to raise money, gerrymandered districts to favor one party over another, free mailing privileges for incumbents, et cetera," Poshard said. "It's why challengers win less than 5 percent of the time. People aren't given a fair choice of their representation under the present system, so just saying that the people have the ability to change their representatives every two years if they want isn't true. The system doesn't allow it. As long as our election system remains the way it is, then I will favor a limit on the number of terms a congressperson should serve."

Increasingly, Poshard heard this question from the people of the Nineteenth District: What would he do when he left Congress?

CHAPTER 15

# Keeping a Promise

On a typical day while in Congress, as the Washington, D.C., sunrise uncovered the majesty of cherished national monuments, Poshard was already at his congressional office. That was a routine he began when first elected. He continued the practice in 1996 as he finished his fourth term and carried that work ethic into his fifth term in 1997. His small apartment near the Capitol and the used furnishings he purchased essentially served as a place to sleep. Most evenings, Poshard arrived at the apartment by 10 p.m. His routine was to have something to eat, watch the 11 p.m. news, then retire for the evening. By 6 a.m. he was in the House gym, getting in his morning exercise, and at 7 a.m. he was beginning the day in his congressional office, prepping for staff meetings, committee hearings, and related scheduled tasks.

Back in the district, Poshard's last congressional campaign was a rematch against Republican Brent Winters. Winters backed the Republican "Contract with America" and questioned Poshard's support for a balanced budget. But his campaign never gained traction. Poshard won a fifth term with over 60 percent of the vote.[1] Poshard was endorsed by media throughout the district. "A tireless, articulate man, Glenn Poshard literally works night and day trying to help solve problems for his constituents," wrote Bill Hamel in the *Mattoon Journal Gazette.* "He is one in a million."[2]

Wrote the *Decatur Herald and Review*: "Poshard has been, and will continue to be, a legislator who places the needs of his district above all else."[3]

In January 1996, a focus was on competing plans to balance the federal budget. Poshard was one of about two dozen moderate Democrats who met with President Clinton, advocating for lower tax cuts and more protection for Medicare. The spending plan ultimately approved was a compromise that included money for black lung clinics and a 2 percent increase in veterans' health care. For his part, Poshard returned to the treasury unspent funds allowed for his offices. From 1989 to 1995, the amount totaled $1.2 million.[4]

The ongoing protests over the cleanup of Crab Orchard Lake continued into September 1996, with protestors rallying outside Poshard's office against the incineration of contaminated soil at the Crab Orchard National Wildlife Refuge. "Poshard believes everything the EPA tells him," they contended. He repeated his assessment of the importance of completing the work in a timely fashion while it was front and center on the EPA agenda. "As I had indicated on many different occasions, I felt incineration was safe, and I didn't want to risk EPA dropping the project from their priority list and perhaps never getting the cleanup completed. We went ahead with the project; it got cleaned up, and it was safe."

In his town meetings, Poshard said it was the most partisan time he had ever known. Of the seventy-five new members brought in by the Gingrich revolution in 1994, many took the approach "It's my way or no way." Poshard said it was almost unbelievable to see these people stand up and say, 'I'm not wrong; I'm always right.'"

As Poshard sees it today, "1994 was the beginning of gridlock in Congress, and it continues until this day with the Tea Party/Freedom Caucus making it impossible for Republican leadership to lead their caucus. Just ask John Boehner and Paul Ryan how difficult their jobs were trying to please people who won't compromise to find middle ground on any issue. Nancy Pelosi is now experiencing much of the same situation with ultraliberal members of her caucus."

At that same meeting in West Frankfort, Poshard praised President Clinton for reducing the deficit from $300 billion to $160 billion. "Democrats always get blamed for being big spenders, but under Clinton's leadership the deficit was entirely eliminated, and we were paying down the national debt."

Poshard hosted his first electronic town hall meeting at Lake Land College in Mattoon, speaking to an interactive network that simultaneously connected him to seven communities.[5] In another town meeting, he broke down where federal revenues were spent by category. Another series of meetings focused on the impact of the Farm Bill. In other meetings he discussed legislation he cosponsored to establish a new system of national trails.

Poshard was one of the dignitaries celebrating the groundbreaking of the Olmsted Locks and Dams project. In the news release dated April 19, 1996, Martin Lancaster, assistant secretary of the Army, is quoted as saying, "While there has been broad based political support for this project, let me congratulate and pay specific commendation to Congressman Glenn Poshard, who has devoted literally hundreds of hours to the Olmsted project and has tenaciously kept this project on track legislatively, all the while insisting on maximum local participation. Without the consistent and persistent efforts on behalf of local workers by Congressman Poshard, we might not have the same sense of optimism and bright view of the future which is evident today as we break ground on the Olmsted project."[6]

Poshard remembers those years of work. "It was the most significant and largest federal inland waterways project in the entire country, and it was in my district, and I wasn't going to let it fail. Ed Smith, the Southern Illinois Laborers' leader, and I worked nearly ten years on this project to bring it to fruition. It was one of the highlights of my career to attend the opening last year with my good friends Senator Durbin and Ed Smith and recall how many thousands of good-paying jobs and increased economic activity the locks and dam brought to one of the poorest regions of our state."

In the never-ending controversies surrounding the Shawnee National Forest, Poshard backed legislation that prevented below-cost timber sales by the U.S. Forest Service. Over objections from environmentalists, he succeeded in clarifying that the Forest Service could remove pine trees so as to allow reforestation of hardwoods that were native to the area.

At about the same time, Poshard was among about forty House Democrats who led an effort to recognize their pro-life position as Bill Clinton sought reelection to the presidency. The group accepted the fact that a majority of Democrats supported the pro-choice position. Their objective was to ask the party to acknowledge a significant number of Democrats with a contrary view.

"We are faithful to the party and will continue to be," Poshard said. "This is not an adversarial position that we're taking at all. But the Democratic party should acknowledge that millions of Democrats who have made great contributions to this party over all the years of their political or public life also ought to be recognized as having a conscience on this issue that they consider every bit as valid as the conscience of the pro-choice majority."

In explaining his personal position on this issue, Poshard gave a lengthy speech on the House floor. He had been brought up in a family and a faith that felt strongly in favor of the pro-life position. "I struggled with this issue as a public servant. How much should one's personal faith inform his public position? When one holds such a position consistent with their faith, many who hold the same view expect you to speak out forcefully in favor of your position. That wasn't me. I am not by nature a confrontationalist, and I held the highest respect for members of both political parties. I never proselytized others with my views on pro-life. I voted my conscience and tried to stay consistent with my family and my faith on this issue."

In January 1996, Poshard arranged for Jesse Jackson Jr., who was in his first congressional term at age thirty, to appear at a Democratic fundraiser in Decatur. The invitation was a way to help Jackson reach beyond his Chicago roots in his young, promising political career.[7] "I felt at the time that Congressman Jackson had a great future ahead of him, and I wanted to try to help him in any way I could," said Poshard.

Congress, in 1996, considered workplace protections for lesbian, gay, bisexual, and transgender (LGBT) people, extending federal civil rights protection in the workplace. Poshard's position was one he later changed, after significant internal debate over many years. He said he learned more about the issue in later years and that it worked against him when he ran for statewide office.

"When I went to Congress in 1988, over thirty years ago, many questions about the LGBT community, which have been settled since that time, were rarely being discussed in positive tones even among leaders in my own party. Same-sex marriage and the HIV crisis were among them. Coming from the most conservative end of the state and never having run statewide before my race for governor in 1998, I was ill-prepared on this issue. I think that had I followed Christ's teaching on love more closely, I would not have made some of the votes I made in Congress. It wasn't until I became vice chancellor of administration at SIU Carbondale in 1999 and came into contact daily with students struggling with their sexual identity, that I had the conversations I needed to learn and understand the needs of the LGBT community. One of my closest friends during this period of time was a woman named Paulette Curkin, a leader on the SIUC campus, who took the time and had the patience to help me see the need for love and respect for this vulnerable community. I will forever be indebted to Paulette for her friendship and teaching she shared with me."

Poshard also found himself involved in another labor dispute. Trailmobile locked out employees at its Charleston, Illinois, plant. As the bitter dispute persisted, Poshard joined Charleston mayor Dan Cougill in bringing the parties back to the negotiating table. In June 1996, Poshard and Cougill mediated a twenty-hour bargaining session. Union members rejected that offer but, about a month later, approved a three-year contract. Poshard wrote a lengthy letter to the *Times-Courier* newspaper outlining his assessment of the talks and why he involved himself in labor matters. He said he's seen too many jobs lost in these kinds of disputes. It's worth the political risk, he said, to try to bring the sides together to find common ground. At least one employee wrote a lengthy reply outlining why employees didn't trust the company. Trailmobile shuttered its Charleston plant in 2001.[8]

In Congress, Poshard kept abreast of the news in Illinois. He followed budget debates. He stayed in contact with friends in state government. He discussed state issues with colleagues in Congress and friends back in Illinois. While solidly Democratic now, Illinois in those days was a swing state. Republicans had dominated the governorship, but Democrats more often than not had majorities in the General Assembly. Republicans Jim Thompson (1977–91) and Jim

Edgar (1991–99) occupied the governor's mansion. Democrats dominated Chicago city politics. Republicans dominated suburban Chicago. Downstate was a battleground, with generally more conservative voters. In those general terms, "downstate" refers to almost everything outside Chicago and the five suburban collar counties.

Though he had made no announcement, many thought that Edgar wouldn't seek a third term as Illinois governor in 1998. That would create an opportunity for Democrats. Poshard had no second thoughts about his belief that self-imposed term limits were best for Congress. But he enjoyed campaigning. He enjoyed the legislative process. He enjoyed being around voters. Increasingly, a question arose: "What are you going to do next?"

Representatives Bill Lipinski and Jerry Costello remember a meeting over pizza in Poshard's office in which Costello, Lipinski, and Congressman Lane Evans promoted a Poshard run for governor. "I thought it was time for a conservative Democrat to run," Lipinski said. "He was an honest, sincere man."[9]

Costello and Poshard sometimes flew back and forth from Washington to their southern Illinois districts on the same flight. They served neighboring districts. "Glenn was always true to his words and principles," Costello said. "No matter how much pressure he received, on matters of principle he didn't change a vote. . . . He said to voters he was only going to stay for 10 years in Congress. That's exactly what he did."[10]

With the encouragement of his colleagues, Poshard actively explored a gubernatorial run. One thing was an immediate casualty. He gave up his Washington, D.C., apartment and began sleeping in his congressional office.

"I was being encouraged by some of my colleagues from Illinois in Congress, as well as many people at home, to run for the governorship. I knew if I decided to run, every minute of my time would be needed to campaign across a large state and keep up my work in Congress. I now lived nearly ten miles off the Hill in an apartment complex that had no assigned parking spaces. Getting home at ten o'clock at night, I often had to park a considerable distance from my apartment. It was time-consuming and tiring. Fighting the Washington traffic every day was bad enough. Now, I had no time to spare.

As soon as votes were over, I had to rush to the airport and get back to Illinois. I canceled the contract on my apartment, got rid of a bad parking situation and rush-hour traffic, bought myself an air mattress, brought some extra suits for the closet in my office, and began sleeping there. The House gym was a five-minute walk from my office with hot showers, lockers, and a dressing room. It was a great situation for me. I saved time and money, and alleviated a lot of stress during a very stressful year."

# PART 3

# A RACE FOR ILLINOIS GOVERNOR

CHAPTER 16

# Pitching Lunch Bucket Populism

"Is there room," Poshard wrote as he entered the governor's race, "for the police officer, health care worker, small business owner, or salesman to make a contribution and run for office if the price of admittance is so high?" His reference was to a system in which two funding sources dominate: political action committee contributions and self-financing by wealthy individuals. Poshard was neither independently wealthy nor willing to change his practice of refusing PAC money. His guest column in the *Southtown Star* newspaper ends by noting his goals "to be part of the solution on education, economic growth, and opportunity for all of our people. I will address each of these issues specifically. But I hope to make a contribution on all of them by being part of the solution on campaign finance reform."[1]

To make a statement on the oversized role money plays in politics and policy required what he considered a modest, reasonable, and workable financial plan. He told supporters he could raise $1.7 million for the primary, then more than double that in the general election with help from the Democratic Party. That was considerably less than his best-financed opponents. Yet it would buy some television ads and targeted direct-mail pieces. It would be enough to pay for staff, travel, and other necessary expenses. "Today," Poshard says, "twenty years down the road, I look at our present political climate in America, and from the courthouse to the White House, money is almost the only factor that counts. Primarily, money to destroy your opponent through negative ads. I wanted to do it differently. The amount of money you've raised basically determines if you can even qualify to debate, no matter how deep your experience or how important your ideas. Is this really the principle on which we want the democratic process of electing our leaders to stand?"

Poshard would deploy his formula, which included developing relationships with key local and regional leaders. He would work hard, communicate directly, debate vigorously, and promote solution-oriented plans. He realized it would be his biggest challenge in politics. The end result he envisioned would show a moderately funded educator from the least populous region of the state leading to change the political narrative.

Formally, he entered the race on March 10, 1997, with a five-city fly around to Chicago, Moline, Springfield, Cahokia, and the Williamson County Airport.[2] Congressional friends Bill Lipinski and Danny Davis of Chicago, Lane Evans of Rock Island, and Jerry Costello of Belleville were among those who joined him at the various stops. They led the core group that encouraged Poshard to run on the idea he could win a contested primary by doing well downstate and finding pockets of support in Chicago with their help.

In the primary, Poshard's goal was 45 percent in the ninety-six counties outside metro Chicago, which equated to about 60-plus percent in southern counties and 35 percent in central Illinois. Overall, he thought 30 to 32 percent would win. With about 1.2 million votes cast in the 1994 primary, that meant he needed about 350,000 votes. He needed about 18 percent in Cook County. "Lipinski believed he could get me five of the biggest wards in Chicago," Poshard said. With other endorsements including those from Forty-Seventh Ward committeeman Ed Kelly and former state Senate president Phil Rock, Poshard thought he could win pockets of Chicago while positioning himself for general election success. In the general election, the winning formula was to do well in the Chicago Democratic stronghold and outperform recent Democratic candidates across the rest of the state.

His Washington routine changed. Every minute was needed to balance his congressional responsibilities with the emerging opportunity in Illinois. In early 1997 he began visiting counties across the state on weekends. That network ultimately resulted in ninety-plus endorsements from the 102 Illinois counties. "Downstate will vote for Glenn Poshard," Rock Island's John Gianulis, who headed up the Democratic County Chairs' Association, was quoted as saying in the *Quad City Times*.[3]

Poshard, while working to establish Chicago roots, repeated to his staff that the primary would be won downstate. "That was a major deal to get that base of support behind you in a primary," he said. Some pundits underestimated the impact of Poshard's downstate support and considered him a little-known long shot in the population centers.

Others saw his candidacy as great potential for his home region. "If Glenn Poshard is our next governor, it would be the greatest thing that has ever happened to Southern Illinois," West Frankfort mayor John Simmons was quoted as saying in the *Daily American* newspaper on February 15, 1997.[4] Still others viewed a downstate candidate favorably. *Chicago Sun-Times* columnist Steve Neal wrote that a winning formula is to run a downstater who would win Chicago and hold his own elsewhere.[5]

From the outset, Poshard sought to mitigate areas where his record veered from traditional Democratic positions. In making his announcement, he highlighted support from thoughtful people who strongly disagreed with him on an important issue such as abortion but saw him overall as the best candidate. In Springfield, Poshard was introduced by State senator Penny Severns, a pro-choice woman who described Poshard "as honest as the day is long." Severns, being quoted by Copley News Service, said Poshard represented a "moderate voice" along with "a tough mind and a tender heart." The *Decatur Herald and Review* report used this Severns quote: "Anyone who underestimates [Poshard] doesn't know him. He is the people's representative. He really does bring honor to the Illinois arena."[6]

In Chicago, he spent time with Congressman Davis in places like the Cook County General Hospital. Poshard described the experience as eye-opening. He said it helped him understand why urban voters viewed gun control differently than voters in his southern Illinois district did. Poshard agreed to drop his opposition to an assault weapons ban, making a point that he would rethink some views using a broader lens. "I'm trying to see the picture for the whole state," Poshard told the *West Frankfort Daily American*.[7]

His campaign style resembled the formula that worked for him in the past. He accepted speaking engagements across the state. He met with individuals and groups. He worked long hours. His supporters rallied with and followed him. His wife Jo, who had spent every summer of the congressional years in Washington escorting constituents on White House tours, was still teaching, but now her evenings and weekends were spent on the campaign trail. She spoke at various rallies for Poshard and engaged in debates all over the state of Illinois, including Springfield and Chicago. Although sometimes attacked for her husband's conservative position on particular issues, Jo was prepared for the criticism, never responding in kind but holding her own in the forums and debates. She was always received well and was, by far, Poshard's best campaigner.

As the campaign got underway, almost every flight for Poshard from the nation's capital was to Chicago. So much of the campaign had to be focused on the city. Thankfully for Poshard, Jo's sister Karen and her husband, Dr. Frank Ferraiolo, lived in Des Plaines, and shared their home with him for the entire campaign. In making sure that Poshard ate well, had ironed shirts, and got up on time to make early appointments downtown, Karen saved the campaign a ton of money.

Two other individuals were integral to the campaign. Elvis Nolen and Jim Williamson had been a part of Poshard's political success for years. Nolen was the regional superintendent of schools in Franklin County, Illinois, and Glenn had been a program manager in his office in the early 1980s, when Poshard had become well known in the Democratic Party and made the decision to run for the state Senate. A group of political heavyweights had visited Nolen's office and pressured him to get Poshard out of the race. They had another candidate they wanted to support and needed Poshard to back off. Nolen listened quietly to the group, all of whom could cost him political support in his next race. He turned to Glenn and asked him what he wanted to do. Poshard said he wanted to run.

Poshard remembered Nolen's words verbatim. He told them, "This is America, and if a person wants to run for office, nobody should stop them, and I will be backing Glenn." From that day forward, Nolen was Poshard's closest political ally and friend. In his race for governor, he was the campaign treasurer and handled all finances.

From the beginning of Poshard's Senate years and through the governor's campaign, Jim Williamson was Poshard's right-hand man. Jim worked for the Williamson County Highway Department and, every Saturday morning at six o'clock, met Poshard at his home and drove him through the entire congressional district for the weekend. Poshard came home nearly every weekend, and with a district that stretched 265 miles from north to south and five to six meetings a day, he totally relied on Williamson to get him to the various sites safely and on time. "Jim was an excellent volunteer and friend."

On June 28, 1997, a Saturday, Poshard made a statement in an atypical fashion. His southern and central Illinois base rallied for and with him in downtown Chicago. In southern Illinois, people were up before dawn, loading a caravan of charter buses, vans, trucks, and cars that began what for some was a 350-mile one-way trip to Chicago. Along Interstate 57 the caravan grew. By 1 P.M., a crowd estimated at five hundred to a thousand dressed in blue or white T-shirts saying "Pack the Plaza for Poshard," began congregating on Daley Plaza in the Chicago Loop. At 2 P.M., an old-fashioned political rally commenced, starting with a prayer and the pledge of allegiance, and then twenty-four speakers made endorsements leading up to Poshard's address. "These people who are here today don't represent any special interest," Poshard said at the time. "They represent all kinds of interests."[8]

The rally underlined Poshard's core support. It highlighted Chicago-area politicians endorsing him. It showcased Poshard's strength as a speaker. It reflected the kind of grassroots effort he intended to use to overcome his financial disadvantage.

The rally also highlighted a Poshard position that hurt him with Democratic core voters. While he moderated his position on gun control, his heart wouldn't change his pro-life position. At the Chicago rally, a small pro-choice group voiced their opposition. Poshard told reporters later that when people look at his entire record on gender equity, he would outperform his opponents. A single-issue litmus test, he said at multiple points in the campaign, is a losing position.

"In the state Senate, I had worked to end investments in the immoral Apartheid government of South Africa. I championed legislation to expand educational opportunities for children, particularly Head

Start, Pre-K, and all-day kindergarten. In Congress, I worked to support the Civil Rights Act of 1991, the Family and Medical Leave Act, the Voting Rights Language Act, the National Motor Voter Registration Act, the Legal Services Corporation Reauthorization, expanded Medicare and Medicaid coverage, and critical access hospitals for the poor in rural and inner-city America. I was a Democrat in every way, but unless I changed my position on something fundamental to my personal faith, I could never be worthy of the vote of many in my own party. Did it hurt that I had supported hundreds of pro-choice candidates my whole career with my finances, my endorsements, and my campaigning throughout the state and never once criticized their position on abortion? It did hurt, especially when I needed their support, and it wasn't there for me.

"As I tried to explain to pro-choice groups that refused to endorse me, the same conscience that compels me to hold a personal belief on this issue consistent with my faith also compels me to allow you to hold a completely different view not subject to my criticism, and as governor I would uphold the Constitution of our country which has established choice as your right. It wasn't enough. Despite the fact that I had worked for every liberal Democratic candidate for years and, except for this one position, had an excellent voting record on women's issues, the constant criticism and demonstrations at so many of my meetings became exhausting, and I am certain that my pro-life position cost me the election in November."

The internal Democratic debate parallels the ongoing exchanges about what should be the party's central waypoint. Is it social issues? Is it economic opportunity? Is it foreign policy? Poshard's record emphasized long-held Democratic fundamentals of fair wages, access to affordable health care, educational opportunities, and a safety net for those most in need. A 1995 *Los Angeles Times* article described Poshard like this: "In many ways, he's a throwback to the lunch bucket populism that defined the Democratic Party before it was carried uptown by the social upheavals of the 1960's."[9]

An early internal draft of Poshard's policy positions led with this quote from Robert F. Kennedy: "The future does not belong to those who are content with today, apathetic toward common problems and their fellow man alike, timid and fearful in the face of bold projects and new ideas. Rather, it will belong to those who can blend passion, reason, and courage in a personal commitment to the great enterprises and ideals of American society."[10] And Poshard could articulate the issues with passion and courage. Few politicians in the state could match his oratorical and debating skills. He was fearless and gained converts at every meeting.

As expected, three opponents emerged: John Schmidt, a former Justice Department official and former chief of staff for Chicago's mayor Richard M. Daley; Roland Burris, a former attorney general and state comptroller in Illinois; and Jim Burns, the U.S. attorney in Chicago. Like Poshard, Burris and Burns were from southern Illinois, though both had moved to Chicago. Burris was the only African American candidate. Schmidt was favored by Daley. Burns was considered the favorite of Mike Madigan, the Illinois House Speaker. Burris had the highest name recognition, having been twice elected to statewide offices.

Poshard knew that his stands on abortion and gun rights provided ammunition for his opponents. He knew, too, that he needed to work hard in metropolitan Chicago. A four-way race, though, could work to his advantage if downstate voters were energized. He thought his core support was stronger than that of the other candidates and thus would be particularly important in a primary.

An early decision Poshard faced was hiring a campaign manager. He had to get someone from Chicago because eventually, if he were able to survive the primary, the general election would be decided there. He felt confident he had secured the party support downstate for the primary and needed to focus on the city. Congressman Lipinski, Poshard's closest friend in the Chicago delegation, insisted Poshard hire Joe Novak as his campaign manager. Novak's reputation for being a smart Chicago pol and a "no-holds-barred gut puncher" caused Poshard some concern, but such was the nature of Chicago politics, and Poshard needed somebody who knew the ropes and could get the campaign organized quickly. Early on he had been pushed by downstate friends to hire someone more familiar, more his style, but he was relatively unknown in the city, he had little time to waste, and Novak knew the ropes. The campaign was underway.

Early in the process, some party leaders attempted to avoid a divided primary. The idea was to form a dream ticket. Poshard would be slated as secretary of state. "There were people in the party who initially talked to me about running for secretary of state," he said. "From the beginning, Bill Lipinski, who was a good friend in Congress, wanted me to run for governor. I thought I could win. I didn't have interest in being secretary of state. It's an important position and a good stepping stone. But it didn't have anything to do with policy or problem-solving, which were the only things in government that interested me, and that's why I ran for governor."

In August, Governor Edgar declared himself a lame duck, saying he would neither run for reelection as governor nor for the U.S. Senate. Poshard thought he would be running against Edgar and that he could be successful, but he was glad the governor opted to retire. "I had a great deal of respect and admiration for Jim Edgar. I didn't want to run against him." In early September, Secretary of State George Ryan became the leading Republican candidate. Poshard expected Ryan's candidacy and welcomed the potential opportunity to contrast his vision for Illinois with Ryan.

As he spent increasing amounts of time in Illinois, his near-perfect congressional voting record suffered. In Washington, he supported the Patient's Bill of Rights legislation and women's health care initiative. He voted against a Republican proposal for health maintenance organization (HMO) reform. He advocated strongly for protection of the Social Security Trust Fund, critical care access to hospitals, increased Medicare funding, and a balanced budget. Every weekend he was back in Illinois.

The campaign had its share of ups and downs. He was surprised when one of his close friends whom he had helped get an important government position with the Department of Agriculture turned out to be a strong supporter of John Schmidt and whose daughter became Schmidt's campaign coordinator for southern Illinois.

"I made several trips off the Hill to meet with Secretary Espy to advocate for my friend to receive the appointment. My staff person waited outside with the car running, and I had to rush back to the Capitol twice so I didn't miss an important vote. Of course it came as a shock when I picked up the *Southern Illinoisan* a couple of weeks later and read the announcement of my good friend's daughter becoming the coordinator for my opponent, but that's politics, I guess. I had much the same feeling when I learned that several friends had held a fundraiser for my opponent only a few miles from my home, friends I had helped many times with various needs. You realize in those moments that there are 'friends' and there are 'political friends.' As a candidate you have no right to expect that political friends are always going to support you. Even though you assume because you help somebody, they are going to help you, you may never know the one area in which you come up short that overrides all the good you have done for someone and causes them to vote against you. It happens all the time in politics, and you learn to not take it personally and to go on about your business."

Over time, however, the campaign developed much to Poshard's liking. He won a coup in January 1998 with the endorsement of the Illinois AFL-CIO.[11] That was telling, particularly with Madigan, who also had strong labor support, having been thought to support Burns. Some media reports at the time concluded that the endorsement was evidence of Madigan moving away from Burns toward Poshard. Poshard said he considers his longstanding support for organized labor and relationships with people like Mike Carrigan of Decatur, Eddie Smith of southern Illinois, and Margaret Blackshere of Arlington Heights as key to the endorsement. "I don't think the other candidates had the same standing."

Perhaps Poshard's biggest obstacle had nothing to do with his three opponents. The challenge started one evening in the House gym, where Poshard regularly exercised. The legislative session was over for the day. "After working out, I got a drink of cold water, and my heart just started flying. I was dizzy and felt faint. I walked to the security station still in my exercise clothes. I told them, 'I think I need an ambulance, there is something wrong with my heart.'"

He remembers paramedics referring to a heart rate of 240-some beats a minute. The initial efforts at the hospital to shock his heart back into rhythm were unsuccessful. It took a couple of days before the hospital released Poshard to stay with his legislative director's family. He felt weakened at a time he most needed energy. The diagnosis of atrial fibrillation, or A-fib, typically includes irregular and often faster heartbeats, heart palpitations, shortness of breath, and physical weakness.

On his first trip back to Illinois, Poshard remembers an A-fib episode as the plane approached O'Hare International Airport. "There was a delay in landing, and as we were circling out over Lake Michigan, my heart went into an arrhythmia that left me weak and dizzy. I was able to finally leave the plane without drawing much attention to myself, avoid a couple of reporters, and meet staff, ready for a busy campaign schedule. There were several [A-fib] episodes during the rest of the primary and the general election. Atrial fibrillation has now been a part of my life for over twenty years. I manage it with the help of my doctors and live a perfectly normal life, but in its early stages, when I didn't understand it and knew I had a grueling campaign ahead of me, it was pretty scary."

While all of Poshard's opponents had a core of support, Schmidt had the most financial backing, which allowed him to hire top advisors, including David Axelrod, who years later became known as an architect of Barack Obama's ascendency to the presidency. Axelrod had worked for Poshard in his successful campaign for Congress in 1988, filming all his commercials and providing valuable advice on managing the campaign. Now, however, he was working for Poshard's opponent.

One of Schmidt's campaign ads played a Poshard speech in slow motion. The effect was to exaggerate expressions and movements, like an outstretched right arm. *Chicago Tribune* reporter John Kass wrote that Schmidt wouldn't say he was proud of the ad, only that it was necessary. "In the hands of Schmidt's storyteller, the gesture is warped and made to look like a fascist salute," Kass wrote in the March 16, 1998, edition.[12]

Poshard considered the ad out of bounds. He explained, "Members of my family have served in the United States Army for generations, including during World War II. One of my uncles was a POW-MIA fighting against Hitler and the Nazis. Anyone who looked at that ad could not fail to get the message. It made me look like I was giving a Nazi salute, and because I wore a moustache at the time, it tried to make me look like Hitler. It was disgusting, and had I not fought back against it, I would have felt like I failed my family and my country."

A March 14 *Chicago Tribune* article highlighted a Poshard-Schmidt exchange after what was billed as the tenth and final debate between the Democratic candidates. Poshard had pushed back against Schmidt's campaign ads with a television commercial and targeted direct-mail piece that portrayed Schmidt as a lakefront liberal who worked on corporate mergers that led to employees being tossed out of work. The ad also said Schmidt supported same-sex marriage, at the time a negative even among many Democratic leaders, and that he supported partial birth abortion.

"This sounds to me like a kind of last-minute diversionary tactic to try to get away from my record and the issues, [when], at this point, it looks like I'm going to win the election Tuesday," the *Tribune* quoted Schmidt as saying.

"I don't think so," the *Tribune* quotes Poshard as responding. "There is absolutely nothing in the ad that is untrue whatsoever." The news account said Poshard told Schmidt that for six weeks Poshard watched ads that portrayed what Schmidt perceived as reflective of Poshard's record. This, Poshard said, was a look at Schmidt's record.[13]

Earlier in the campaign, at one of the debates, Poshard drew a contrast between the number of women in administrative positions in his office compared with the number of female lawyers in Schmidt's firm, which were very few. Poshard contrasted that with his own record of promoting women to key positions and supporting women's health care issues, pay equity, and family issues. "My chief of staff in Washington was a woman, my district manager in southern Illinois was a woman, women headed up three of my regional offices, and the majority of my employees were women," Poshard said.

Poshard developed a campaign theme as a whole-life Democrat that highlighted his consistently broad support for women's issues and equality. As he reflects on the campaign twenty years later, many highlights are memorialized with news articles glued in a maroon book whose pages are held together with a string. The title says, simply, "Scrapbook." There are no frills. A few handwritten notes from supporters and related correspondence are mixed between news accounts, political commentary, and a few articles about his opponents.

A couple of pages include campaign literature with headings like "Five Reasons Why People Support Glenn Poshard."[14] The number-one reason is no PAC money. The number-two reason is fiscal responsibility. The number-three reason is hard work, citing his record in supporting major infrastructure needs of his district. Numbers four and five are responsibility and accountability, highlighting his voting attendance record, his constituent outreach, and the economical way he ran his congressional offices. Poshard considered these reasons as the foundation to help voters understand how he would lead Illinois.

On election night, results were better than expected. He won 37.5 percent of the vote, an even more convincing victory than optimists predicted. Burris was second with about 30 percent, and Schmidt third with about 25 percent. The front page of the *Southern Illinoisan* showed Glenn and Jo Poshard, their joined hands held high as they greeted supporters. The feeling resembled the satisfaction in other political victories. But it was one step of a multistep process. The way forward would be even more challenging.

In 2018, Poshard made numerous primary appearances on behalf of winning gubernatorial candidate J. B. Pritzker. After the primary win, Pritzker's opponents immediately offered their support of his candidacy. That prompted Poshard to think back to the 1998 unity breakfast. "People came and pledged their support for the ticket," he said. "I was grateful for that." But, according to newspaper reports, there was little enthusiasm in the room.

Poshard believes his pro-life position was paramount in a lot of people's minds. "I'm sure it was a shock to pro-choice groups when I won the primary."

Saying enthusiasm was lacking is one way to characterize the mood. Another interpretation went like this: "It was like a morgue."

CHAPTER 17

# Liberal Fallout, Lost Opportunity

One Sunday while speaking at a Chicago church in an African American community, Poshard remembers seeing a familiar figure rise from his seat and walk down the aisle. The tall, thin man joined Poshard at the podium. State senator Barack Obama put his arm around Poshard and endorsed his candidacy. "I remember it well," Poshard said. "He said some nice things about me. He was genuine. I really appreciated that." The endorsement during a church service exemplifies one way Chicago politics differ from downstate. Influential pastors and community leaders, particularly in the African American community, openly engage in the course of their church services. For a white candidate from a rural area, support from Obama and others like him became critical.

Key aldermen, precinct captains, and other influential leaders endorsed Poshard, which helped combat the way George Ryan immediately began defining Poshard through thirty-second television commercials. One featured black smoke billowing from a factory to highlight Poshard's vote against the Clean Air Act, which had devastated his rural coal mining district and which Senator Paul Simon had opposed also. Another ad ended with a flag burning. A third ad placed the words "No Gun Control" and "Anti-Environment" and "Higher Taxes" next to a Poshard picture. Ryan set out to cast Poshard as a gun-toting rural extremist.[1]

Poshard moved to consolidate support among the Democratic ticket by organizing a downstate bus tour. This action, he hoped, would help unify urban and rural, introducing his upstate colleagues to downstate constituents. Perhaps synergies would emerge, and Democrats would help each other.

The unity tour started in Springfield, ended in East St. Louis, and included stops throughout Poshard's southern Illinois stronghold. The tour included U.S. senator Carol Moseley Braun, who was in a tough reelection campaign, Poshard, lieutenant governor nominee Mary Lou Kearns, secretary of state candidate Jesse White, attorney general candidate Miriam Santos, state treasurer candidate Dan McLaughlin, and state comptroller nominee Dan Hynes.[2]

Stops included Taylorville, Shelbyville, Effingham, Newton, Olney, Carmi, Harrisburg, Marion, Cairo, Jonesboro, Murphysboro, Chester, Belleville, Edwardsville, and Caseyville. Poshard was in in his element at union halls, county courthouses, restaurants, and a library. An advance team worked ahead of the bus, introducing local candidates. When the bus arrived at each stop, candidates were introduced for brief remarks to the crowd, typically by a county chairman, state central committeeman, or local official. "We want each stop to have a feel of a meet and greet rather than speech-making," the tour playbook says. "People should feel comfortable coming up and meeting their candidates, posing for pictures, and asking questions."

"I had worked very hard for many years over two congressional districts which covered over a third of the state, and I wanted our candidates to do well there," Poshard said. "They were all Chicago area natives, and I wanted to help them win as well as gain an appreciation of southern Illinois."

Poshard had hoped for reciprocation in kind. In a written note on the itinerary, one supporter complained some did not return the same sentiment for Poshard. "I genuinely liked all of our statewide candidates but for some, I was just too conservative, and at least one spoke openly in other parts of the state for George Ryan."

Mayor Daley traveled to southern Illinois in June to formally endorse Poshard at a $100-a-plate fundraiser.[3] "He has resisted at all times to divide the state by region, resisting to pitting Chicago against downstate or the suburbs against Southern Illinois," the *Southern Illinoisan* quoted Daley as saying. "The issues are the same. You have job losses. We have job losses. You have education problems. We have education problems."

House Speaker Mike Madigan from Chicago's Southwest Side was another leading Democrat who provided valuable support. "Once the primary was over, Mike Madigan helped me considerably," Poshard said. "He never told me an untruth or exaggerated what he could do or would do. He was always very helpful to me."

Many leading Democrats privately told Poshard he would need the PAC money to win. He needed to push back earlier with television advertising. Poshard resisted. Like the abortion issue, he saw it as something on which he couldn't compromise. In handwritten notes, Poshard wrote, "Do you think voters are concerned about candidates having too little money, or too much money? Do not tell me I cannot be competitive because I do not embody what is wrong with our current system."[4] Poshard noted that his campaign would challenge conventional wisdom. He had done it for five terms in Congress, and he believed he could do it in the race for governor.

He followed that theme in his early television advertising. "There is a candidate for governor who has a record of following his convictions despite political consequences. There is a candidate for governor who will end the insidious influence of money and special interests on state government. There is a candidate for governor who will tell the voters the truth and act according to his lifelong values."

An early position paper outlined Poshard's focus on five broad areas: education; trust in government; protecting the vulnerable; fiscal responsibility; and the economy. Family issues included his support for women-and-children issues like childcare subsidies, family leave, sexual harassment, workplace equity, stalking, deadbeat dads, domestic violence, and DCFS reforms. Aside from abortion, Poshard's record in support of women's issues was clear. He called it being a whole-life Democrat.[5]

That message was difficult to sell in some key places. Jo Poshard was among those who learned that lesson firsthand as she embraced a regular speaking role. She was part of all of Glenn's campaigns. In the governor's race, that meant being out front more. She discovered that if a group cannot get the candidate, the next choice is the candidate's wife.

Because of the demand for more appearances, she made an exception and took a leave of absence from teaching. She had her own driver and schedule, often packing the back of the car with a change of clothes and campaign material. At one party function on the affluent suburban North Shore, a man approached her before the event. "I just want you to know I'm going door to door in my precinct and telling everyone not to vote for your husband," he told her.

"This was at a Democratic meeting; it happened on occasion, but thankfully, not often," said Jo Poshard.[6] At another function, in downtown Chicago, a woman listened to Jo's prepared remarks, then asked from the audience about abortion: "What do you have to say about this?" With staff members giving the signal to remain silent, Jo thought it best to speak.

"Is being pro-choice going to be the litmus test for being a Democrat?" Jo asked, noting her husband's long record of supporting important issues for women and families. He wasn't going to change the laws protecting abortion, she said; it was the law of the land, and he would swear to uphold the Constitution and to enforce the law. To her, it was clear which candidate would advance women's issues. Further, she said in retrospect, "If I was going to represent him, when the occasion called for it, I had to stand up."[7]

To this day, Poshard shakes his head at the Illinois Education Association's endorsement of Ryan, who twenty-five years earlier as a lawmaker voted against collective bargaining for teachers. Poshard, as a former teacher and union member, seemed the logical choice. He had already been endorsed by the Illinois Federation of Teachers. In the endorsement interview, Poshard said there were multiple questions about the abortion issue, even though he and Ryan had the same position. Ken Bruce, the brother of Terry Bruce, who Poshard defeated in the 1992 Democratic primary, was still in a key role with the IEA, which didn't help either. "On nearly every issue concerning education and support for teachers, my record was far superior to George Ryan's," said Poshard. "He literally killed the Equal Rights Amendment in Illinois and did everything he could to stop teachers from collective bargaining. Quality education had always been my top priority and headed my list of goals as governor of the state."

Jo, an IEA member for over twenty years, was present at the announcement of the IEA endorsement of George Ryan. She was stunned that Poshard's record on education and women's issues had been pushed into the background in favor of questions on abortion, especially since Ryan had been anti-abortion his whole career. "But the records didn't matter," said Poshard. "Local IEA chapters in central and southern Illinois still supported me, but the endorsement committee made its decision, and that was it. I am certain that the IEA's affection for Governor Jim Thompson enabled Thompson to gain their support for George Ryan. They gave George Ryan a half-million dollars and put thousands of people on the street to go door to door for him."

In time, some of the liberal leaders in the party vocalized support for Poshard. After Ryan made a statement to the press saying, "I did the right thing by killing the Equal Rights Amendment in Illinois," Poshard highlighted that Ryan didn't advocate for equal pay for women, voted against maternity leave, against granting family and medical leave, against minimum wage increases, against HMO reform, and against collective bargaining for teachers. In a Poshard news release, liberal state representative Barbara Flynn Currie was quoted this way: "The real George Ryan has now emerged, and he is no choice for women, no choice for progressives, no choice for labor, no choice for reform."[8]

There was another issue that put Poshard at odds with progressives. Like Ryan, Poshard had opposed LGBT rights in areas like discrimination in housing, benefits for domestic partners, and same-sex marriage. Ryan, however, supported a move to prohibit discrimination against LGBT people in the secretary of state's office, a policy Poshard had embraced and practiced every year in his office since being elected. But Ryan successfully used his newfound policy to court the LGBT vote while attempting not to alienate conservative Republicans.

In a letter to Congresswoman Jan Schakowsky, Rick Garcia of the Illinois Federation for Human Rights asked her as a leader of the Democratic Party to ask Poshard to modify his anti-LGBT positions or distance herself from his campaign.[9] "His previous positions may have been based on his assumption that they reflected his constituency in Illinois' nineteenth congressional district," Garcia said. "As governor of Illinois, his constituency would be much broader and certainly include not only a large number of gay and lesbian residents but also Illinoisans who believe that all should be treated fairly and equally."

Over time, after his years at SIU, Poshard saw the LGBT issues differently. "Garcia was right; this is an area where my upbringing and my faith weighed too heavily on my decision-making. While the two congressional districts I served broadly endorsed one opinion on this issue, my conscience, not immediately but gradually, began to reflect a different opinion. Darin Johnson, a young gay man, worked in my Washington office. We all loved Darin. He was a hard worker, a professional in every respect. He quietly challenged me to consider the moral and ethical issues of judgment surrounding gay men and women. He came from a position that no matter what my faith had taught me or my district accepted as truth, love was the only valid response to judgment. I didn't learn the lesson quickly enough and continued to hold onto my views through the campaign for governor. Mental assent to changing my viewpoint just to help myself become governor wouldn't have worked either. My heart still had not caught up with my changing conscience. As I became associated with members of the LGBT community at my alma mater, SIU, and observed the respect they had for themselves and others, I worked with them to effect changes to build a more loving and accepting community for all of our students."

Poshard hoped his earlier support for Jesse Jackson Jr. and his support for equal rights for African Americans in the state Senate and Congress might help him merit Jackson's support in the gubernatorial race.

One of the big issues in Illinois was debate about air traffic in the Chicago area. O'Hare International Airport was the second busiest in the country. Midway Airport served an important secondary role. Some, including Representative Jackson and his father, the Reverend Jesse Jackson, thought the region should add a third airport in suburban Peotone southeast of the city, which, among other things, would bring many jobs. Mayor Daley opposed the third airport. In April, Poshard appeared at a rally in Peotone and said he opposed the third airport but left open the possibility of investigating the need in the future.[10]

Poshard knew from serving on the Aviation Subcommittee of the Transportation Committee in the House that the costs and related issues to developing a new airport had no chance of passage, and hundreds of millions of dollars of transportation dollars were not available. "I didn't think it was an idea that would work. First of all, not a single major airline would commit to using a third airport. Second, airline schedules at O'Hare and Midway easily accommodated those airlines. Hundreds of millions of dollars to build light rail from Peotone to O'Hare and Midway to accommodate passengers' schedules would never be justified by the Federal Aviation Administration, considering that Congress had just invested millions of dollars in a new airport immediately across the state line in Gary, Indiana. Plus, the fact that a new airport in Belleville, Illinois, which cost hundreds of millions of dollars to relieve pressure on Lambert Airport in St. Louis, was vastly underutilized. Now, twenty-two years later, the airport still hasn't been built and for all the reasons I articulated in 1998. I was roundly criticized by the south suburban newspapers, but I made my decision based on the facts and what was possible at the time."

Poshard sought a meeting with the Reverend Jackson. As first the minutes and then hours went by, Poshard sat in the waiting room, canceling appointments. Clearly, Jackson wasn't in a conciliatory mood. The rift with Jackson hurt Poshard with a great many people in the African American community.

There was another relationship that became difficult to manage. Poshard first met President Clinton in the late 1980s. They were both southern Democrats who preached fiscal responsibility. Clinton, it seemed, should be positioned to help Democrats take back the Illinois governor's mansion.

Poshard welcomed Clinton's support. The Clinton headlines, however, often dealt with impeachment and the Monica Lewinsky scandal, neither of which were helpful. The president's problems often occupied prime real estate in newspapers and the newscasts that otherwise may have gone to the governor's race.

On September 26, the president came to Chicago for a fundraiser for Poshard. On the date of the Chicago fundraiser, House Speaker Dennis Hastert scheduled an important vote on Social Security that forced Poshard to make a choice. Poshard can't prove it but suspects the timing of the vote was intentional. Hastert, who was close friends with Ryan, essentially gave Poshard the option to miss a key vote in Congress or be absent for his own fundraiser with the president. Either way, it wasn't going to look good. Poshard chose to vote, explaining the importance of doing his legislative job.

Headlines about Clinton persisted. Poshard remembers the day he was riding in his campaign van on the Eisenhower Expressway when the radio news headline became Clinton's admission of his relationship with Lewinsky. "I stayed with President Clinton. I thought he was doing a good job as president and the charges against him came nowhere near the Constitutional requirements for impeachment, but the proceedings galvanized the American press and the public for months."

On one point, the Poshard and Ryan teams agreed. Poshard was the superior orator and debater. Thus debates were a place Poshard could score points with voters. A Ryan aide was quoted as saying the best time to debate would be Easter Sunday about the time sunrise services begin. Ryan ultimately agreed to two debates.[11] One was hosted at the University of Illinois and shown on public television. The second was taped on a Friday evening and shown on a Chicago television station at 7 AM on a Saturday morning. The *Chicago Tribune* criticized Ryan for his poor performance in the U of I debate. Hardly anyone watched the second debate.

In early September, unfavorable polls plagued Poshard. That further limited his fundraising. While he remained optimistic, the path to victory seemed narrow. Every day was sixteen hours long, and the schedule filled with as many events as possible. Much later than he hoped, key liberals publicly offered support. John Schmidt, one of his primary opponents, joined Poshard outside domestic violence court in Chicago. At their appearance, Poshard advocated an increase by $5 million in funding for shelters for battered women and reiterated his support for anti-domestic-violence measures.

"People are going to focus on the real George Ryan, and then they're going to get to know the real Glenn Poshard," the *Sun-Times* quoted Schmidt as saying.[12] About three weeks later, other leading Illinois liberals, including former senators Paul Simon and Adlai Stevenson III, U.S. Appeals Court judge Abner Mikva, and 1994 Democratic nominee Dawn Clark Netsch backed Poshard at a Chicago press conference. The support came about the same time as conservative national newspaper columnist George Will wrote about Poshard and conservative southern Democrats as an endangered species. Will's column ends like this: "Poshard, some of whose constituents live closer to Jackson, Mississippi, than to Jackson Boulevard in Chicago, is testing liberal Democrats' belief in 'diversity.' They seem determined to demonstrate, redundantly, that they believe in diversity in everything other than ideas."[13]

The press conference came at a time internal polls showed Ryan's support among white liberals running at close to 50 percent. The press release from the four Democratic leaders emphasized Poshard's democratic values. "We have become increasingly concerned that voters in the Chicago area are not getting a true picture of the Glenn Poshard we know," they wrote. "When we look at the broad arc of Glenn Poshard's career, we find an outstanding record in defending and advancing the values that so many of us share" in areas like "support for education and child care; equal rights for women and minorities; concern for the environment, and protection for the vulnerable."[14]

In some ways, similar to what we see today, there still raged an internal party debate about what it takes to be a Democrat. Poshard checked nearly all of the boxes. Was it enough? Were words from leading liberals enough to swing votes Poshard's way? While he preferred to have had their support earlier in the campaign, he welcomed it. He had worked for Democrats all his life. He supported people he disagreed with on some key issues. Democrats, he thought, embraced broad ideals with broad appeal.

The portrayal of Poshard by Ryan and some Democrats as an extremist too often overshadowed the view put forth by the nonpartisan *Almanac of American Politics*, which in this quote used by the liberal Netsch described Poshard as "a moderate on the issues and an earnest reformer whose sincerity is not in doubt."[15]

By early fall, media reports across the state highlighted potential corruption in the Ryan campaign. One speculation that continued to surface was the accusation that a horrific traffic accident north of Chicago that took the lives of six children had involved a driver who obtained his license illegally by paying a bribe to the Ryan campaign. From what Poshard's campaign already knew, Poshard believed it was appropriate to run a campaign ad highlighting the accident and the growing questions around secretary of state offices selling commercial drivers' licenses.

"The FBI wants answers," a narrator says in the 1998 ad. The ad notes the launch of an extortion probe against Ryan's secretary of state office as well as arrests of Ryan employees. "And George Ryan wants to be our governor?"[16]

Weeks earlier, Poshard had dinner with the Reverend Duane and Janet Willis in their south Chicago home. Over dinner, they discussed the six Willis children killed in an automobile accident involving a truck driver who illegally obtained his commercial driver's license in exchange for money that ended up in Ryan's campaign fund. While traveling on the Interstate north of Chicago, several people tried to warn the driver, Ricardo Guzman, that a taillight assembly was about to fall off his truck, but he kept driving. When the assembly finally fell, it lodged under the van of the Willis family and the van exploded, killing six of the Willis children. Poshard watched videos of the children's parties and related events, heard about their developing lives cut short in the fiery accident.

"I watched these good, decent people pour out their hearts over the loss of their children. I understood their grief at a certain level because I remembered the loss of my sister and four good friends when I was young, but no one can really understand the grief of a loss this profound. I don't know how Duane and Janet were able to get through it, knowing the injustice of it all, except for their devout faith. They knew beyond any doubt that they would see their children again. I shared with them that people from Secretary Ryan's office had secretly sent us copies of the check stubs showing that Ricardo Guzman had his driver's license paid for with a $500 bribe at the McCook driver's license facility. The bribe ended up in George Ryan's campaign fund. But they knew already that a crime was being covered up, because the secretary of state's office had closed the file on the accident and wouldn't open it. Sharing that evening with them was one of the most difficult things I had ever done. I showed them the ad, and they agreed that I could run it. Everything in the ad was absolutely true."

The *Tribune*'s editorial board saw it differently. The editorial page called Poshard "cruel" and "mean spirited" because he had insisted that Ryan's corrupt activities had resulted in the traffic accident that killed the six Willis children. "They said I should 'examine my conscience' and ask myself if 'the governor's office is worth defaming your opponent and trying to ride the deaths of six children to victory?'"[17]

Headlines filled the final weeks of the campaign with the unfolding scandal. For three weeks, Poshard's television ads featured the accident. Some Democrats, including U.S. senator Paul Simon, contended the ad was "over the top and should be pulled." Poshard did so, against his better judgment, in light of the criticism Simon's assessment had brought to his campaign.

Two years later, with Ryan on the edge of indictment after the federal investigation, the *Tribune* apologized.

"An apology is necessary and probably overdue. Along with others, we took Poshard severely to task for a campaign commercial that put then–Secretary of State Ryan at one end of a chain of cause and effect that led to the deaths in a November 1994 traffic accident of the six children of Duane and Janet Willis. If only we had known then what we know now. . . . It is no exaggeration to say that the Willis children, who were incinerated when their family's van hit a part that fell from a truck driven by a man who bought his commercial driver's license, were victims of that corrupt atmosphere in the secretary of state's office."[18]

Months earlier, Poshard called for investigations into wrongdoing. Both the secretary of state's inspector general and the state police investigated. They told Poshard they found nothing. Poshard's office received anonymous documents to the contrary. "There was nothing we could do," said Poshard. "The investigations said they found no wrongdoing."

Poshard accused Ryan's office of using state employees and equipment for campaign purposes and for requiring employees to sell fundraising tickets for George Ryan. "We didn't manufacture this information. It came to us by way of George Ryan's own people. And both the State Police and the Secretary of State Inspector General said they found nothing, but all of it turned out to be true."

Years later, Poshard was on the phone with a reporter who had covered the race. "The reporter needed to tell me something that had caused guilt for a long time. After an interview with investigators about lack of any findings, for some reason, the phone didn't hang up properly, and the reporters were hearing derisive laughter about how Poshard had been played for a fool. The recorders were still on, taping the remarks. They couldn't use it, of course, because they didn't have permission to tape the extended conversation, but it showed how absolutely false the investigation had been and how far they would go to cover up for the governor."

Ryan's campaign deployed other what many described as dirty tricks. In one, a stranger came up to Poshard at the Taste of Chicago festival. The man pulled out a sign that read "Guns = Freedom, Vote Poshard," and someone snapped a picture. The photo appeared in a last-minute brochure produced for the Ryan campaign and was distributed widely in Chicago.[19]

In the run-up to the 1998 election, it was an unfolding story that would be far from complete by election day. Voters would not know what would be uncovered in the months and years ahead. How would they interpret all of this? Baffling to Poshard was the response of U.S. attorney Scott Lassar, whose office handed down the indictments. Lassar said Ryan was not a target of the investigation.[20] How, Poshard wondered, does he know where the investigation will lead? "In my judgment, this was an unconscionable act on the part of Lassar," said Poshard. "George Ryan was secretary of state. He was responsible for his campaign and his office. Plenty of evidence had already been brought to Lassar's attention. How could Ryan not be a target of the investigation? This, in effect, cleared Ryan of any wrongdoing before the facts were even in."

In the closing months, Poshard continued to attempt to leverage his financial disadvantage. A news release on October 25 noted that Phillip Morris contributed $45,000 to Ryan in two weeks. Ryan, the release said, raised $74,000 a day from October 9 to October 22. A Poshard spokesman put it this way: "George Ryan isn't running for election—he's conducting an auction."[21]

Polls consistently showed Ryan with a double-digit lead. Polls for the *Chicago Tribune* showed Ryan ahead by more than twenty points right up to the end. Poshard never believed the polls. He felt the polls made it more difficult for him to raise money and caused a lot of support to wane. A late poll published by the *Chicago Sun-Times* showed Poshard closing to within two percentage points of Ryan, but it came too late to help with fundraising.[22] Poshard's campaign was critical of the *Tribune*'s coverage and its position that political reporter Rick Pearson could fairly cover the campaign while Pearson's wife was a secretary of state employee. Despite the obstacles, Poshard in his gut felt an upset was possible.

In an election eve column on November 2, the *Tribune*'s John Kass wrote this: "I understand Poshard's heart. I've seen the courage it takes for him not to sell his soul for votes. I've seen the price he has paid. I've been saying that character is important. . . . Moral courage counts with me."[23]

As it turned out, Poshard was closer than many thought. But he didn't garner enough votes in Chicagoland. Ryan won with 51 percent of the vote to Poshard's 47.5 percent. On election night, Poshard was gracious. "No purpose is served by anger or resentment. No good is served by dropping out of the system in the future. The time for disappointment is only for this evening. Tomorrow we go back to work."[24]

Poshard remembered, "The first polls after the March primary had Secretary Ryan at 52 percent and me at 30 percent. Despite all the advantages the Ryan campaign held, we came up nearly eighteen points in the final election and they lost a point. No one worked harder than my staff, my family, and I did. We gave it everything we had. When Michael Jordan was asked about the championship Bulls teams and their grit, he would always say, 'We left it all on the floor.' So did we. It's just that the referees turned a blind eye to the fouls that were right in front of them."

Poshard handily won downstate. Larry Woolard, his longtime friend and former colleague in the state Senate, played a lead role in organizing his downstate effort. Woolard said he called Poshard on election morning with reports that some in Chicago who claimed to be handing out "Vote Poshard" cards also carried a second handout without Poshard's name. That lack of enthusiasm by more liberal Democrats who Poshard had supported over many years was telling.

Woolard also feels that Poshard was mistaken not to accept PAC contributions from his friends in labor and other key constituencies. "Had he won, everything would have changed in the dynamics of the state," Woolard said. "In my opinion, the 'good guy' Glenn, by his decision to make a change [in election financing], cost him the election. Had he taken the union money, he could have won and then made the radical changes that needed to be made."[25]

His friend Eddie Smith supports the view that Poshard should have taken contributions from unions, as does SIU political scientist John Jackson. The movement in the final month had been toward Poshard and away from Ryan. Looking back, it's easy to wonder whether the outcome would have changed if only one or two things had gone differently.

In this race, perhaps, one thing that could have impacted the outcome had nothing to do with the campaigns. In January of 1997, near the end of the legislative session, Illinois Republicans, who controlled both chambers, successfully moved through the General Assembly the elimination of straight-party voting. The single punch had always benefited the Democratic Party, particularly in the city of Chicago, where there may be over one hundred judge races that nobody wanted to vote on individually. The year 1998 would see the first Illinois election without straight-ticket voting since 1891. Voters would have to individually mark ballots in each of the races. Looking at the results showed that many Chicago voters filled out the ballot for U.S. Senate and a few other statewide races but passed over the race for governor. Straight party votes could have added as many as 122,000 votes.[26]

Months earlier, in an outline of one of his campaign speeches, Poshard stated why he wanted to be governor. The document cites ensuring quality education for every child, regardless of where they are raised; prioritizing schools over prisons; protecting the vulnerable, including babies without proper nutrition and elderly people without money to pay utilities; standing for high wages and economic justice; balancing budgets; maintaining integrity in government; taking a balanced approach to the environment; granting affordable access to health care; ensuring equality for women in the workplace; and promoting a work ethic second to none.

These issues represent the kind of bread-and-butter matters that Poshard first learned in the southeastern Illinois hills, following his dad through the precincts. He took to heart the speeches he memorized and often recited. The policies he advocated emerged from years in the state Senate and the Congress. He knows better than to dwell on "what if," but it's hard to ignore.

Still disappointed in the result, Poshard appreciated the experience of running for Illinois governor. The sting of the loss doesn't evaporate; neither does the drive to press on. Jackson, a political scientist at SIU and longtime faculty member, administrator, and observer of Illinois politics, has known Poshard from the first days of his political life to the present. Jackson later hired Poshard as an SIU vice chancellor; then he closely followed Poshard's years as SIU president. Jackson said Poshard is defined by four core values:

First, Poshard has a strong sense of public service obligation, a commitment to good citizenship. Second, Poshard has a strong sense of patriotism. Third, he holds a strong sense of religious values and commitment. He doesn't wear religion on his sleeve "but is as deeply committed as any I've ever seen." Finally, Poshard clings to the identity developed in White County, what Jackson referred to as an FDR commitment, meaning that Poshard always identifies with ordinary people. Said Jackson: "None of it is fake with Glenn." He went on to say that "Poshard had been highly effective, that he [Jackson] had recognized how smart he was early in his career. Not as flamboyant as Kenny Gray. Not as international as Paul Simon. It's hard to outwork Glenn. He fits as the kind of Democrat who could win in southern Illinois. Now no Democrat can win down here."[27]

In postelection assessment, the following reasons were cited for Poshard's loss: Poshard could not overcome the liberal wing of his party's opposition to his pro-life position, even though Ryan held the same stance. Their support came too late in the campaign. Poshard was outspent by Ryan $15 million to $4 million. He wasn't able to overcome the flood of negative advertising. That there was no straight party ticket voting cost him important votes in Chicago. Poshard did better downstate than any Democrat since Dan Walker, but his margins in Cook County were well below par. The heavy coverage of the Clinton scandal and impeachment occupied prime real estate in news coverage that otherwise may have gone to the governor's race. The coverage was particularly critical to Poshard because of the gap in campaign funding. The issue of a potential third airport in the Chicago area hurt with key constituents like the Reverend Jesse Jackson and Representative Jesse Jackson Jr.

With it being Poshard's last campaign (he considered running in the 2002 Democratic primary but opted against it), the assessment was an act of clearing the slate. In the moment, he felt the best possible decisions had been made. He had thrown every bit of his energy into a two-year campaign for a job he believed he could have done very well.

The campaign cleared in his mind another slate that, until this book appeared, existed silently in the background. Since his mental health treatment in 1972, he concealed his fear of discovery of his diagnosis and treatment being revealed. The details were known by few. With each new campaign came renewed unease someone might find out and use the mental health issue against him.

A little more than two months before the November 1998 election, Poshard attended a barbecue at the colonial-revival-style home of John and Wanda Rednour on the Du Quoin State Fairgrounds. Constructed in 1942, it is one of two mansions built by fair founder W. R. Hayes for his sons.[28]

At the barbecue, Einar Dyrhkopp, from nearby Gallatin County and a national Democrat committeeman, pulled Poshard aside for a one-on-one meeting. The clear inference of the ensuing conversation was that Republicans asked Dyrhkopp to deliver a message. They revealed to Dyrhkopp the shock therapy treatment Poshard received in 1972.

"Glenn, you have to get out of the race," Poshard remembers Dyrhkopp saying. "They've got your medical records."

"I stood there in stunned silence," Poshard said. "My worst fear had come true only two months before the general election. Jo and I had lived with this fear for years, but I had never developed a concrete plan in my thinking to counter this possibility. For a moment, I saw everything as being lost. But in that moment, I just relinquished control over the whole situation. I felt a calmness come over me and I said to Einar, 'I am not getting out of this race. You can tell those people they need to do whatever they need to do.' It was the most freedom I had experienced since my time with Dr. Longwell. I was not going to live in fear anymore."

At that point, personally, Poshard won. He was at peace with whatever emerged. The issue never came up in the campaign.

Still, he opted not to voluntarily disclose the matter publicly. The account in this book is the first. All these years later and with Poshard retired from public life, the decision to include it still was difficult. It underlines that while nearly one in five Americans experienced mental health issues this year and one in twenty adults experienced serious mental illness, honestly dealing with those issues in helpful ways is elusive.

"If my life can stand as an example to help one person struggling with a mental health issue, then it's worth it."

## CHAPTER 18

# Meeting the New Governor

In March 1999, just four months after the November election, Poshard was in the Illinois Capitol, in the Illinois governor's office, for a meeting with the governor and a top aide. All were dressed in suits, ready for business. They exchanged pleasantries and got down to their task as Poshard took the seat across the desk from the chair he had sought in the election. It was uncomfortable for Poshard. But both he and Ryan, being seasoned elected officials, were amicable toward each other.

Poshard had returned to education as special assistant to the president of John A. Logan College, in Carterville. One of his tasks was to generate support for two new buildings, a community fitness center and a workforce development building. "Ryan had told me that if I ever needed anything to give him a call," Poshard said. "So I went to see George. I told him about the projects and said we needed state support. He gave us the money for both buildings."

The commitment amounted to more than $12 million for two new buildings. In his follow-up letter to Ryan, Poshard wrote in part, "Again, Governor Ryan, this center will enable us to tailor job training efforts to meet the needs of any prospective new business or industry which may locate here and to continue serving the needs of existing businesses." In closing, Poshard wrote, "My family and I continue to hold you up to the Lord in our prayers and wish you much success in your administration."[1]

From Poshard's standpoint, this was vintage Ryan. The governor was known as a dealmaker who could make things happen. The projects were good ones that would help southern Illinois. Poshard's involvement clearly wasn't a negative factor for Ryan, and probably was key. What other assistant to a community college president could schedule a personal meeting with the governor?

The second major goal President Ray Hancock asked Poshard to develop was a campaign for a much-needed property tax increase for the college. Property tax increases were failing all over the state, and the task to pass an increased levy was formidable. But Poshard knew how to organize campaigns, and Logan had a great product to sell. It had been ranked as one of the top community colleges in the country and was held in high esteem by the people in its district. Everyone was given a role to play, and the entire college pitched in. An effective television campaign was developed, and faculty, staff, and students went door-to-door to convince their neighbors of the need. The increased levy passed with room to spare. Poshard had met both of the president's goals, and other doors were soon to open.[2]

A month later, Poshard's gubernatorial campaign made news. Rich Miller, a journalist who covers Illinois politics, wrote that while Poshard claimed his campaign desperately needed money in its final push, he had enough to immediately pay down debt days after the election. The implication was that Poshard didn't put all available resources into the final weeks.

"Just two days after he lost to George Ryan, Poshard wrote a $100,000 check out of his supposedly impoverished campaign account to pay off a bank loan that he had personally guaranteed earlier in the year," Miller wrote in *Capitol Fax*. "That same day, Poshard's campaign also paid off $50,000 of a $100,000 bank loan that the candidate's brother had guaranteed. Poshard gave his entire staff a full week's pay after the campaign ended." Miller's source said the campaign's finances were kept in southern Illinois, away from the

Chicago staff, who contended the money could have been used for much-needed television ads.[3]

The criticism deepened Poshard's still fresh wounds. His response was a three-page letter addressing each point in Miller's article. Poshard wrote that he pleaded for funding in the campaign's final month in efforts to win the election. The appeal had success, particularly after a *Chicago Sun-Times* poll showed Poshard within two percentage points of Ryan.[4]

Poshard said, however, that much of the cash came only days before the election, when it was too late to buy any reasonable time slots on TV. He said he used all the money he could. After the campaign, he asked his treasurer to repay as much debt as possible, which resulted in repayment of $150,000 of the $345,000 he owed. The staff was paid as a reward for months of hard work and long hours. Finally, Poshard wrote this: "After Miller's source inaccurately charged us with hoarding money, the article asserts that I may have done so because I knew I couldn't win. Every day from March 1997 through November 1998 we focused on winning 100 percent of the time.

"There was never a moment when I didn't believe I could win. I worked twenty hours every day, my wife quit her job to campaign full-time, we borrowed every penny we could to put into the campaign, and we didn't campaign just for ourselves, we campaigned for the entire ticket. To say we weren't giving everything we could to win was simply not true."

Poshard's postcampaign transition soon would take another path. A month later, he became a candidate for vice chancellor of administration at SIU Carbondale. At the same time he was preparing to be part of a U.S. State Department delegation for the International Convention on Climate Change in Bonn, Germany, from May 28 to June 12.

Delegates from 146 countries attended the conference, the purpose of which was to establish timetables for compliance with environmental proposals developed at the Kyoto Conference in 1997. Poshard was selected for his background in clean coal technology, his efforts to preserve wilderness and natural wetlands, and his work on land use and forestry matters.

"I had put in so many hours in Congress working on issues concerning the development of clean coal technologies," Poshard said.

"Because of our outstanding research center at SIU, I had become very knowledgeable of the newest research on pre- and postcombustion technologies to clean high sulfur coal. Combined with all the other work I had done on environmental protection, the State Department thought I would be a good fit for their delegation to the Bonn Conference. I was honored by this appointment and very excited to be able to help."

Before his departure, Poshard was told by SIU Carbondale chancellor Jo Ann Argersinger that the search had been terminated and she didn't know when the vice chancellor position would be filled. He later learned that Argersinger and President Ted Sanders were at odds, and his candidacy for the position complicated the deeper clash of top administrators. This was puzzling to Poshard, because only a couple of years before, Sanders had brought Argersinger to his office in Washington, D.C., and he seemed excited about her becoming chancellor. But in June, Argersinger was fired. John Jackson, a prominent and respected political scientist who was vice chancellor for academic affairs and provost, was appointed interim chancellor. Jackson told Poshard to stay at the conference. When he returned, the interview would be reopened for Poshard to be considered.

In Germany, Poshard said there was a bomb threat every day at the conference center. In many ways, the experience was unlike anything in his past: day after day of meetings, back and forth, looking for openings that might lead to progress.

"The Chinese delegation was very, very aggressive toward us," Poshard said. "Their attitude was, 'You're talking to us in negotiations, trying to get us to stop using coal, when you've been polluting the whole globe for years, and now you don't want us to do the same thing you've been guilty of doing yourself.' They were tough negotiators, and they had many third world nations on their side."

Poshard was pleased to be selected as part of the United States delegation and appreciative of the experience, but he was eager to pursue the opportunity at home.

# PART 4

# SOUTHERN ILLINOIS UNIVERSITY LEADERSHIP

CHAPTER 19

# Vision and Action on Campus

As often as twice a week, Poshard left his Anthony Hall office as SIU Carbondale's vice chancellor for administration and stepped into the driver's seat of a university van to spend the day with recruiters and university staff making high school visits. They traversed every corner of southern Illinois, places Poshard knew well, meeting with counselors, students, and parents. Sometimes they had assemblies; other times, small group sessions. Everywhere people knew Poshard. "I did that because I wanted students in this region to know what a great university we had, and I enjoyed it so much," he said of the high school visits.

Having spent nearly two years introducing himself across Illinois, there was comfort getting back to his roots. On campus, he looked for ways to enhance the student experience by addressing physical needs. While nature has been kind to southern Illinois and its university campus, over time buildings show wear. Early in his tenure, Poshard helped identify places to add more than a hundred parking spaces, a move that resulted in a favorable editorial in the student newspaper, the *Daily Egyptian*, headlined "Poshard Is a Man of Action."[1]

He helped lead the updating of the Touch of Nature Environmental Center, or TON. "TON was one of the first special needs camps in the country," Poshard said. "Eunice Shriver came in and made a speech. That's one of the places I went as a student. It was falling into disrepair, and we began fixing up the place." The Jewish Federation, area laborers, and other groups joined the effort as Poshard and the center's staff developed a plan to increase usage and long-term viability of the 150 acres along Little Grassy Lake. Inside the buildings, updated wiring allowed students and faculty to connect and use what were modern computers at the time.[2]

At the direction of Interim chancellor John Jackson, Poshard initiated a campus-wide infrastructure assessment, chairing a twelve-person committee with Phil Gatton, director of physical plant operation, as vice chairman. The resulting land use plan became one of the defining pieces of Poshard's tenure in SIU administration as vice chancellor, as a member of the board of trustees, and then as president. "This was one of Dr. Jackson's main goals, and he had enough confidence in me to move it forward," said Poshard. "I was very grateful for that."

Substandard lighting, outdated signage, labs that begged for modernization, and the need for new buildings were just some of the items identified. The *Daily Egyptian* said Poshard made steady progress addressing campus needs. "More parking spaces, competitive technology, consistent attention and funding devoted to our aging buildings demonstrate Poshard's administrative efficacy at SIUC." Not since President Morris left in the early 1970s had there been such a focus on campus infrastructure.[3]

Student residence halls were far behind in the wiring required to accommodate the latest computers that students needed to keep up with their studies. In just one semester the rewiring was completed and students enjoyed the latest technology in completing their academic and research requirements. It was an important step forward for a university proud of its research reputation.

The committee's initial purpose in 2001, Gatton said, was to move away from an individualized approach of each department doing its own thing. The goal was to develop a cohesive overall campus approach with a comprehensive, long-term view. "People recognized," Gatton said, "that one of the greatest assets is the natural beauty of the campus."[4]

Some also recognized that beyond the natural beauty, certain things didn't look good. Gatton, an engineer and an architect but also the parent of two children assessing college options, had the necessary perspective to ensure prospective students would appreciate the improvements. The dormitory arrangement developed in the 1960s was a turnoff to children of Gatton and many others. Classrooms lacked technology. Labs were old with worn-out equipment. Sidewalks were cracked. The library needed upgrading. The Woody Hall shuffle was still in place after decades. Student health services were still in a cramped dorm far from the center of campus. A new building was needed to centrally locate student services. Athletic facilities had deteriorated. The campus lacked appropriate signage. Some departments were scattered among several different buildings and needed their own space in one location.

The goal was to upgrade facilities to what students were seeing at other locations. Gatton said before the improvements, his son wouldn't consider SIU. That changed when he saw the renovations, things like the seventh floor of the library, which included technology improvements on par with or better than other institutions.

The committee developed a series of questions such as, "Do you want more parking? Green spaces? New labs? Modern dorms? The resulting plan became a map of what the campus could look like.

The committee placed big boards full of ideas on campus and around town. People placed color-coded stickers that showed their preferences. "Below each campus goal are seven ideas for reaching that goal," material from the project says. "Place a dot next to what you think are the best two ideas for reaching each goal. Students are to use red dots, faculty orange dots, and staff yellow dots. Place a blue dot next to any ideas you strongly oppose." More than six thousand people provided feedback. The committee met multiple times a month to review progress and determine next steps.

The team produced a Power Point presentation to show the board of trustees how the campus could be shaped long-term. "We put in timelines for things that could be done quickly, like signage," said Gatton.[5] Minor steps at first helped people realize the plan was working. The improvements included new buildings, upgraded labs and technology, renovated classrooms and lecture halls, library renovation and expansion, and countless other improvements to the campus.

In time, changes came in the way Thompson Point residence halls were organized. The housing arrangement moved away from high-rise dorm-style living and toward an apartment-style arrangement. Some of the older housing was torn down to make way for quads with restrooms for each apartment. "Through Dr. Poshard's leadership, we created a completely different learning environment," Gatton said.

One contentious issue among the committee was the football stadium. "Many on the committee didn't like football," Gatton said. "It required finesse on Glenn's part to get support for that. He knew how to compromise, knew how to get people on board. He was so passionate about what he did. People trusted him."[6]

There was no dispute about the deterioration of McAndrew Stadium. The question was the value of investing in new athletic facilities. Half of the committee didn't want to put any more money into the program, let alone build a new stadium. "McAndrew Stadium was old and an embarrassment to the university," Poshard said. "Locker rooms would flood, the electrical system could hardly be maintained, the bleachers were rusting out, the press box was the joke of the conference, and SIUC hadn't had a winning program in years. While the committee vote wasn't binding on anyone, it did represent how divided the campus community was on this issue, and that's certainly something the board of trustees would have had to take note of." The proposal survived by one vote cast by Poshard, opening the door for the most successful period in SIUC football history, under coach Jerry Kill.

Through student fees, a city sales tax for which Poshard personally lobbied, and state support, the $83 million athletic renovations included a new football stadium, a renovated basketball arena, and a new baseball field. "Without the support of Mayor Brad Cole and the City of Carbondale, it would have been very difficult to finance new athletic facilities for SIUC. Their participation made our job so much easier," said Poshard.

Poshard credits trustee Roger Tedrick with helping shape the final layout of the athletic complex. "Working with Chancellor Walter Wendler, it was Tedrick who suggested the new football stadium be built next door to the arena instead of where we placed it in the land use plan, on the site of the old stadium. He also suggested that the renovation of the arena be done simultaneously to the construction of the football stadium so an economy of scale could be accomplished to cut down on building costs. The east side of the campus was referred to as Saluki Way. Even though it was only a renaming of a small part of the land use plan, which had already designated new athletic facilities, it held a much more inviting and emotional appeal to potential donors. Roger and I worked closely with Dr. Duane Stucky to find the financial resources to rebuild and renovate the SIUC campus, a job of which I will always be proud."

Leading the plan development and then seeing it come together remains a point of pride for Poshard. It is part of his long-term relationship with SIU, dating back to his days as a student. "It would be hard for me to explain how deep my love for SIU has been over all the years," he said. "The opportunities it gave me as a student, a poor kid from the hill country of southeastern Illinois, and working with the SIUC administration for so many years in carrying important legislation for the university in Springfield and Washington, as well as holding important administrative posts, were life-changing experiences for me. But nothing I've done surpasses the sheer joy and excitement of leading this committee to develop an entire land use plan for our beloved university that would guide its future development for decades to come. With maximum input from the entire university community, we tackled every part of needed development. New buildings, including an expanded Morris Library, a new Transportation Education Center, a new Student Services Building, a new Student Health Services Building, new residence halls at Grand and Wall, renovated labs and classrooms, new sidewalks, new signage, and multiple new athletic facilities."

The Transportation Education Center brought together two of SIUC's most nationally known programs, the Automotive Technology and Aviation Technology programs. Poshard worked with former state senator Larry Woolard, who was then the governor's economic development director for southern Illinois, to include funding for the center in the 2009 Capital Construction Bill and later negotiated an agreement to build the center on SIU-owned property at the Southern Illinois Airport. The plan changed the campus experience with long-term implications. It is one of the defining parts of Poshard's years in SIU leadership. In July 2022 the SIU board of trustees voted to name the facility the Glenn Poshard Transportation Education Center.

In late summer of 2000, rumors started that Poshard might soon announce plans to run for governor in 2002. "I thought about it," he says now. "The polls showed a double-digit lead. But I couldn't change on taking PAC money. I knew there would be pressure to accept big money. I wanted to send the opposite message. Jo and I were still in debt, and when we weighed and balanced everything, I just said I couldn't do this again." The decision found favor with the *Daily Egyptian*. One headline read, "Poshard's Decision to Stay Brings Stability to SIUC Infrastructure."[7]

The governor's race rumors resurfaced in 2001, this time suggesting Poshard was preparing to accept PAC money. SIU trustees were asked about the developments after a board meeting. Poshard assured the board and the media that he was not running again. He enjoyed his job at SIUC.

Another event that year stood out personally. In October, Poshard was named Illinois 4H alumnus of the year, an award that recognizes major contributions through outstanding career accomplishments, leadership, and responsibility in civic and community affairs and citizenship. "In my quarter century of public service, I consider this to be among the highest honors I have received," Poshard said at the time, which included recognition at a University of Illinois football game and a reception hosted by President James Stukel and Chancellor Michael Akin. Poshard and his wife Jo both grew up participating in 4-H programs, Jo also winning statewide 4-H awards.

University president James Walker initiated two major reports in 2002. The first was a "2020 Vision," led by retired senator Paul Simon.[8] Simon sought input from external leaders on how SIU could remain at the education forefront in a rapidly changing world. The second report, led by distinguished SIU alum and former trustee William Norwood, dealt with collaborative opportunities between campuses in Carbondale and Edwardsville. The task force's purpose was to identify "ways to foster greater cooperation and collaboration among our various campuses maximizing our resources and the strengths of SIU as one university." That report would have implications in years to come. A few years later, when Poshard became president of the university system, he followed both reports as nearly as possible in governing SIU.

In 2003, Illinois had a new governor, Rod Blagojevich, a former congressman from Chicago. Poshard supported Paul Vallas, a former Chicago school superintendent, in the Democratic primary, much to the dismay of many of his supporters. Some wrote him strong letters questioning his loyalty and judgment in backing Vallas. "There were several Democratic meetings," said Poshard, "where I was not welcomed. I kept a file of letters from outraged Democrats, many of them my close friends, who couldn't believe that I was backing Vallas, one of the smartest people with whom I had ever worked in government."

Governor Ryan didn't seek reelection as controversies grew from investigations into the illegal sale of driver's licenses, use of state equipment and employees for political campaigns, and related matters. A federal investigation into the automobile accident that killed six Willis family children and had been central in Poshard's gubernatorial campaign made headlines. Since the 1998 election, Poshard had many opportunities to comment on scandals emerging around Ryan that verified charges Poshard made during the campaign but had been rejected at the time. Poshard declined those opportunities to comment until March 2003, five years after the election.

In an extensive interview with Jim Muir of the *Southern Illinoisan* newspaper, the headline read, "It's Time for Me to Tell My Story."[9] Poshard talked about his view of unfolding indictments, which at that point didn't include Ryan. Poshard described how his campaign staff turned over to investigators documents showing money from illegal sales of driver's licenses going into Ryan's campaign. He described details of use of state equipment and employees for campaign purposes. He expressed his disappointment that separate investigations by the Illinois state police and the secretary of state's inspector general turned up nothing. Now, years later, a federal investigation uncovered wrongdoing that resulted in prison sentences. "Ryan was using state equipment and state employees," Poshard was quoted as saying in the article. "We know that to be a fact now. And still, two state police superintendents conducted investigations and couldn't find anything wrong."

Poshard said in the *Southern Illinoisan* article that he could accept it if voters knew the candidates and their positions and chose his opponent. It's now clear, he said, that the voters didn't have facts about the candidates. "I don't want George Ryan to go to prison," he was quoted as saying. "For me to run for governor of this state, that was a truly wonderful and great experience. I felt like I had a dream taken away from me based on lies and corruption."

Jackson, no longer the interim chancellor but still a key figure on campus, cautioned Poshard to be careful about his comments. Public discussion of such issues by administrators could jeopardize SIU funding. Hazel Loucks, the deputy governor for education and workforce development, reinforced that message. During an appearance on campus, she pulled Poshard aside at a meeting in the Dunn-Richmond Economic Development Center after the lengthy interview appeared in print. She said he should not talk to the press anymore; it might jeopardize SIU.

"Louck's comments really upset me," Poshard said. "I loved SIU. It was my alma mater. I had devoted much of my time in the Illinois Senate and the U.S. Congress to protecting and supporting it. I would never do anything to harm my university. But here was a deputy governor serving George Ryan telling me to be quiet about things I had said were true, and were proven to be true, or I could be harming the university. It felt like it was just a continuation of the threats we endured during the campaign. After nearly five years of silence, I had the right to tell my story, and I did." It was a frustration that would not go away easily.

In 2006, Ryan was convicted by a federal jury of eighteen counts of wrongdoing related to the scandal. The governor knew, for example, that incriminating documents were shredded so that investigators wouldn't see them. The former governor spent more than five years in prison.[10]

Poshard had followed the indictments, convictions, and imprisonment of Ryan and key staff members over ensuing years. On a regular basis, Poshard heard friends and others say Illinois would be a different state now had he been elected. Speculation proves nothing. It only adds to the enduring pain. "The only thing that bothered me was that people never got to know the truth," Poshard said. "I trust the people when they have the truth to consider. Short of that, an election is pretty meaningless."

One of his last acts as vice chancellor was to advocate for funding for key initiatives like Alzheimer and Parkinson disease programs and development of a cancer institute for the medical school. He felt comfortable back on campus and enjoyed his work. He also felt it was time to move on.

In July 2003, Poshard, age fifty-seven, retired as vice chancellor. The *Southern Illinoisan* published a twenty-page tabloid section about his years at SIU and his public service, titled "A Salute to Glenn Poshard: Patriot, Servant, Friend." The section included articles on many highlights from his career. The campus hosted a retirement picnic in which people from across the region wished him well.

He wouldn't sit still for long. In the fall, he helped facilitate the end to a thirty-five-day teachers' strike in Benton.[11] Other opportunities would soon follow.

CHAPTER 20

# Trustees Turning Inward

Southern Illinois University was at a crossroads, trustee Ed Hightower remembers. Legislators representing the SIUE area were submitting bills to break up the system and give SIUE its own board of trustees. Retaining the system governance approach was increasingly an issue. Budget matters called for growth in some areas, consolidation in others. Each campus faced significant building needs. Student recruitment required fresh approaches. As the board assessed the best way forward, it felt Poshard was uniquely qualified.[1]

His life and career revolved around the southern Illinois region, governance, and SIU. His connections would help fund growth initiatives. He had a grasp of the campus issues, having served as vice chancellor for administration at SIUC and then being appointed by Governor Blagojevich to a six-year term on the SIU Board of Trustees in January 2004. In March 2004 Poshard was named the board chairman.

President James Walker had come to SIU from Middle Tennessee State University, where he had built a modern campus and was revered in Tennessee higher education circles. He brought stability to

SIU in a chaotic time. But shortly into his tenure, he became ill with advanced-stage prostate cancer. Poshard supported Walker while he battled cancer, filling voids created by the president's illness. The board of trustees appointed Duane Stucky as the interim president after granting Walker extended sick leave, hoping he could recover from his illness. "When Roger Tedrick and I went to visit Dr. Walker to offer him the sick leave, we were stunned by his appearance," Poshard said. "He had lost a tremendous amount of weight and seemed very fragile. He had been a fine president for SIU, but it was clear his health was failing him fast, and we wanted to help relieve the stress."

When it became clear that Walker would not be able to continue his presidency, a discussion was held at a board of trustees meeting on the East St. Louis campus of SIUE about starting a search for a new president. Poshard was asked after that meeting if he would be a candidate. "Even though I had my doctorate in administration of higher education, had served as vice chancellor for administration at SIUC, had been a member of the board of trustees, had served on the Education Committee in both the Illinois state Senate and the U.S. Congress, where I had given 100 percent support to SIU, I answered the question by saying I would not be a candidate; I hadn't even had time to think about it. The next day I got a call from Dr. Walker asking if I would come to see him. I went to meet with him, and he immediately told me that I should be a candidate for the president's job and gave me all the reasons he felt that way." After talking it over with his family, Poshard resigned from the board in June 2005, and announced he would seek the presidency.

"We were looking for someone with impeccable character and a long reach, political connections to move the system forward," Hightower said. "It was our desire to turn to Glenn, not something he pushed. . . . Glenn was and still is such a visionary. He forecast that the system should plan for reduction in student enrollment because of declining state revenues and the loss of Illinois students to other states. He saw the need to build SIUE in the next phase of growth. SIUE was a commuter campus, which is what some wanted it to remain. Now it has housing, Division 1 athletics, doctoral programs. He and Chancellor Vaughn Vandegrift were a great team to make those things happen.

"On the Carbondale campus, he saw a different concern. He said we have to make it affordable because it's a rural area. We have to change the marketing plan to compete with neighboring states, and we have to implement the land use plan he had developed as vice chancellor of administration there."[2]

In November 2005, trustees unanimously voted for Poshard as SIU president, beginning in January 2006. He set the tone for how he would operate by the way he organized his office. The SIU president's office is in the Stone Center, which was constructed as a presidential residence in 1971. It's named after W. Clement Stone, who donated $1 million to dampen complaints about higher-than-expected costs.

Sliding glass doors behind the president's desk open to a concrete patio suitable for an open-air meeting or a moment of reflection. The grassy lawn slopes downward toward a grove of trees that burst in colors each fall. In the spring you can walk down to the edge of the meadow or beyond and perhaps take in the unique odor of skunk cabbage or the sweeter odor of mayapple. Inside, a multilevel bookcase requires stretching one's arm to reach its top. Two maroon chairs face the president. A long conference table comfortably accommodates twelve to fifteen people. As the president sits at the desk, a long wall, some four paces long, provides space for a visual, a piece of artwork perhaps.

Poshard asked the university's physical plant to erect an oversized white board. Phil Gatton, director of plant and service operations, remembers it as a custom board, essentially three large boards pieced together, covering about fourteen feet. The board is an enduring memory for multiple people who worked closely with Poshard. The board had the operating plan for SIU, with action steps supporting key themes, from the budget to diversity. Poshard regularly updated the board. It became a reference point for discussions at the conference table. It was a waypoint that helped leaders focus on what's most important.

The Stone Center became central in another way. For various reasons, dating back many years, the building had served as not only the office of the president but also home to other university organizations, doubling as an entertainment center for the system and the campus. Jo Poshard brought new energy to the Stone Center by using the building to accommodate the entertainment expectations required of a university president.

"This beautiful architectural marvel, with its spacious dining room, elegant reception hall, large patios, and manicured lawn and flower beds could showcase educational, cultural, and charitable events," she said. She believed the Stone Center should be alive with activity that would benefit the university and the broader community. Art auctions, artistic and musical performances, and the gatherings of educational societies soon became the norm for the center under Jo's leadership. The SIU Women's Club, the American Association of University Women, Friends of McLeod Summer Playhouse, and Carbondale Community Arts were some of the organizations that were hosted by Jo Poshard at the Stone Center.

One priority the board of trustees set out for President Poshard was to foster a team-based approach. Poshard identified staff he would rely on as partners. In the finance area, he enjoyed a close relationship with Stucky, a veteran administrator. Poshard asked John Haller, vice president for academic affairs, to delay his planned retirement, to which Haller agreed. General counsel Jerry Blakemore served as a key advisor. In Springfield, Poshard worked with Dave Gross to help move SIU priorities through legislation and work with state agencies. Gross had been one of Poshard's top staffers when he served in the Illinois Senate, and Poshard knew how effective he would be for SIU. Managing flow to and from the office was Paula Keith, assistant to the president. Poshard spoke weekly with Roger Tedrick, who succeeded him as board chairman.

Based in Springfield, Gross was a bridge between the campuses and state government. Tall and slender, with neatly parted graying hair, Gross was a veteran around the statehouse. Wearing Saluki maroon in Carbondale and Cougar red when in Edwardsville, Gross shuttled between the campuses, lawmakers, and state agencies. Those Springfield connections were critical to execute the plans on the whiteboard. Keith, who it seemed knew every administrator on both campuses, formed a team with Gross and Poshard in making sure that the SIU story was always front and center in Springfield and Washington.

Nine months into his presidency and for the first time since Morris led SIU, Poshard had a formal inauguration to further set the tone for SIU's future. "I really was unsure about a formal inauguration ceremony, but several key advisors on both campuses felt we should reestablish the tradition," Poshard said. "After all, there were only two systems in the state, and the University of Illinois had never broken its tradition. Perhaps SIU shouldn't have either, was the thinking."

On September 28, 2006, about twenty-five hundred people gathered at the SIU Arena; among them were state Senate president Emil Jones, attorney general Lisa Madigan, and several lawmakers.[3] In his remarks designed to outline a vision for the future, Poshard cited the Morris inaugural multiple times. Morris, Poshard said, saw opportunity for the region and country and for the leading role of the university to deliver in areas of teaching, research, and service. Poshard said the renewed vision for SIU "must begin with our traditional values of accessibility, affordability, and citizenship preparation." He quoted from the Robert Frost poem "Reluctance" in saying the university shouldn't yield to those who say our best days are in the past.

*Ah, When to the heart of man*
*Was it ever less than a treason*
*To go with the drift of things*
*To yield with a grace to reason*
*And bow and accept the end*
*Of a love or a season? (19–24)*[4]

At SIU, Poshard said, there will be no acceptance of "the drift of things." Early in his remarks he cited Morris's question: "To what are our children born? To poverty, to poor health, to ignorance, or to hope and promise?" In closing, Poshard answered Morris's question this way: "To hope, to opportunity, to the future that only our Southern Illinois University can offer."

Haller said you could feel the speech, which Poshard wrote, as was his custom. Haller said the formal inaugural set the tone for the aggressive, optimistic, forward-looking focus outlined on that whiteboard. Sitting in a wide Morris Library hallway near an original drawing of Old Main, Haller recounted how the plans turned into action. "His plans were very real. He held people's feet to the fire in terms of those objectives. And we all knew it."[5]

Poshard was the seventh SIU president, or ninth if interim presidents are counted. Haller served six of the nine. "Of all those presidents, Glenn is the most impressive to me." Haller served not only the university presidents but also worked with trustees and the Illinois

Board of Higher Education. His long experience at SIU and higher education administration provided Poshard with a needed experienced voice and perspective. In the book *Southern Illinois University at 150*, Haller wrote this of Poshard's presidency: "Anyone who has spent time with Glenn Poshard is aware of his interpersonal and leadership skills, his magic with legislators in both Springfield and Washington, and his genius at strategic thinking."[6]

Keith, administrative assistant to the president, whom Poshard credits with much of his success at SIU, managed the schedule and activity flow. She described Poshard as humble, well- connected, strategic, passionate. Poshard didn't flaunt his connections. Rather, he used them strategically. Keith said having the president ask to put the governor on the line, or a key contact in Washington, was typical.[7]

Another key Poshard partner was Vandegrift, the chancellor at SIUE. Vandegrift said in one of their initial meetings Poshard presented ideas for the campus. "I said, 'Mr. President, give me fifteen minutes and I'll show you where I think Edwardsville can go.' " Vandegrift described an SIUE future for an inclusive, premiere metropolitan campus with high standards. "Glenn listened to me for fifteen or twenty minutes and then said, 'Chancellor, forget what I said to you and do everything you just said. I think it's a strong plan, and I'm here to help.' "[8]

SIUE was growing beyond its commuter school roots. It was ready to become a residential university, prepared to grow and enhance its regional reach. "I loved Chancellor Vandegrift," Poshard said. "He was so committed, so passionate about SIUE, and he was exactly the right person to take the university to a higher level. In the eight and a half years I was president, there was never a time we disagreed on the goals or the future needs of SIUE. I was so thankful I got to work with him on building new labs in the dental school, developing the school of pharmacy, developing one of the finest schools of nursing in America, and building new science and technology buildings, all part of his vision for his university."

Politically, Edwardsville's growing stature created a challenge. State Representatives Tom Holbrook and Jay Hoffman, both representing the Metro East area, introduced legislation to separate SIUC and SIUE so that each would be independent, with its own governing board. They contended that by separating governance from the flagship Carbondale campus, Edwardsville would receive more state support. With Poshard's appointment, however, they put their efforts on hold and, out of respect for the new president, provided him time to show he would be fair to both campuses.

"One of my first tasks after becoming president was to sit down with Representatives Holbrook and Hoffman and assure them I would work to help both campuses develop in the best way I could and would not treat Edwardsville with less respect than Carbondale. I believe our mutual friendship over the years enabled them to trust me in working toward that goal, and they withdrew their bills to split the system."

It helped to have Hightower, the school superintendent in Edwardsville and a high-profile college basketball official, and Metro East lawyer John Simmons on the SIU board along with Marquita Wiley, who had an outstanding career in finance, Mark Hinrichs in construction management, Tedrick in insurance, and Keith Sanders, a former SIU dean and vice president in the University of Wisconsin system. "This was an outstanding board of professionals who worked as a team and provided me with the best advice and guidance I could ever hope for," said Poshard. "They had risen to the top of their professions, understood the board's role of governance and policy, and stayed away from trying to micromanage the university."

Gross helped supply legislative support. "They wanted to grow academically," Gross said of SIUE. "Vaughn helped Glenn through the thickets."[9] The priorities outlined by Vandegrift and endorsed by Poshard took shape. "Our science building was so crowded, we were teaching classes on Sunday," Vandegrift said. "Glenn took responsibility to get a science building. He went around the state and talked about the importance of a capital bill for higher education. He could see how to get things done."[10]

In remarks in September 2006 at an SIUE town hall meeting, Poshard noted several Edwardsville assets, including a 330-acre research and technology park that includes a corn-to-ethanol research center and an international trade center that provided expertise to entities across southern Illinois. The pharmacy school, which opened in 2005, the dental school, and the nursing school all combined to make SIUE a leader in health care education for downstate Illinois, Poshard told the gathering.

As to management style, Vandegrift described Poshard as "directive but not prescriptive. . . . He could do things for Edwardsville that were going to improve our university but not be involved in day-to-day operations. We needed a spokesperson and champion for the politicians and the public, and Glenn was certainly that person."[11]

The progress at SIUE strengthened Poshard's oft-repeated theme that all in the SIU system were better together. Separating individual pieces would weaken them all. Talk of separate governance dissipated.

Poshard's 2006 performance review showed high marks across the board, including increasing presence in Springfield and Washington, D.C., expanding diversity, developing an SIUC master plan, building support for SIU as a system, building a collaborative atmosphere, and improving campus infrastructure across the system.[12] Not everyone saw the progress. An editorial in the *Daily Egyptian* had nothing good to say about Poshard's first year other than his hopeful inaugural.[13]

In February 2006, Poshard and the campus mourned the death of President Walker, who was credited with bringing stability during a challenging time. "Dr. Walker came to SIU after a highly contentious time for the Carbondale campus," Poshard said. "Tensions between Dr. Ted Sanders's presidency and Chancellor Jo Ann Argersinger flared into the open. It was into this atmosphere that Dr. Walker brought his calm, moderating demeanor for the time he served, even though the feelings and attitudes from the Sanders era continue to the present day."

In Carbondale, enrollment, affordability, and promotion of the university's regional role were top issues. Several articles on affordability are among the documents Poshard retained from early in his presidency. One, written by Haller and titled "The American Dream: Alive but Ailing," outlines key metrics that Poshard consistently used as themes in his remarks.[14] The themes include showing that the benefits of higher education are both economic and social drivers of the regional and national economy.

In early 2007, Poshard wrote eleven typewritten pages on the need for affordability. He cited statistics showing those from low-income households are far less likely to attend a university. He noted southern Illinois is a low-income region, and this has a direct bearing on the university's ability to recruit students from its own region. He cited benefits to students and society of a university education, such as better health, improved quality of life, better consumer decision-making, higher salaries, increased quality of civic life, greater productivity, and more charitable giving, among several others.[15]

The solution, he wrote, has multiple facets, including increases in student aid like Pell grants, the Stafford loan program, and the Perkins loan program; flexibility for Illinois universities to waive the difference between resident and out-of-state students; flexibility for more needs-based scholarships for Illinois students; the creation of an "SIU achievement scholarship" targeted to those with a family income below the median; and creation of a local tax beginning with the state's lower thirty counties for students attending community colleges and public universities.

Blakemore recalls a Saturday morning call from Gross, who said Poshard was going to meet with the governor about student aid, and there might be legal issues. "I got off the treadmill, showered, and spent the next couple days there," said Blakemore.[16] They met with Senate president Emil Jones and other legislators about scholarship programs for first-generation students, a program that had been cut by the federal government. Poshard persuaded Jones to add to the SIU budget scholarships for these students.

In July 2007, Poshard and SIUC published a two-page newspaper advertisement outlining SIUC accomplishments and the university's regional impact. The more than seventy-one hundred employees were greater in number than those of the top ten other industries in southern Illinois combined. The $495 million operating budget was cited as one of the most important drivers of the regional economy.[17]

Poshard spoke in February 2007 at a community leaders' breakfast in which he outlined plans to promote the university across the region.[18] In September 2007 he announced openings of service centers at community colleges to promote the transition to SIU, to promote dual credit offerings, explore night and weekend classes, and build on existing relationships.[19] "I devoted a great deal of my time trying to reach out and strengthen relationships with our community colleges. I honestly felt the university had not done enough to cement those relationships over the years, and by the time I became president, many of the community colleges had developed programs with other universities, and some of them were out of state. I am a strong believer in the community colleges and wanted to make every attempt to work closely with them and give them assurance that SIU was there to meet their students' needs. Key to this outreach to community colleges and southern Illinois were two top staffers, John Davis and Brian Chapman. Davis and Chapman helped build positive relationships for the SIU system throughout the region and in Springfield."

The Vandegrift partnership and Poshard's relationships with senior administrators at the Stone Center formed a core with the administrative teamwork envisioned at his hiring. Working as a unit toward common goals was vital to meeting objectives. The biggest challenge proved to be finding the right fit to lead SIUC as chancellor. Early in his tenure as president, Poshard demoted SIUC chancellor Walter Wendler for being insubordinate and not a team player.[20] Poshard and Wendler had enjoyed a good working relationship as chancellor and vice chancellor for SIUC, but when Poshard became chairman of the board of trustees, a board directive to include benefits to same-sex partners became a major issue between them. Poshard said it was the right thing to equally extend benefits to same-sex couples. It had been brought to the board of trustees by Chancellor David Werner, who strongly favored the policy for SIUE. SIU had been the last university in the state to make the decision to extend those benefits, and the board mandated the change in policy. Wendler publicly disagreed on multiple occasions and spoke to the issue from his own personal religious point of view. This conflict became a divisive issue on the campus, with Wendler viewing it as a moral issue and others as an issue of equality. It made newspaper headlines all over the state, a controversy the Carbondale campus could ill afford at the time.

"I liked Dr. Wendler, and I believed I had served him well when I was vice chancellor for administration. But when I became board chairman and later president of the university, the relationship changed. I gave him good evaluations but privately had many conversations about his failure to communicate and his constant applying for jobs elsewhere without my knowledge. The issue of benefits to same-sex partners was only one of several issues that divided us."

The ensuing national search led to Texas, where the SIU committee received strong reviews while vetting Fernando Trevino, who was introduced as chancellor in May 2007.[21] The reviews received in the search process didn't match with what Poshard and others experienced at SIU. In April 2008, SIUC reassigned Trevino to a professorship at the School of Medicine in Springfield, which he declined. Poshard had placed Trevino on administrative leave in March 2008, saying Trevino didn't fulfill requirements outlined in his contract.[22] "The search committee's recommendation of Dr. Trevino was a strong recommendation, and several members of the committee visited his university in Texas. They received glowing reports from the people with whom they met. The other two finalists were not highly qualified, with one being objected to by the faculty union for his anti-union position on many issues. I hired Trevino and soon found out that we were all wrong. The man simply failed to perform, even minimally, his responsibilities. He sued us for several hundred thousand dollars and wanted a large settlement. I flatly rejected it, and we won the suit. He didn't get a penny."

To stabilize the position after departures of Wendler and Trevino, Poshard and the board turned to Sam Goldman, who had a long and successful relationship with the SIUC community. Goldman arrived on campus in 1980 as dean of the former College of Human Resources. He served the campus in multiple ways and on many committees, developing relationships with faculty, staff, and students. With a smile, he remembers sitting in a dining hall listening, interacting with students. At one point, a student surveyed him and asked something like this: "Now who are you again?"[23]

The familiarity with the campus and the faculty allowed Goldman to immediately step into issues. He and Poshard agreed on a set of goals for the Carbondale campus. Among Goldman's accomplishments were starting the School of Nursing at Carbondale by joining with Edwardsville, which already had the needed accreditation. Goldman also worked through challenging budgets that led to consolidating programs and no pay raises caused by reductions in operating revenue.

"The state, under Governor Blagojevich, was cutting back significantly on funding higher education, and our office began implementing spending restrictions that affected both campuses," Poshard said. "It was hard making the cuts while at the same time experiencing inordinate delays in state funding, but Dr. Stucky and I stayed with our plan for sound fiscal management. Dr. Goldman and Dr. Vandegrift handled these spending restrictions well and worked cooperatively with each other."

The budget and enrollment would be a focus for the next chancellor. Like other Illinois universities, SIU faced multiple challenges to attract and retain students. In the late spring of 2010, Poshard took a phone call from the chair of the chancellor search committee. Poshard was disappointed the search committee recommended just one candidate, Rita Cheng. Typically multiple names would be forwarded to the president, who ultimately made the decision. "After the interviews, however, I concurred completely with the committee's decision. I thought Dr. Cheng was an impressive candidate, and she was hired for the job."

Cheng had a record of building enrollment at University of Wisconsin–Milwaukee. Her background in accounting and business administration would be helpful in addressing budgetary issues. Coming to the campus at a time when new buildings and infrastructure needs were already being addressed by the land use plan passed ten years earlier, the new chancellor could focus on other, more pressing issues.

In her first two years, Chancellor Cheng began some important initiatives. The board of trustees had agreed that in light of the turnovers the campus had experienced in that office, she should be allowed to build her own team and put forth her own plan for future success. One of her earliest decisions in addressing the enrollment issue was to restructure the office of vice chancellor for student affairs, essentially eliminating that position, while creating a University College to coordinate advisement and support services, particularly for new freshmen and transfer students.

Larry Dietz, who had held the position of vice chancellor for student affairs, decided to move on, which later led to a successful seven years as Illinois State University president before his retirement in 2021, after more than fifty years in higher education. "Dr. Cheng, in evaluating the effectiveness of the University College, believed strongly that it helped halt the enrollment decline, and in her fourth and last year at SIUC, the enrollment had begun to rise again," Poshard said. "I had serious personal reservations about the chancellor's decision to push Larry out. As vice chancellor for student affairs, Larry had responsibility for student enrollment, and enrollment had fallen. But it had fallen in nearly every university in the state, and SIUC had fared better than most in keeping up its numbers. Despite those facts, the chancellor was convinced that a change was needed. Larry and I had started working together as colleagues and friends when Dr. John Jackson was interim chancellor, and that relationship continued under Chancellor Wendler. I had great respect for Larry's ability and integrity. At the same time, however, I did not want to be micromanaging the campuses, especially high-profile personnel decisions."

In putting her administrative team together, the chancellor hired Gary Minish as the new provost. Minish had been a highly effective dean at the SIUC College of Agriculture, and many applauded the chancellor's decision, believing he and Cheng would make an excellent team to lead the campus. But in less than two weeks, Minish had resigned the position and would not return. "It was stunning," said Poshard. "I had several conversations with Dr. Minish, pleading with him to return and give the relationship time to build. He was adamant. He responded, saying not only that Dr. Cheng was overly authoritarian and did not respect his relationship with the deans but also that their opposite leadership styles would never allow them to work effectively with each other.

"The loss of these two people, Dietz and Minish, was very difficult for me because I knew them both as excellent administrators and good friends, and I hated to see them leave. Given the ongoing circumstances at SIUC, it would have been inappropriate for me, regardless of my feelings, to become involved in personnel decisions that were clearly within the authority of the chancellor to decide.

"To her credit, Dr. Cheng made some tough choices with which I agreed," Poshard said. "She made decisions which upset a lot of people: cutting expenses and redirecting resources to priority areas to balance the budget. Her decision in November of 2010 to enact furloughs to save jobs and bring financial stability to the campus brought strong resistance from the faculty union and would prolong negotiations on a new contract well into the next year, culminating in a strike led by the faculty union that divided the campus and the region.

Early in Poshard's tenure, the campus received the results of the Simpson Scarborough Report, a review by an outside marketing firm that concluded resources were insufficient to be a top-seventy-five public research university, which had been the goal of the SIU at 150 Plan, and also to maintain the desired focus on undergraduate teaching. "The SIU at 150 Plan was ten years old when Dr. Cheng became chancellor, and many parts of it had proven to be unattainable. To become a top-seventy-five research university as the plan proposed was simply beyond the university's resources to achieve," Poshard said. "During her first two years, she led a campus committee to develop a new plan, Pathways to Excellence, which met with broad approval from faculty and staff.

"Dr. Cheng held important positions with the NCAA Governing Board and, I believe, advanced SIU's athletic programs while she served in that capacity," Poshard said. "Chancellor Cheng had considerable talent, but during the last year or so of her administration, the president's office received constant complaints about her autocratic leadership style. I had discussions with Dr. Cheng about implementing a more democratic approach to leadership. I wanted her to succeed, but my advice didn't work and eventually led to a serious division between us. I was retiring at the end of June 2014, and before I left, I learned that she had accepted a position as president at Northern Arizona University."

Strong administrative relationships continued at SIUE, where Julie Furst-Bowe was appointed chancellor in July 2012. In her prior position as associate vice chancellor for academic and student affairs at the University of Wisconsin–Stout, she had been prominent in leading that campus to receiving the prestigious Malcolm Baldridge National Quality Award in Higher Education. She was a sought-after international speaker in science and math education and had spoken at conferences in Singapore, Dubai, Azerbaijan, Bahrain, Thailand, Canada, England, India, Mexico, Japan, and other countries.

"In my discussion with Dr. Charles Sorenson, the chancellor to whom she reported in the Wisconsin system, he had the highest praise for her ability and desire for quality academic improvement," said Poshard. "SIUE was a growing university, and it needed a leader who emphasized the academic growth to keep up with the increased student enrollment. I felt Dr. Furst-Bowe fit that bill nicely and agreed that the search committee had made a sound choice."

In her first year at SIUE, the faculty evaluations made it clear that Dr. Furst-Bowe had open and transparent communication with campus constituencies. Her democratic style of leadership fit Poshard's own style and continued the excellent relationship between chancellor and president that had existed with Chancellor Vandegrift. Furst-Bowe continued the work on completing the science and art and design buildings and began the creation of a new Instructional Design and Learning Technologies Center, which greatly complemented the campus's ability to expand its online programs and a new strategic plan for summer course offerings.

"Unfortunately for me," said Poshard, "the last year and a half of my administration as president was drawing to a close, so I never got to work with Dr. Furst-Bowe extensively. I thought she was making good progress in her goal of enhanced academic improvement at SIUE and, given appropriate administrative support from the system, would bring the campus to an even higher academic level."

While the Carbondale and Edwardsville campuses often are the focus, the Springfield-based medical school has a long reach that impacts much of the state. One of Poshard's documents relating to the medical school is a handwritten single sheet that cites six goals: to fund finishing the cancer center, restore Alzheimer and Parkinson research funding, promote telemedicine, promote Medprep, and expand patient care clinics and children's health programs. Founded in 1970, the medical school sometimes misses the headlines received by the Carbondale and Edwardsville campuses. The school's mission is to help meet health care needs in central and southern Illinois via education, patient care, research, and community service.

"I had absolute faith in Dr. [Kevin] Dorsey and his staff to run the medical school appropriately, to build on its growing reputation, and he did," Poshard said. "The medical school reported directly to the SIUC chancellor, and it was the president's job to advocate for and maximize its funding from the state and federal government, which we always tried to do. During my administration and under Dr. Dorsey's leadership, the medical school saw tremendous growth and trained hundreds of young doctors to serve the needs of medically underserved areas of our state and nation."

When the medical school sought a donor to contribute more than $10 million toward a new cancer center in Springfield, trustee John Simmons asked to go along to hear the pitch to potential donors, including a major drug company. The companies who heard the pitch declined. But Simmons was interested. He took the idea to partners at his law offices.[24] The result is the Simmons Cancer Institute, which Simmons describes as being designed to focus on the patient, bringing providers to patients in a single location. "The SIU Cancer Institute is just the tip of the iceberg of all the philanthropic efforts that John Simmons and his wife Jayne have made over the years to promote southern Illinois in a hundred different ways. They are some of the most generous people with whom I have worked in my career."

Poshard was comfortable and effective working with the medical school leaders to help promote the cancer institute. One reason such tasks fit Poshard is because of the depth of his feelings for the university and important projects like the institute. Blakemore, who later moved on to positions with Northern Illinois University and the University of North Carolina–Greensboro, said the defining characteristic of Poshard is his passion for SIU developed over his lifetime, beginning as a student. "He approaches issues from where his character is," Blakemore said. "He cared as much for the people who scooped snow to clear the parking lots as he did the highest-paid professor and administrator."

On a personal level, Blakemore said when his appendix burst, Poshard visited almost every day. "He helped put me in the car leaving the hospital. He treated everyone like a best friend, and he knew almost everyone. He was equally effective in the classroom," said Blakemore, who had Poshard speak to his law classes on different occasions.[25]

Bigger picture, Poshard's appreciation for the region helped link SIU with a broader vision. "Public higher education never had the type of advocacy and support that Glenn Poshard brought to it because of his public service and what education did for him," Blakemore said. "He brought a passion and advocacy for higher education that was very much needed then and now."

CHAPTER 21

# Not a Job

As Poshard moved into his third year as SIU president, trouble brewed in Springfield. Governor Blagojevich was at odds with about everyone, including leaders of his own party. A federal investigation ultimately led to his impeachment in January 2009. In June 2011 he was convicted of seventeen charges that included wire fraud and conspiracy to solicit bribes.[1] He was sentenced to a federal prison term that ended in 2020, when President Trump commuted the balance of his term.

In March 2008, Blagojevich sought to strengthen his weakening position with a capital construction program. Capital construction is a staple for lawmakers. High-profile projects help drive employment in construction, make a positive public impression, and have a long lifespan. Constituents like seeing projects in their region, and lawmakers appreciate happy constituents.

Blagojevich, recognizing the difficulty for him to personally lead the effort, asked Poshard and retired U.S. House Speaker Dennis Hastert to assess needs and develop a plan and a way to pay for it.[2] Poshard and Hastert brought credibility. They covered both ends of the state and both political parties. Poshard's background in regional and statewide public policy made possible the appointment, which was viewed as an opportunity for the SIU system and higher education across the state.

Some key players, however, weren't convinced that the timing was right for a capital plan so long as Blagojevich remained governor. Gross remembers that Hastert missed a meeting. When asked why, the reply was, "I got a call," that is, from the powerful House Speaker Mike Madigan, who said he didn't trust the governor.

"I got a call, too," was Poshard's reply. Poshard sought to move forward, as, ultimately, did Hastert. With Gross and others helping drive the process, they brought together interested parties, identified needs across the state, and set out a plan to have money raised for the program to be separated from other state funds and placed in a lockbox that could be used only for capital expenditures.

"The Senate passed the bill by a good margin, but it was killed in the House," Poshard said. "I had been cautiously optimistic, because the Speaker's office had participated in all of our meetings over the past several months, and we felt they were supportive of the bill. But on the day it was scheduled for hearings by House committees, I received a call from my good friend Congressman Bill Lipinski. Bill was the Speaker's congressman, and he simply said to me, 'Glenn, go home; the bill is going down tonight.' Unfortunately, later that day, Mike Carrigan and Tim Drea, president and vice president of the Illinois AFL-CIO, joined me in a meeting with the Speaker, who told us there was no support in the House for the bill. We knew what this meant without asking. There had just been too much water under the bridge between the Speaker and the governor, and the Speaker was not going to give Blagojevich this bill. I also knew, as disappointed as I was at the moment, that you don't burn bridges with the Speaker. There would be a later time when he would help us, but this wasn't the time."

The capital bill didn't move while Blagojevich was governor, but much of the task force's work was used by the General Assembly and Governor Pat Quinn, who signed the $31 billion plan in July 2009 with SIU among the beneficiaries receiving about $168 million in projects.[3] The SIUC list included a $60 million Transportation Education Center, completion of the sixth and seventh floors of Morris Library, planning and design for an $80 million communications building, and deferred maintenance. SIUE received funding for the new science building and several deferred-maintenance projects. Poshard gave the credit to area legislators with whom he had worked on every project. In the Metro East, Senators Bill Haines and Jim Claiborne, along with Representative Jay Hoffman, championed SIUE, and Senators Dave Luechtefeld and Gary Forby, along with Representatives Brandon Phelps and Mike Bost, did the same for Carbondale.

While oversight of construction projects falls to campus leaders, Poshard remained involved in continuing implementation of the land use plan developed by the committee he led as vice chancellor. The capital funding from the state was pivotal in significantly advancing major pieces in the plan. Having the detailed plan in place facilitated multiple projects making the final list.

"From the time interim chancellor John Jackson saw the need and instructed me to put a plan together in 2001, we found a way to get the funding to build a new Student Health Center; complete the beautiful Morris Library; build a Transportation Education Center, a new Student Services Building, new athletic facilities, new residence halls; upgrade our technology; and receive start-up funding for a new $80 million communication building for which the final construction funds are waiting to be released," Poshard said. "The land use plan was a central focus and a labor of love for me for which I will always be grateful, but I was only one member of the team. This plan was Dr. Jackson's vision from the beginning and should be recognized as a part of his legacy to the university."

As noted above, Poshard's involvement came as vice chancellor, as a trustee, and then as president. "In those positions, working with the chancellor, I tenaciously clung to the development of the land use plan, and today, nearly two decades later, 90 percent of the plan has been completed. None of it could have been done without the tremendous leadership of Roger Tedrick, the chairman of our board of trustees and such outstanding board members as Keith Sanders, Ed Hightower, John Simmons, Marquita Wiley, Mark Hinrichs, Bill Norwood, and John Brewster. Tedrick's love for SIU and his service to the university in so many voluntary capacities over decades is unmatched by anyone I know.

Jackson, after his retirement from SIU, is now a visiting professor in the Paul Simon Public Policy Institute. "Glenn's proud of that plan. I'm proud of it. There hadn't been one since Delyte Morris. Most of the things have either come true or are viable possibilities."[4]

"The land use plan was a strategic plan, an aspiration," Jackson said. "After careful and inclusive consultation on campus, it then had to be implemented. Poshard and others like Phil Gatton were able to turn the plan into concrete, bricks and mortar, buildings and grounds. And it all took money, lots of money. The money required effective politics to obtain the funds. That took a careful and compelling presentation of the university's case in Springfield and Washington, which Poshard did persuasively and often. As an undergraduate and later a graduate student and then during his long tenure in a variety of increasingly important offices, Poshard was able to see the university and its evolution from a unique perspective. It was a key part of his vision for the Carbondale campus, which he helped to make a reality."

By 2013 the campus was opening another centerpiece described as the front door to the university, a $36 million, four-story Student Services Building that created a one-stop opportunity for students to take care of enrollment, registration, bursar, and other needs and put an end to the infamous Woody Hall shuffle. Poshard, in his remarks at the ribbon-cutting ceremony, acknowledged the members of the land use plan committee, crediting them for their vision in making this building a reality.

Another key player in facilities development was Kevin Bame, the SIUC vice chancellor for administration and finance. Of Poshard's role, he said, "He was respectful to my chain of command. He would call and say, 'I need to run something by you. What do you think?' He would typically ask, 'Where do you think we need to go?' If he thought differently, he would say, 'Help me understand your position.' He was good at drawing that out. The goal was that students would have a clean, safe, modern campus."[5]

Most all of the SIU senior staff spent time with Poshard in Springfield. Stucky said one reason Poshard was effective was he knew everyone from the custodian to the governor. In the governor's office, most of the staff called him by name. If he had a few minutes he might greet the staff, then sit at a table and work on remarks he would later use before the respective committees. "He was kind of notorious with coming up with remarks at the last minute," Stucky said.[6]

On one trip to Springfield, Haller and Gross joined Poshard in the basement rathskeller of the Capitol for a meeting with the director of public health. That meeting resulted in a $1 million grant to the Rural Health Care Center at SIUC to assist in medical transportation in deep southern Illinois, which had lost much of its ambulance services. Another trip with Gross to the Illinois Department of Transportation for a meeting with the director followed Poshard's same pattern. After a warm greeting, Poshard would quickly get to the point. "Director, what is there in your agency that my university or my region can help you with?" He would go on to explain the things the SIU system could do with their research and scientific innovations. He would meet with agencies at the state and federal level. Paula Keith, Poshard's administrative assistant, kept a file for these lobbying efforts, which shows an additional $10 million to $13 million a year generated to the SIU system by Poshard beyond the normal appropriation process.

Keith said Poshard worked hard to maintain good relationships with Black and Hispanic leaders in Chicago and Springfield, many of whom had graduated from SIU. "If a legislator needed him to meet with a group of his or her constituents, he would jump on the 7:30 A.M. train, make the trip to Chicago, hold the meeting, and return on the 4 P.M. train, all on the same day," she said. "There was a constant stream of legislators coming through our office, and he always had an 'ask' ready for them."[7]

Gross said the three key skill sets for Poshard were negotiation, people skills, and political savvy. "He is a really smart guy. He hid that some, kept that to himself. But he is one of the smartest guys I ever met." "He was here [in Springfield] all the time," Gross said. "He was on the phone all the time. You can't sit down with the guy and listen to his vision without being a cheerleader for him."[8]

Haller and Keith said Poshard was equally effective in Washington. After Poshard's first trip to the nation's capital as SIU president, Poshard essentially became the top university lobbyist. Keith indicated SIU had several lobbying firms employed when Poshard became president. "Two of them totaled right at $200,000 per year in fees to the university, and, after evaluating their effectiveness, President Poshard eliminated both and completely took over their duties himself. He knew more people in Springfield and Washington than they did."[9]

"We kept one firm in Springfield," Poshard said, "which was equally effective with both sides of the aisle, but we had Dave Gross as our governmental affairs director, and he was the absolute best. Dave had been a senior staff officer for the Senate president, knew every legislator personally in both houses, and had the highest reputation for integrity under the dome. What Dr. Stucky, Dr. Haller, General Counsel Blakemore, and Paula Keith were soon to find out was something I had known since Dave worked with Senator Severns and me as a young staffer in the mideighties; he was a brilliant problem-solver. Dave not only knew how to get our agenda passed in the legislature but also knew how to avoid the minefields and kill off legislation that opposed us. But it was so much more than just his work in Springfield. He was an integral part of our team decision-making on every important issue concerning the welfare of the university."

Gross saw something else, a firsthand experience of Poshard's empathy. Poshard didn't support Blagojevich in the Democratic primary. But they repaired a relationship. Gross remembers that Poshard was in an intimate, private setting with the governor on one of the governor's dark days. The governor reached out in an unexpected way. "He knew that Glenn had deep faith," Gross said of Blagojevich. "He asked Glenn to pray with him."[10]

Poshard obliged. Gross remembers the scene well. It was a moment that would have been surprising had it been anyone but Poshard and a key staffer. The governor, like many others, knew of Poshard as someone in whom he could comfortably place trust.

Most everyone close to Poshard has a story about the influence of his faith or about Poshard the humanitarian. Bame remembers the time when Poshard learned of a woman, at that time not an SIU employee, who received a cancer diagnosis. Her husband was deployed overseas. Poshard quietly reached out to his contacts, arranging for the husband to be home to help with the difficult early treatment days.[11]

Haller recalls calling Poshard when Paul Sarvela, who took Haller's place as vice president for academic affairs when Haller retired, was on his death bed. Sarvela, who had been serving recently as interim chancellor at SIUC, had been ill, but the timing wasn't expected. "Glenn and Jo were on vacation in Tennessee with friends," Haller said. "They rented a car and returned to Carbondale immediately."[12]

Religious faith and a reflective nature open the door to an emotional side Poshard typically doesn't show in public. In private, colleagues say Poshard sometimes lets emotions flow. Tedrick was a sounding board. The two talked at least once a week. Like Poshard, Tedrick's SIU roots run deep. Tedrick moved to Carbondale at age two, living in a three-story rooming house. His family housed fifteen college boys. "I saw most of the campus built," he said.

At the outset of Poshard's tenure, Tedrick said, Poshard enjoyed solid faculty support. "He was seen as fair-minded. You knew if you disagreed with him, it was because he felt he was doing the right thing."[13] The faculty-president relationship was bound to be tested. In 2004 an assistant professor who had sought promotion at SIUE was fired for plagiarism. Administrative handling of the matter was contested. A lawsuit ensued.[14]

In 2005 chancellors at both Edwardsville and Carbondale were accused of plagiarism by a group of friends of the fired professor who called themselves the Alumni and Faculty against Corruption at SIU (AFAC). They refused to reveal their names but accused Vandegrift of plagiarism for public remarks he made at a Martin Luther King luncheon. They also accused Wendler of lifting material from Texas A&M in documents used in the SIU at 150 plan. Multiple other plagiarism accusations came forth against many SIU personnel from Dr. Joan Friedenburg, an SIUC professor who had ties with the AFAC group from SIUE.[15] When Poshard refused to reinstate the fired professor and defended the chancellors after investigating the charges, the group came after him.

Poshard had been forewarned by the general counsel's office that they had received a message from a concerned professor who had overheard a conversation in a faculty gathering that "something big was about to happen to Poshard." In short order, the student newspaper, the *Daily Egyptian*, accused him of plagiarizing his 1984 doctoral dissertation. In a September 10, 2007, article in the *Southern Illinoisan*, Darrell Dunham, a Carbondale lawyer and official in the Jackson County Republican Party, conceded he had taken a copy of Poshard's dissertation to the *Daily Egyptian* but refused to acknowledge where he obtained the dissertation.[16]

"It tore him up," Haller said of the plagiarism charge against Poshard. "It was as if someone sucker-punched him. There were days he wanted to quit. There were days when he almost insisted on quitting."[17]

Said Paula Keith: "His integrity was being challenged. That was hurtful."[18]

Stucky put it this way: "You couldn't do anything worse than challenge his integrity. Accused of being dishonest hit him hard."[19]

The allegations dealt with attributions in the thesis. Most all the allegations were in the chapter titled "Review of Related Literature," not in his original research. Given the timing that the allegation closely followed the firing of the SIUE professor and the subsequent allegations against the two chancellors and others, some considered it a political move designed to embarrass the president and the university. Poshard sat down with *Daily Egyptian* reporters who had a copy of the dissertation in which specific places had been identified as problematic. The story received widespread play across the state. Plagiarism is a serious charge that potentially could end a presidency. Personally, Poshard felt confident in his academic work. He knew, too, that this would be difficult to deal with and certainly would distract from other initiatives.

Haller was responsible for organizing the investigation into the allegation. "To be credible, I thought I had to get faculty to do it. I recommended we go with the elected leaders of the faculty. They accepted the task. They found a few problems but not at the level of plagiarism."[20]

Blakemore engaged former Missouri U.S. senator John Danforth to lead an outside inquiry that arrived at the same conclusion. "Their opinion was there is no issue here," said Blakemore.[21]

Several people close to Poshard, including Goldman, consider the attribution shortcomings in the dissertation something faculty should have addressed in 1984. "The committee approved it," Goldman said. "They should have had him revise it at the time. He fixed it. . . . I think he has a high reputation. He's honest to a fault. That hurt his reputation."[22]

Poshard made multiple trips to the archives, reviewing theses and dissertations from the same college completed during the same 1974–84 period. He found that many of the works were produced under the same standards and used the same attribution style. That finding also was the conclusion of Gerald Nelms, an SIU professor with background in researching plagiarism, who defended Poshard to the faculty committee, composed entirely of research professionals.

"I brought thirteen of these dissertations with me to my hearing," Poshard said. "I showed them to the committee as we went over every single charge in question, and I gave a full defense of the charges made. I brought corroborating material that I had used, letters from prominent faculty who had assisted in my dissertation, expert opinion from former professors, in order that the faculty leadership committee could see, in complete detail, my writing and the fact that there was no intent to deceive anyone.

"In their final report, the committee indicated that they too had looked at several dissertations from my college written during the same time period and found many, besides the ones I had presented to them, using the same attribution style I had used. Nevertheless, the recently adopted university guidelines called for my mistakes to be termed inadvertent plagiarism, meaning they were unintentional. In compliance with the committee's request, I went back and updated my dissertation to present standards. In my retirement years, I had hoped I would benefit from my service, but the accusation proved powerful enough to prevent me from realizing those opportunities."

Looking back, Poshard considers experiences with SIU as a student, as a lawmaker, as a campus administrator, as a board member, and as president as central to his life. He maintains a deep affection for the university. He continues to make substantial financial contributions. The plagiarism charge stands out as one high-profile issue whose deep wounds left permanent scars.

"This was the most painful experience of my professional life," Poshard said. "I had been in the public arena for decades and was accustomed to making difficult decisions that brought intense criticism. I had learned to handle it as part of the price of holding public office. But this was different. In all those years I had never been accused of taking credit for someone else's work . . . never been accused of trying to deceive the public. I went before the university and took full responsibility for my work and my mistakes. I wasn't angry at anyone. Not the underground faculty. Not the *Daily Egyptian* reporters. No one. But I was overcome with sadness.

"I thought of the first day I walked onto campus, January 3, 1966. I had just spent three years in the U.S. Army. I had recently turned twenty, and I was now the first in my family going to my favorite college. I had a job as a student worker in the physical plant, and it was already dark when I got off work and walked across campus to the upstairs bedroom I rented in a small house on College Street. I could remember that walk like it was yesterday. Past the stately old Baptist Union, the Pulliam Hall clocktower silhouetted against the full moon shining down on the grassy knoll now covered with snow. The sheer exhilaration I felt at being alive at that moment. So lucky. So blessed.

"In 2007, over forty years had passed since then, and in all the intervening years, I thought of the love SIU had poured into me and the love I had tried to return to her. My failing seemed so small compared to this love affair I have carried all my life with my alma mater. Irony of ironies. Love gives and love takes away."

In April 2011, Governor Pat Quinn appointed Harrisburg businessman Roger Herrin and two others to the SIU board, a move that led to highly publicized conflicts.[23] Administrators who worked with Poshard describe the matter as an extreme case of board overreach into operations. The role of board of trustee members in higher education has to do with policy and direction, not getting involved in the day-to-day operation of the university as it pertains to personnel and other operational tasks assigned to administration.

From the outset, the new board members, who had no prior experience in higher education governance, were critical of SIU's enrollment and financial management. These areas, which always make campus whiteboards and are often complex and difficult to grasp, had been misrepresented to the public by some board members. At a time when enrollments were declining at universities all over Illinois and appropriations were being cut by the state, SIU was being accused of failing compared with other universities, and that portrayal was false.

The enrollment challenges included sluggish and declining enrollment numbers at many rural high schools, and increasing competitiveness of universities in neighboring states. Another challenge was continuing to attract students from metropolitan Chicago. Affordability was part of the equation, as universities weighed merits of raising tuition in times of decreasing state support. The declining support makes it more challenging to offer programs and facilities that meet and exceed those of competitors.

Poshard is proud of the results under his administration. He notes that each public university in Illinois annually publishes a fact book detailing relevant information. Examination of the fact book from each of the public universities in Illinois published between 2006 and 2014, the years Poshard served as president of SIU, full-time equivalent (FTE) enrollment was as follows:

- Eastern Illinois FTE enrollment declined by 30 percent
- Northern Illinois FTE enrollment declined by 18 percent
- Western Illinois FTE enrollment declined by 16 percent
- Chicago State FTE enrollment declined by 15 percent
- Northeastern Illinois FTE enrollment declined by 12.3 percent
- SIUC FTE enrollment declined by 12.1 percent
- SIU system FTE enrollment declined by 5 percent
- Illinois State FTE enrollment stayed the same
- SIUE FTE enrollment increased by 5 percent

The analysis excludes the University of Illinois, which as the flagship university turns down many more students than are admitted. "Their enrollment never is in doubt," Poshard said. "Overall, despite SIUC facing extraordinary challenges that other universities do not face, such as being surrounded by three neighboring states whose universities aggressively recruit students from southern Illinois; seeing increased competition from its sister school in Edwardsville; being more than three hundred miles from Chicago, a traditional drawing base for SIUC students; and being in an area with the poorest regional economy in the state, a declining high school population, and an excellent community college system that draws heavily from middle- and low-income families, SIUC trailed only SIUE and Illinois State in maintaining the number of full-time equivalency students. And overall, the SIU system lost far fewer students than most other universities in the state, with SIUE being the fastest-growing university in the state during my tenure. Some board members, however, refused to acknowledge that while we were losing students at SIUC, we were maintaining our enrollment at a higher level than almost every other university in the state. This misperception led to misinformation being dispersed to the public."

In the five years after Poshard retired from SIU, the Carbondale campus lost several thousand students. A February 5, 2021, article in the *Southern Illinoisan* about enrollment stated that SIUC enrollment declined by fifty-six hundred students from 2015 to 2019, or about fourteen hundred per year.

Financially, Poshard credits Stucky with leadership that made the best of a difficult situation at that time, and, while not known then, an even more challenging state financial picture was about to get worse. To navigate the changing financial climate, the SIU system identified priorities to fund while also moving to reduce or eliminate programming in other areas. That created internal debates among the different colleges for scarce resources.

Underlining the sensitivity of the issues was a weeklong faculty strike in Carbondale in November 2011. A significant tuition increase was among the possible solutions, but that would lead to more enrollment declines. Throughout his career, Poshard talked about finding balance in assessing difficult problems. That was the objective in these matters: to strike the best balance among multiple competing forces.

In assessing the options, Stucky said one could disagree with Poshard without finding him argumentative. "It was more conversational, part of the process," Stucky said of deliberations. "One thing you felt good about is he would not compromise his integrity. You were never going to be asked to do something that was ethically going to be hard to do."[24]

A report by Bain and Company on the financial health of public and private nonprofit higher education institutions ranks favorably SIU's navigation of the choppy financial waters. Both SIUC and SIUE were ranked in the highest category among the top 20 percent of all institutions reviewed.

The Bain report described financially sound institutions like SIU as "among the most innovative" and as having "strong financial statements through prudent financial management."[25]

"The rankings," Poshard wrote, "were based on the pattern of change in two ratios between fiscal years 2005 and 2010: the 'expense ratio' and the 'equity ratio.' The expense ratio gives the ratio of expenditures to revenues. A decline in the expense ratio signals movement to stronger financial health. The equity ratio gives the ratio of equity, that is, assets less liabilities, as a percentage of assets. An increase in the equity ratio signals movement to stronger financial health. Over the five-year period, both SIUC and SIUE showed substantial movement to stronger financial health in both ratios with declines of 2 percent and 9 percent, respectively, in the expense ratio and growth of 5 percent and 8 percent, respectively, in the equity ratio."

Poshard highlighted the report in a campuswide email in which he also cited the Higher Learning Commission, which in August 2011 said, "SIUC gives strong evidence and detail regarding the University's ability to address its financial challenges effectively. In spite of the challenges posed by the state's financial uncertainties, SIUC has taken sound and well-considered measures to assure its continued financial health."

When he began his presidency, Poshard handwrote sixteen challenges to be addressed. They were numbered like this: 1, attitudes and silos; 2, transportation education center (SIUC); 3, science building (SIUE); 4, contract negotiations; 5, Morris Library renovations; 6, student health center; 7, state agency contracts; 8, lobbying for capital spending bill; 9, land use plan; 10, lobbying for tuition tax credit; 11, lobbying for HUD loan conversion to grant; 12, more minority participation; 13, SIUE school of nursing renovation; 14, Simpson Scarborough report; 15, declining state aid; and 16, rapidly rising tuition.[26]

Almost all of these challenges had been positively addressed during his administration; others were ongoing. All touched on the goal of making SIU an attractive, affordable institution.

Diversity was another focus that Poshard considered a priority. Bringing people of different backgrounds to SIU enhanced the educational value of a degree by exposing students to multiple perspectives, from which they can learn. It also was good economically. Further, Poshard found it beneficial regionally to bring varied viewpoints to an otherwise nondiverse region.

Poshard said when he accepted the presidency, he didn't consider it a job. He loved SIU, loved the region. It was an honor to be able to work toward furthering its long-term interest.

He felt he would know when the time was right to step aside. In July 2013, Poshard gave trustees notice he would retire June 30, 2014. "There comes a time when you weigh and balance things," Poshard was quoted as saying.[27] "I'll be nearly 69 years old by the time June 30 rolls around next year, and, you know, it's time for me to step down now."

When he left, both campuses had significant reserves to get through some rough times, and he was proud of that. When asked the one thing he was most proud of in his tenure as president, Poshard responded, "The fact that every year we kept tuition the lowest in the state. SIUE was always the lowest among the master's degree granting institutions, and SIUC was always the lowest among the doctoral degree granting institutions. I was able to come here as a poor student in 1966 because tuition was low, and I could get a quality education. I wanted to keep it that way for future students."

The foundational role SIU played in his life is visually underlined in the Poshard home. He received recognition from many organizations throughout his career. Various plaques, newspaper front pages, military citations, maps of the nineteenth and twenty-second congressional districts and related items are hung on a wall in his garage. Key themes emerge, including support for organized labor and education, initiatives to preserve the environment, support for rural health care, a hand-up to children in need. When you look at the collection of awards, something else becomes prominent. The awards are arranged in a way that unfolds the letters SIU.

Poshard had almost no contact with his successor, Randy Dunn, who was forced from the presidency in 2018.[28] After the 2018 election of J. B. Pritzker as the new Illinois governor, Tedrick, Hightower, and Simmons were reappointed to the SIU board. The board, along with board chairman Phil Gilbert, recognized that the university was far better because of Poshard's service. In December 2019, they took time to acknowledge not only Poshard's eight and a half years as the SIU president, the second-longest term in history, but also his many contributions over his career, conferring on him the title of president emeritus (see appendix C).

In accepting the title, Stucky said, Poshard showed the character that defines who he is: when things went well, Poshard shared the credit. When times were tough, the buck stopped with him. Of the president emeritus designation, Stucky quoted Poshard: "This belongs to the staff in the Stone Center." Stucky countered, "Well, it doesn't belong to the Stone Center. This belongs to him."[29]

Former President Jimmy Carter shook hands with Poshard at a Capitol Hill reception. Photo from congressional photo staff.

Several dignitaries including Poshard stood with Democratic presidential nominee Bill Clinton and his running mate, Al Gore, at a campaign stop in Cairo, Illinois during a campaign bus tour after the 1992 Democratic National Convention. Photo from Glenn Poshard personal file.

Poshard greeted Nelson Mandela at a Capitol Hill committee meeting. Photo from congressional photo staff.

Jo and Glenn with President Bill Clinton at a lawn party at the White House. Photo from William J. Clinton Presidential Library.

Jo, President Bill Clinton, First Lady Hillary Rodham Clinton, and Glenn at a White House Christmas party. Photo from William J. Clinton Presidential Library.

Poshard spoke with President Clinton on Air Force One. Photo from William J. Clinton Presidential Library.

Poshard with grandchildren Maddie and Tucker with state Senator Barack Obama, while Obama was campaigning for the U.S. Senate. Photo from Glenn Poshard personal file.

*Above*, Jo Poshard with granddaughter, America, prepared to campaign during Glenn Poshard's race for governor. *Left*, Harrison was with his grandfather, Glenn Poshard, on Obama's presidential campaign trail. Photo from Glenn Poshard personal file.

Poshard spoke at a gubernatorial campaign rally at the Daley Center in Chicago. Photo from Glenn Poshard personal file.

Jo Poshard campaigned in the Chicago area during the gubernatorial campaign. Photo from Glenn Poshard personal file.

Jo and Glenn Poshard hosted a social event at the Stone Center at Southern Illinois University. Photo from Glenn Poshard personal file.

Glenn and Jo Poshard stood in front of the Glenn Poshard Transportation Education Center at SIU-C after the formal dedication In October 2022. Photo by Britni Bateman, printed with permission courtesy of SIU Foundation.

PART 5

# RETURNING TO ROOTS

## CHAPTER 22

# The Right to Rise?

Educational opportunity for all is one of the defining themes of Glenn Poshard's life. But for influential teachers, but for the GI bill, but for the life-changing perspective of a university experience, Poshard would have lived a much different life. He was particularly passionate that neither income nor status should set educational boundaries. He saw higher education as a vehicle for growth academically and for developing citizenship.

On October 2, 2013, Southern Illinois University president Glenn Poshard spoke to these issues in Chicago as the guest speaker for the City Club luncheon. Founded in 1903, the club describes itself as the "longest running civic forum in Chicago," a nonpartisan group interested in firsthand information regarding important issues.[1] The talk was complete with Poshard's protocol for coming prepared, for having practiced, and delivering a message with passion.

Wearing a white shirt and gold tie, with hair neatly parted, Poshard used the opportunity to highlight a troubling higher education trend. At the outset of his thirty-five-minute talk, he quoted President Abraham Lincoln who, in signing the Morrill Act of 1862 that set aside land for development of public universities, described the initiative as representing the "people's right to rise." Poshard explained, "Until that time, higher education in America was almost exclusively for the children of wealthy parents who attended private universities usually associated with one religious denomination or another."[2]

That "right to rise" opened wide the doors of opportunity for many Americans. "The great land-grant universities were started and were open for the sons and daughters of the lower and middle economic classes," Poshard told the club. "The promise of a brighter future for their children now lies within the grasp of the farmer, the miner, the factory worker, and thousands of American families who had been denied access to the private universities."

Opening his talk, Poshard referred to his own parents, who each had a third-grade education. They worked for less than a dollar an hour during the Depression and depended on WPA programs to sustain their family. "They understood one powerful thing—to break the cycle of poverty, their children had to get a good education. With the help of the GI Bill and an incredible university, I was the first ever to get a college degree in my family after five generations in America."

For Poshard, his time as an SIU student made possible his job as a teacher, as an elected official, and now as a university administrator. But, Poshard told Chicago business leaders, data from a 2008 Illinois Board of Higher Education map titled "The Geography of Wealth in Illinois," suggests growing questions about "the right to rise."

The report, he said, points to two states of Illinois. One Illinois is prosperous and growing, with per capita annual incomes ranging from $29,000 to $62,000. This Illinois lies mainly in the wealthy suburban areas surrounding Chicago as well as parts of northern and central Illinois that have the best farmland in the world. In the other Illinois, prosperity is uneven and declining, with per capita annual income of $10,000 to $20,000.[3] This Illinois comprises the inner city urban areas of the state as well as deep southern Illinois. "This prosperity gap, which also leads to a disturbing educational gap, is wide and growing," Poshard said, with the trend beginning by the fourth grade.

Further setting up his point, Poshard cited data that shows other countries surpassing American students in educational achievement. "We used to be first in every category," he says, gesturing with his right hand to emphasize the point. "Those other countries," he said, "invest in places where the need is greatest. That is not so in Illinois and America. Can anyone actually justify the quality of a child's education depending on the value of the property where that child is born and raised?" he asked the group. "Does it make sense that children from the one Illinois get three times the amount of money spent on their education as do children from the other Illinois?"

Poshard referred to the inaugural address of Delyte Morris when Morris was installed as SIU president in 1949. Speaking about the southern Illinois region, Morris said in part. "To what are our children born? To poverty? To poor health? To ignorance? Or to hope and promise . . . ?"

Moving ahead to the modern day, Poshard quoted from a *Wall Street Journal* op-ed written by former defense secretary Bob Gates and a former U.S. senator, David Boren, who at the time was president of the University of Oklahoma: "State budget decisions are returning America's system of public higher education to a pre-1862 luxury available only to the well-off or those willing to assume life-changing debt."[4]

Poshard told the audience the increasing disparities in income and educational opportunity fall along multiple areas, including race, ethnicity, and region. Southern Illinois has the lowest family income, the highest unemployment rate, and the most limits on health care access in the state.

Going back to the higher ed board's report, Poshard noted two primary goals for students: increase accessibility and affordability. Yet both of those goals seem more elusive as the trend grows for more well-off students, mostly white, to choose more selective private institutions rather than open-access colleges and universities, leaving the students in those universities and their middle- and low-income families to shoulder more of the costs of running the institutions.

Poshard said higher education provides students the personal benefit of making themselves more employable. It also offers the public benefit of making them better citizens. He explained, "The college and university setting is where we learn how to be good citizens in a democracy. Here, we are exposed to people of different ethnic, religious, and racial backgrounds. We meet people from different social and economic backgrounds. We learn to appreciate the differences, the diversity. Here's where we truly learn to 'get along' with one another despite our differences. When we leave the university and take a job somewhere, the people we work with, the people who live next door to us, in all likelihood, are going to reflect that diversity, and we will have been prepared at the university for the requirements that good citizenship demands to be a contributing member of a pluralistic, democratic society."

Yet, at SIU and other institutions, state budget payments show the state doesn't place a high value on these attributes. State payments to SIU totaled $248 million in 2002, Poshard said, and were on time. In 2014 the payments totaled $203 million and were several months late. Noting the higher education board goals of increasing accessibility and affordability, Poshard asked this: "Does the right to rise still exist?"

These comments came nearly two years before a multiyear state budget impasse that had a crippling impact on higher education and fueled a trend of increasing numbers of high school students leaving Illinois to attend colleges and universities in other states. Poshard closed his talk describing multiple accomplishments of SIU students coming from communities with populations as small as 420. SIU, he said, represents equality of opportunity. "My job is for students to get the same opportunity today that SIU offered me forty years ago."

## CHAPTER 23

# Professional Baseball in Southern Illinois

Beginning as a youth and continuing through his life, Poshard loved baseball. It was among the enjoyable activities in the hills. Listening to the St. Louis Cardinals on the radio was a welcome part of the day for Poshard and many other youth. Years later, I experienced the same enjoyment. One time, I remember staying awake for twenty-plus innings as the Cardinals battled the New York Mets.

In 2004, Poshard was out of elected office and recently retired as vice chancellor but remained a prominent figure in southern Illinois. A group of southern Illinois leaders brainstormed on the possibility of bringing minor league baseball to the region. They paid for an extensive feasibility study. Elected officials sometimes are asked to put their name on a regional project like this one to help provide credibility and prominence. Poshard took this a step further, playing a lead, though behind-the-scenes, role. The effort initially received too little support and was about to fall into the abyss.

Just home from church on a Sunday morning, Poshard was ready to enjoy an afternoon reading and relaxing. His Marion residence on Wildcat Drive was across the street from Marion High School, a multistory complex that generated significant activity the rest of the week. Typically, Sundays were peaceful. Poshard had placed a phone call to his friend John Simmons, an attorney based in Alton, and was hoping to hear back from him soon. The phone rang. It was Simmons.

Simmons, whose undergraduate degree is from SIU-Edwardsville, is a personal injury lawyer with offices in Alton, Chicago, New York, San Francisco, and Los Angeles. He first made his mark with a $34.1 million verdict in a case that involved mesothelioma and followed that with a $250 million verdict. Those cases established Simmons and his firm in the financially lucrative field of asbestos litigation, leading to many billions of dollars in settlements since 1999.

Poshard explained to Simmons that he and his son Dennis were helping on a project to bring professional baseball to southern Illinois and were looking for investors. Would Simmons have an interest? The baseball franchise referred to efforts by William Hays, a physician in Herrin, and Ken Crews, a local banker, to put together a group that would build a modern ballpark and buy a minor league franchise for southern Illinois.

They commissioned the Leib Group to complete a feasibility study. The ninety-seven-page report backed by multiple exhibits outlines in detail the challenges and opportunities in bringing baseball to southern Illinois. Poshard and his son helped promote the plan, which was about to be scrapped. "Dr. Hays, Crews, and their group asked Dennis and me to help with their efforts. Dennis, working with Emily Carter at the SIU Dunn-Richmond Center, helped write a plan to seek financial support for bringing a team here. We made out a list of fifty potential investors, developed our sales pitch, and proceeded to make the calls. These were all people with significant financial resources and mostly people who I had known for years in my work in government. We were hoping for a large participation rate with a significant investment in a 'citizen-owned team.' Only one person, Harry Crisp of Marion, who owned the Pepsi distributorship for the region, offered to invest. No one believed professional baseball could make it in southern Illinois." Seemingly, there was no viable route forward.

Poshard briefly discussed the feasibility study with Simmons and asked if they could get together to talk some more. Simmons agreed.

Poshard asked when he would be available. "How about this afternoon?" Simmons said. "I'll meet you at the McDonald's in Nashville in two hours." Nashville, Illinois, population 3,109, was about an hour's drive for both Poshard and Simmons. Poshard called Dennis, told him to drop whatever plans he had for the afternoon, and bring the baseball plan.

Simmons brought a partner, and the four men reviewed the details of the plan for about two hours. While not certain of the next step, Poshard left the meeting knowing that Simmons's interest could make the project possible.

The next morning, Simmons was at St. Louis Lambert Airport waiting for a flight to South America. He called Poshard at 7 A.M. "I'm going to buy a team and build a stadium in southern Illinois," Simmons told Poshard. "I don't want partners."

Poshard's response? "I was blown away." For the first time since 1948, southern Illinois would have a professional baseball franchise.

Dennis helped identify potential locations. Simmons considered sites around Southern Illinois, including Nashville, Mt. Vernon, and Carbondale before settling on a spot just off Interstate 57 at Illinois Route 13. The location was easily accessible and visible from the Interstate. Perhaps more important, it made a good first impression at a heavily traveled location that served as a gateway to Southern Illinois University, the VA Hospital, and related southern Illinois attractions. From the beginning, the vision for the baseball complex went beyond providing evening entertainment through the summer. The ballpark on which Simmons and his wife, Jayne, spent $20 million would become a magnet for related events and a source of regional pride. The facility features thirty-four hundred chair seats and lawn seating for two thousand. The design makes it a functional multipurpose venue that hosts concerts, banquets, and other regional events throughout the year.

In their inaugural season in 2007, the Southern Illinois Miners led the Frontier League in attendance with 259,392 fans filling the stadium. The team followed that opening by leading the league in attendance each of the next three seasons.[1] Jayne Simmons served as team owner, leading an operation that has expanded its baseball, softball, and hospitality functions.

When Poshard retired as SIU president, Simmons hosted a retirement party at the ballpark, complete with Poshard bobbleheads. Near the end of 2021, the Simmonses sold the stadium to a local economic development group and ended the most storied franchise of professional baseball in southern Illinois history.

# CHAPTER 24

# Rend Lake Turnaround

Personal, potentially reputation-damaging risks often are repelled by former members of Congress. Poshard was different, both in and out of office. During his terms of office, he volunteered to intervene in labor disputes. As he left the role of vice chancellor at SIU, he was approached about an even riskier task. This one involved a sensitive management turnaround at a high-profile southern Illinois organization.

"Glenn, can you help us?" Those were the words from Pete Micheletto, the board chairman of the Rend Lake Conservancy District.

"We're having a big problem with bad management," Micheletto said. "The board wants to know what it would take to get you."

Poshard didn't hesitate. "I said I don't want anything [salarywise]," Poshard replied. "But I need the board's authority."

With that, Poshard started daily trips to the Rend Lake headquarters, about a forty-mile drive each way, to dig into the issues. To the casual traveler, Rend Lake is an attractive body of water along Interstate 57 where fishing boats often dot the landscape. At the Whittington exit, a few of the twenty-seven golf holes are visible. A motorist with an eye for detail might notice the golf-ball design on the water tower.

The district's reach, however, goes much farther into southern Illinois life. Thirty-five towns and water districts purchase treated water that moves through two hundred miles of pipes across seven counties. The smaller wastewater treatment operation services the Big Muddy prison and two nearby communities.[1]

Constructed in the late 1960s, the lake has 162 miles of shoreline that open doors to fishing, hunting, and related outdoor activities. The lake is a hub for tourism, one of the most important southern Illinois industries. Its $12 million-plus operating budget ranks near the top among governmental entities in southern Illinois.

Poshard's arrival was unwelcomed by some board members and senior employees. "We had some very stormy meetings," Poshard said. Purchasing protocol, expense reporting, and overall management structure were among the issues.

Poshard placed a call to William Holland, the state's auditor general. Holland had been Senate president Phil Rock's chief of staff many years ago when Poshard served in the state Senate. He knew Holland was a straight shooter and went by the book. Poshard asked Holland to audit the district and provide recommendations. The agency's internal audit and subsequent state audit led to firing the general manager amid allegations of hundreds of thousands of misappropriated funds.[2] In August 2004, Poshard, then the interim general manager, met with Holland to review the more than two-hundred-page state audit. The audit called for a full-time staff attorney, full-time engineer, accounting changes, and an overhaul of internal practices.

Poshard called the state audit a blueprint for future operations that he would fold into a plan for the district. "There will be significant changes out of this audit, significant changes," he was quoted as saying in the *Southern Illinoisan.* "And that's throughout the entire system."

Holland's report concluded, "The Rend Lake Conservancy District has significant deficiencies in virtually all aspects of its management, including planning; water and sewage operations; personnel; contract management; property and equipment management; performance monitoring; and internal controls."

More than seventy corrective actions were recommended. "We developed a short-range and a long-range plan with precise goals and objectives and assigned accountability to implement the recommendations of the state audit," Poshard said. "We had to let go of people who were ripping off the district with unbelievable salaries and expense accounts. We cut expenses to the bone and stopped the practice of some board members and others using the facilities of the district for free. We set aside every available penny in a fund for upgrading facilities and being prepared for any emergency. And most important, after eight months we left the district in the hands of excellent management and a clear path forward."

Poshard's tenure stabilized the operation, and provided a plan for future management and a transition to new leadership. Looking back, he said it was a challenging but rewarding experience. "The district was a mess, but working with some of those members of the board and the employees who really cared about the district, we got it cleaned up."

Another call to turn around an organization in need of an overhaul came in September 2004. Governor Blagojevich appointed Poshard to lead and rebuild a state board that reviews and approves health care construction projects that can reach into the hundreds of millions of dollars.

The board had become corrupted by political cronies in Chicago. The board's chairman prior to Poshard, Stuart Levine, later pleaded guilty to mail fraud and money laundering. Blagojevich asked Poshard to clean up the board, a task that Jeff Mark, the board's executive secretary, said Poshard accomplished.[3]

Health care organizations, including hospitals, nursing homes, surgery centers, and dialysis facilities need a board permit to open, close, build, or renovate major construction projects. Mark, an architect and health care planner, was appointed in 2003 as the board's executive secretary. He called it a "small, but powerful board. . . . Health care is a big, big business. It's a very powerful entity."

When Poshard and two others were named to reconstitute the board, they faced a backlog of cases along with the challenge of repairing the organization's image. "We tried to reestablish the board," Mark said. "Glenn did so with impeccable integrity. He did a great job as chairman in a very, very difficult time for the board." Receiving no pay, he spent two weeks each month poring over hundreds of proposals, some more than a thousand pages long, for health facilities all over the state. From Poshard's questioning, Mark said it was evident he reviewed almost all, if not all, of the material to prepare for the meetings. "I came to admire Glenn very highly not only for his integrity but his work ethic. He had an ability to compartmentalize [that is, focus on a meeting]."[4]

Upon his appointment as SIU president, Poshard asked General Counsel Blakemore to assess whether he could continue in that role. Blakemore wrote that the health board posed potential conflicts of interest because of SIU's association with major hospitals in central and southern Illinois.[5] Poshard followed his advice and resigned.

## CHAPTER 25

# Faith and Politics

Faith plays a role throughout Poshard's life. He wrestles with it personally. From his earliest days, he welcomed opportunities to sit, think, and ponder about what's important. As a grandfather, he wrote a 324-page daily scriptural guide for his family that covered an entire year. As a public official, he took care not to proselytize. His spiritual journey was his. Others were free to go their way. Everyone should feel comfortable approaching their elected representative.

Personally, he weighed the sometimes conflicting roles of his religious beliefs with the high-profile role of elected office. One of his proudest accomplishments was being part of the development of a group in Congress that made time to thoughtfully address related issues. By the way, the moral grounding of his religion sometimes played a role in his votes. The last paragraphs in this chapter highlight one such time.

One way Washington introduces new members of Congress to their duties is a three-hour dinner in Statuary Hall, one of the most visible and visited places in the U.S. Capitol. In the early years of the Republic, the hall was the House chamber and thus a place of great debate. Now, a collection of sculptures of prominent Americans stands along the exterior walls of the two-story, amphitheater-like area that features Greek Revival architecture.

By chance, Glenn and Jo Poshard were seated at the same table as Doug Tanner, a Methodist minister whose wife was chief of staff for Michigan congressman David Bonier, the Democratic floor leader. Poshard and Tanner quickly connected. Their conversation moved along from the typical discussions about family and how they became involved in politics to bigger issues about life itself. They discovered common interests, including a relationship with monasteries, which both men visited periodically for self-improvement.

Poshard and Tanner shared a passion for inquiry and learning. They appreciated and welcomed being part of the nation's political hub, yet they didn't want to be consumed by it. One question that surfaced that night was how to follow Christ's admonition: "Render unto Caesar the things that are Caesar's and unto God the things that are God's."[1]

"Nothing quite represents Caesar, the world, more than Washington, D.C.," Poshard said. "It is the seat of power, position, authority, wealth, all of the things that stand in contrast to the teachings of my faith as a Christian. Christ taught us to be humble, loving, forgiving, not to seek our own way. How, then, as members of Congress, do we live and survive in those two worlds at the same time? And why was I placed next to a perfect stranger that night at dinner who shared the same concerns I had about this important question?"

Poshard and Tanner agreed to continue the conversation. They invited others to join a meeting in Poshard's congressional office that became the first session of what now is known as the Faith and Politics Institute, an established bipartisan initiative. Among the initial invitees were Anne Bartley, a personal friend of and an aide to Hillary Clinton and a former president of the Rockefeller Family Fund, and Joe Eldridge, another Methodist minister who later became a chaplain and a distinguished professor at American University. Eldridge said the group readily connected on the need to explore heartfelt, serious issues, including civil rights. In time, they realized the need to formalize the group, with Tanner as the founder and director.

"Those 7 a.m. meetings in my office every Tuesday morning with Doug, Joe, and Anne proved to be a touchstone for me for the entire week," Poshard said. "We talked about developing a clear understanding of the principles in which we believed. What should the ethical and moral positions be for leaders on issues such as the use of power, compromise, criticism, risk-taking, time demands on family, money and fundraising, patriotism, love, forgiveness, race relations, and many other issues? We helped each other examine our philosophies of life and how these difficult decisions could be addressed while trying to live in both the world of politics and the world of faith. It helped me make decisions that I felt were consistent with both my political and moral beliefs."

Thirty years later, the institute remains a leader. "Since our founding, the institute has offered opportunities for members of Congress and political professionals to cultivate effective public leadership through mutual respect, moral reflection, increased understanding, and honest conversation," the organization's website says in discussing its history. The institute says the word "faith" was chosen rather than "religion," as a way to broaden the perspective to be inclusive of all spiritual traditions. "The Institute encourages civility and respect as spiritual values essential to democracy, and it strives to strengthen political leadership that contributes to healing the wounds of dividing our nation and our world through a range of activities involving members of Congress."[2] A worthy goal in Poshard's judgment.

Civil rights struggles in southern Illinois go through Cairo, a town on the state's southern tip, where the Mississippi and Ohio Rivers converge. Cairo is steeped in history going back to the Civil War. "When I was growing up, Cairo was the place to go," Poshard said. "It featured busy department stores, a vibrant library, wide streets with stately, Southern homes on one side of town. The other side of Cairo was economically poor, primarily African Americans from the South."

In the 1960s, the two Cairos violently clashed. When an African American soldier was hanged in a jail cell in 1967, riots ensued.[3] Tensions continued for years, with gunfire a common occurrence. Poshard remembers working in Cairo as part of his role in regional education in the 1970s, trying to be part of the solution. White families pulled their children out of the public schools, and later pulled children out of a summer program designed to bring together white and African American youth. "I worked that whole summer with Dr. Lynn Byrd and Mrs. Jenolar McBride, two of the finest educators I had ever known, both of whom had a heart for the education and welfare of the children of Cairo. The summer program involved art, music, poetry, and other activities to try to keep the children together, no matter what the adults were doing to divide the community. I would drive down to Cairo in the afternoon or evening two or three days a week as part of my job with the Regional Educational Service Center, and many times I would take my young son with me. We worked with the children in a building over on Commercial Street, but by the end of the summer there weren't many white kids left in the program, and violence in the city became unnerving to me."

Wounds didn't heal. At one point, Poshard remembers he was told by the mayor not to return or try to help anymore. Cairo's decline continued. The city's population dropped from 14,407 in 1940 to an estimated 2,281 in 2017, a shell of its prime. "Prejudice can literally tear a community apart," Poshard said, remembering a cartoon he saw in the *New York Times* that featured flames burning the Los Angeles neighborhood of Watts, Harlem in New York City, and Cairo in Illinois. "It was sobering to think that a small town that we all loved would share that kind of national spotlight with major cities in America."

Over the years, the Faith and Politics Institute has responded to such issues by organizing pilgrimages led by civil rights leaders. This activity includes experiential pilgrimages, reflection groups, United States–South Africa faith-and-politics initiatives, Capitol forums, retreats, St. Joseph's Day breakfasts, and many congressional receptions.

Joe Eldridge said sometimes conversations dealt with issues before the Congress. More often, though, the sessions started with a poem or reading designed to prompt discussions. "And then we would just talk. Everyone drew from the wellspring of our own life experience and brought that to the table. It was about our personal journeys. It was an invitation for discernment."[4]

According to Eldridge, a congressperson's typical daily schedule is divided into short increments, often fifteen minutes apart. The Faith and Politics meeting took an hour. An initial focus centered on race and justice issues that were personal and important to several of the original members. The institute grew in that and other areas as it emerged as a bipartisan initiative by those with varied backgrounds. Institute members now take pilgrimages like the one civil rights pioneer John Lewis had led to Selma, Alabama, almost every year since 1998.

Poshard recalls his friendship with Lewis. "John was elected to Congress in 1986. I was elected in 1988. Not long after my swearing in from the twenty-second congressional district of Illinois, I met Congressman Lewis for the first time. It was 6 a.m. on a Wednesday morning in the House gym. Over the ten years I served in Congress, our little group of congressmen, Pete DeFazio of Oregon, Dick Durbin and I from Illinois, and John Lewis from Georgia met as many times in the House gym at 6 a.m. Tuesday through Thursday as our schedules allowed. It was usually twenty minutes on the treadmill, ten minutes on the weights, shower, dress, and a walk back to our offices. John talks about our little group in his biography, *Walking with the Wind.*

"Since John's office and mine were fairly close to one another, we often walked together. In that hour each day, I never once saw the civil rights icon or the sought-after national leader. What I did see was the personification of kindness and calmness. John never brought up the demonstrations or marches he led . . . never anything about Dr. King or other civil rights leaders. We seldom ever talked about those things except perhaps as the issue related to legislation currently pending before us in Congress.

"John and I shared a common background of growing up in rural poverty, of believing that government could be a force for good. We shared a common love for the powerful principles of the Declaration of Independence and the Constitution. We had many conversations about our families and the small rural churches that were such an important part of our upbringing. We shared the scriptures that we learned from our mothers, and we talked often about Dr. King's 'Beloved Community,' a vision John never gave up on his whole life.

"John became an important leader in our Faith and Politics Institute. Who better than my friend John to help us understand the dynamic relationship between faith and politics? There was a reason he was called the 'Conscience of the Congress.' His conscience manifested itself as courage and kindness and will always be a beacon to all Americans who care about justice."

Eldridge remembers that Poshard stood out for his moral firmness that led to Poshard's refusal to accept money from political action committees and his rejection of playing the game of congressional fundraising. "He was not tempted by lobbyists and the money they controlled," Eldridge said of Poshard. "He was a very unusual guy in that sense. Glenn is a very thoughtful, theologically sound man."[5]

In his book *The Truth Can Set Us Free: Toward a Politics of Grace and Healing*, Tanner offered these words on Poshard's political path. "Glenn's life in politics came to follow the model of Parker Palmer's Möbius strip. He journeyed inward with us to see clearly what he needed to do to be true to himself; he then journeyed outward with integrity and authenticity."[6]

Poshard said the institute was founded on the premise that most everyone in Washington was trying to do the right thing in a complex situation in which many interests were represented. "So let's not stand in judgment; let's help each other."

Poshard calls being part of the institute's founding one of the highlights of his years in Congress. "I think the Faith and Politics Institute has made a big difference in Washington, D.C., over the years. As partisan as the environment has become over the past thirty years, the institute is a constant advocate for civility and respect among our representatives, offering a way forward to regaining the people's trust."

On a personal level, Poshard went a step further. Up to two times a year, he set aside as much as a week to spend with the monks at the Abbey of Gethsemani Monastery in central Kentucky that was once home to Thomas Merton, one of his favorite writers. He relaxed, silently spent time with his thoughts, and walked the picturesque grounds, retiring each evening to one of thirty austere guest rooms simply furnished with a bed, a desk, a chair, and a small nightstand with a dimly lit lamp. A communal bathroom and shower served the entire floor, and often Poshard and a couple of others were the only guests there.

Poshard is not Catholic, and there is no requirement that Abbey visitors be Catholic. Rather, it's a place for anyone to slow down, to appreciate the power of silence, of reflection. Guests typically read, relax, and visit with the monks and work to align or realign their lives with their priorities. As much as he enjoyed policy and politics, as much as he strove to make a positive difference in his district, Poshard relished the time away from the fast-paced world. "I don't know why but I grew up with a contemplative nature," he said. "I love the reflective life. Augustine, Thomas Aquinas, Martin Luther, Wesley, Teilhard de Chardin, Merton, C. S. Lewis, are some of my favorite writers. The library at Gethsemani is full of their writings."

Poshard, in one of his conversations with Brother Bruno on developing concentration in prayer and meditation, received the following note by mail. "The whole point is to keep the mind free before God. If you concentrate on a mantra, for example, nothing else can get into your mind. The mind has to have something it can latch onto; it is not capable of being empty, yet it is most empty when concentrating on something minimal. Concentration actually is to free the mind. Most people think, if you concentrate, your mind is completely engaged; not true. Concentration is pulling together on something limited that actually leaves a good part of the mind free. That is why you should concentrate on something not too complex, such as breathing, or heartbeat, or one word. It is ironical men of science who do concentrate on problems get intuitions. People least susceptible to insight are those completely dispersed. (Father Flavian says he still holds this and finds that it 'works' in practice.)"[7]

Time at the monastery was for personal growth. Poshard said it was never about bringing religious doctrine into the political arena. At times, though, the moral foundation showed in his votes. This was never more evident than on June 27, 1986, in the Illinois Senate chamber. Senator Emil Jones's bill on the divestment of Illinois funds from companies doing business with the apartheid government of South Africa was up for a final vote. The bill and the vote had far-reaching implications, because if Illinois started divestment, other states would follow suit, and the economic consequences would be an important step in breaking the back of the apartheid government of South Africa. Jones had not discussed the bill with Poshard, knowing he was a freshman senator, and a vote for this measure would not be popular in his conservative southern Illinois district. He assumed a "no" vote from Poshard and his fellow southern Illinoisan in the Senate, Bill O'Daniel, and believed their votes could cause the bill to fail.

When Poshard rose to speak on the bill, no one was prepared for the force and the eloquence of his words. He quoted liberally from Martin Luther King's "Letter from Birmingham Jail," making the point that this bill must be viewed as having the moral backing of the eternal perspective, because it sought to right the injustice perpetrated on millions of people by a morally bankrupt government. He sought to bring the attention of Senate members to a "higher law" that deemed apartheid guilty of sins against humanity and implored his colleagues to find other, morally acceptable places in which to invest the state's resources. In the end, Senator O'Daniel sided with Poshard, and their votes assured passage for the bill by the smallest of margins.

When Poshard returned to his office after the vote, there was a Western Union telegram waiting for him. It was from the Coalition for Illinois Divestment from South Africa. It read simply, "Millions of people in Illinois and South Africa commend you for your strong anti-apartheid position. Thank You." The telegram is framed and hangs on his wall in his office at home. "In all my years of public service," he said, "it was the most important vote I ever cast."[8]

## CHAPTER 26

# The Shadow Side of Leadership

Finding common ground is central to Poshard's legislative approach. The ability to find common ground begins with developing respectful relationships. Poshard had and has an extraordinary number of relationships. Have breakfast with him on a Sunday at Bob Evans in Marion and count the people who personally, respectfully speak with him. Meaningful relationships are a foundational part of Poshard's public and private life.

Poshard's son Dennis recently reminded his father of an example of the kind of thinking our world could use more of, thinking that embraces a respectful, inclusive approach.

"When he was eighteen years old, Dennis went to Springfield with me to spend a few days in the Illinois state Senate. He said the most fun he had all week was the ride we shared with Senator Ralph Dunn. He sat in the backseat and listened to Ralph and me discuss issues before the Senate, trade stories about our colleagues, and laugh about our travails with certain constituents. Ralph and I occasionally rode up and back with each other and depended on our friendship and goodwill to fairly represent southern Illinois. Ralph, of course, was a

Republican, and I am a Democrat. Sometimes we differed only slightly on an issue, and at other times, the gulf was wider between us. But through respect for each other and an honest desire to understand the other's position, many times we narrowed that gap.

"My son asked me a question. 'Dad, how did we get from you and Ralph Dunn to today?' I didn't have an answer. Maybe it's not as complicated as it may seem. Loss of respect and goodwill doesn't happen overnight. There is a gradual erosion.

"Maybe it begins with the notion that life is only about wins and losses, so whatever it takes to win is most important . . . the end justifies the means. So we don't have to see the other side, we don't have to compromise, and the chasm grows between us.

"Maybe our fear of public failure or criticism means we don't have the courage to be imperfect so we present a false image of perfection and strength, making it difficult to see others as anything but weak, masking our own sense of cowardice.

"Maybe our intolerance of differences makes enemies of other races, religions, ethnicities, or sexual orientations so judgment becomes more important than mercy or compassion.

"Maybe our sense of self-preservation is so great it prevents us from caring about preserving the life or integrity of others.

"Parker Palmer, one of America's great leaders in higher education, defined a leader this way: 'A person who has an unusual degree of power to project on other people his or her shadow, or his or her light. And this power creates the conditions under which other people must live and move and have their being. Conditions which can be illuminating and uplifting to the people or conditions which can cast them into total darkness.'

"When we believe that winning by any means is all that counts, that others' preservation is not important, that intolerance and judgment are more conducive to the success of our democracy than respect and goodwill, then we will have failed our children and our country. I have witnessed too many times the shadow side of leadership cast people into darkness and have spoken out as forcefully as I could, but without eternal vigilance by the people, the darkness wins."[1]

CHAPTER 27

# Poshard Foundation and Beyond

The first leg of this book takes Poshard through the financial poverty of his youth. He cries for the orphans he left in Korea. He experiences firsthand ways a university experience redirects life. As a teacher and regional educator, he opens doors for students that otherwise might remain closed. In places like Cairo, he sees firsthand how it is difficult to overcome divisive issues like race relationships. As a university administrator, he places priority on creating a culture that facilitates personal growth. When you see Poshard in his own world, his home, his farm, you see the richness he finds in making joy possible for others. Much of the Poshard story comes together in the way he responded to losing the election for Illinois governor. Many of us think Illinois would be a better place had Poshard been elected governor. There is no doubt that southern Illinois is better because of the way Glenn and Jo responded to losing the governor's race.

The day after the 1998 gubernatorial election, in the living room of their Marion home, Jo and Glenn Poshard pondered their future. Jo sat on the couch, Glenn in a chair across the room. For the first time since his appointment to the Illinois Senate in 1984, he would soon be out of elected office. "I remember the conversation clearly," Jo Poshard recalls. "We had poured everything into that race, absolutely everything, our hopes and dreams. In the aftermath of the loss, we went through a lot of soul searching."[1]

Glenn considered the question of what would come next. He thought some more. He paused. Silence ensued. Finally, words emerged. "The only thing I can think of right now that matters to me is helping children."

This was his heart speaking, in the same way it had at key points in his career, like the vote to disinvest in South Africa. From his youth onward, his desire was always to help kids who had suffered real blows in life and to encourage them to experience the joy of overcoming. In his own upbringing, the poverty of the hill country and the physical and emotional toll it took on his family always shadowed his life. As a young adult, Poshard experienced Korean children clutching him and other soldiers for moments of joy, a memory that remains one of the highlights of his life. As a college student, he gave his spare time to mentor minority children and share their joy at seeing them succeed in school.

As a high school teacher, he was able to use an old bus as a vehicle for teens to explore beyond their small hometown. As a regional administrator, he was part of a team that sought to bring African American and white children together for a summer of enrichment in racially divided Cairo. Learning and teaching became hallmarks of his legislative life.

Thus, a desire to help children were the words that emerged from the conversation that day. They became the center stone for the Poshard Foundation for Abused Children. While still wrapping up details of the campaign, Poshard began the process to set up a 501(c)(3) nonprofit organization, pursued where to house the office, what would be the name. In a matter of months, Chicago attorney Dan Kubasiak helped establish the nonprofit. Poshard worked with Ray Hancock, president of John A. Logan College, to arrange office space. The name emerged from a conversation on what would be the central theme, helping abused, neglected, and abandoned children.

"From the very beginning, Kubasiak and Frances Gilliam joined Jo and me as members of our executive board and have remained faithfully serving through the present day," Poshard said.

In the foundation's infancy, Glenn led the activities. Jo, exhausted from the campaign, extended the leave of absence she took in the fall through the spring semester, then returned to teaching. Glenn started traversing southern Illinois highways as if he were on the campaign trail, giving talks, raising awareness, building a support base. A meeting in White County was typical. By Jo's account, "People came because they loved Glenn, and they wanted to be part of what he was going to do next."[2]

Jo described his work of traveling to various children's agencies as similar to the caravan approach he used in his campaigns. He wanted to win support for these children from businesses, labor groups, lawmakers, and the general public, and he was as committed to this campaign as he was to political campaigns.

In Cairo, a town in which he had spent over two decades trying to help the community bridge social and economic gaps, the women's shelter was housed in a building that was borderline condemnable. Thus, the first project became building a new Cairo Women's Shelter. The unmarked shelter has been full since its opening in 2003. It rests on a corner lot next to a row of trees, around the corner from the site of a now demolished housing project. The fenced-in backyard playground provides respite for children dealt an undeserved hand.

"We purchased two lots next to the old building where Jeannine Woods and her staff were trying to take care of abused women and children from the southernmost counties of Illinois, the poorest part of the state," Poshard said. "The building was a fire trap and needed to be replaced as soon as possible. Over the next year our Foundation raised money, purchased hundreds of thousands of dollars in materials, and with the leadership of Reverend John Annable, pastor of the United Methodist Church in Carbondale, and many SIU student volunteers, a new $650,000 shelter was built.

"Every Saturday morning at 8 A.M., ten or twelve carloads of students would leave the SIU Student Center and caravan the sixty miles to Cairo and work a ten-hour day building that shelter. When people today tell me this generation of kids are self-centered, that they don't care about others, I tell them the story of the Cairo shelter. All this generation needs is someone to give them directions, and they'll get the job done. They're great kids with a heart for helping others.

"Union electricians and plumbers wired and plumbed the entire building for us, volunteering their time and labor. Union laborers and painters built the sidewalks and painted the shelter. A local veterans group contributed an entire backyard of playground equipment and put it all together for the children. It was a great team effort, and the building was turned over to Mrs. Woods without one penny of debt.

"On the day the shelter was finished, Mrs. Woods and I were sitting at the kitchen table in the old shelter which would soon be torn down. She received a phone call from the Massac Memorial Hospital in Metropolis, Illinois. A baby had just been born, and they needed the address of the new shelter. It would go on the baby's birth certificate. It broke my heart. A baby had come into the world, and a shelter would be its first home. But I knew in that moment we had done a good thing. It was a new home, and Mrs. Woods and her staff would love the baby like it was their own."

The next major building project took place in 2007. The Night's Shield in West Frankfort was created by converting a nursing home into a safe haven for children in crisis situations. A nursing home owner had built a new facility in a neighboring community and deeded the old nursing home in West Frankfort to the Poshard Foundation. A young lady named Sara Bond had a dream of solving a difficult problem with children who were facing foster care when removed from their homes. Many times, if there were more than one child in the family, the children would be separated into different foster homes, creating double trauma for the children. Bond wanted to keep the siblings together and came to Jo and Glenn with her problem.

Poshard envisioned the remodeling of the nursing home and making it a beautiful building where children could stay together. "He raised $125,000 to begin the remodeling and went to his friends in labor, to Habitat for Humanity, to SIU students, and to private businesses that were willing to help with the renovation," Jo said. "He's excellent at collaborating and bringing people together. He had done that multiple times throughout his career in politics." In a little over a year, the facility was among the best in the state. The Poshard Foundation deeded the building free and clear of debt to Bond and the Night's Shield.

In 2005, Jo retired from her teaching position in Carterville. Glenn was taking on more responsibility at SIU. "It was a natural fit, rather seamless, that I became more involved with the foundation," Jo said. "For many years in the classroom I had seen children without the correct shoes, without coats, without support at home. It was easy for me to direct my attention to the foundation."[3]

From the onset of the foundation, training was deemed critical. In 2001 the foundation had helped form community teams throughout the region to bring awareness to not only child abuse but also domestic violence and how it affects children. Each team was composed of providers, social service workers, educators, prosecutors, law enforcement officials, medical personnel, and other community members. Using the Duluth Model of domestic intervention, the foundation helped communities learn to identify abuse, own it as a problem in the community, and respond appropriately to helping these children become whole.

Speaking at a long conference table down the hall from the foundation office, Jo neatly places her keys to one side, her glasses and purse to the other. She recalls the transition from being a third-grade teacher and wife of a political leader to a more orderly pace of operating a foundation. "I'm more the detail person; he sees the big picture," Jo said. "Glenn is never one to think small. He always thinks with an eye toward the future."

Jo deepened relationships with agencies. "I worked a lot with providers and still do," she said. "I have the utmost respect for the social workers who are on the front lines of protecting our children." She added yearly trainings and increased attendance at the annual fundraiser, moving it out of conference rooms and into the college gymnasium. The foundation was growing and assisting more children, and, with the help of her faithful volunteers, Jo brought excellent organizational skills to meet the future needs.[4]

In 2014 the Poshards' differences in approach were highlighted in their reactions to a proposal from Ginger Meyer, clinical director for the Children's Medical and Mental Health Network, a program of Southern Illinois University School of Medicine, regarding the need for trauma-focused cognitive behavioral therapy in twenty-three southern Illinois counties. Before the meeting, Jo told Glenn to listen; then they would discuss Ginger's proposal and respond later. As Meyer made her pitch, however, Glenn said, "This is exactly what we need," and pledged $100,000 in support for an eighteen-month learning collaborative that trained master's level clinicians across southern Illinois. "Southern Illinois was void of certified trauma-focused counselors," Glenn said. "We had only one in the entire region. Our foundation paid for this highly specialized training, and today we have more than 105 of these counselors available to children throughout southern Illinois. It's been one of our best collaborative efforts."

Over the past six years, the value of these clinicians to a rural area ravaged by abuse of methamphetamines and other drugs that leads to the neglect and abandonment of children has been proven many times over. "How many times have we seen a young couple with good jobs become addicted and abandon the children while they sought out the drugs?" asks Jo.[5] "We want communities to become advocates and protectors of the children, and raising awareness is one of our main goals. We support many organizations that do a great job in protecting the children and speaking up for their interests, including the CASAs [court-appointed special advocates] and child advocacy centers."

In 2020 the foundation began collaborating with the Illinois Education Association and the Education Redesign Lab at Harvard University Graduate School of Education in a project involving child resiliency, helping to support classroom teachers across southern Illinois who work with children in overcoming difficult home and economic conditions. "We are grateful that so many organizations now look to us for help," said Jo Poshard. "No one at the foundation receives a salary or coverage of expenses. We've been fortunate. We can operate entirely on behalf of the children."

In 2019 the foundation hosted its twentieth-anniversary fundraiser, raising $120,000. That marked the time between the "what could have been" from the governor's race and what became a valued resource in changing lives for children most in need.

The foundation's emphasis on children reminds Poshard of moments over many years in which Kristen and Dennis joined him in visiting homeless shelters, crisis centers, and other places where there are poor and vulnerable people, especially the old and the young. "I have constantly reminded my children of Vice President Humphrey's admonition to always protect the most vulnerable. Seeing a poor homeless man with shoes falling off his feet and struggling with mental illness, Kristen wrote the following poem."

### *Shoeless Voices*

*It is not an air of confidence*
*That I hold my head high*
*Looking down is just too brutal to bear*
*Reminding me that I have become "that guy"*
*If shoes really do say a lot about a man*
*These tassels are shouting I'm such a fool*
*Laces strapped so tight knotted again and again*
*Made for the trailblazing of others*
*Not for the unpaved paths where my mind wanders*
*Clacking too loud for the quiet halls that house my most precious memories*
*Shhhh . . . they whisper*
*Big deal, Big deals . . . Big deal*
*Big skies, little stars*
*Big hearts tire of the big doings*
*They open just as wide for the little ideas*
*Take off those shoes*
*Welcome the lumps and bumps that grow over your hands*
*They will still be held*
*Walk slower . . . as slow as you want*
*With a slouch that knows no one is looking*
*No sounds, nothing to say, little ideas*
*Quiet, Peace*
*Barefoot and little.*

While in the final stages of putting together this book, the Poshards became troubled by the emerging rancor, including Facebook posts that promote violence and racism. In multiple cities, disrespect and violence were taking place. A divisive 2020 presidential election was weeks away. Just months earlier, Poshard's friend Congressman John Lewis, arrested about forty times in the quest for civil rights, died of cancer. "I have to do something," Poshard said.

Glenn and Jo organized rallies promoting nonviolence at the courthouse in each of the thirty-nine counties he served while in Congress. Most every weekday for three weeks, they were up by 5 A.M. to be at the first stop by 9 A.M. Glenn and Jo hosted two or three rallies most days. When going to the northern part of the district, they drove their mini-SUV four-hundred-plus miles, arriving home for a late dinner.

At each stop, Poshard wore a black, long-sleeved shirt, on the front of which were these words:

> "To DO JUSTICE
> To LOVE MERCY
> To WALK HUMBLY BEFORE YOUR GOD"

On the back were words from a prayer attributed to St. Francis of Assisi.

> "Where there is hatred, let me sow love
> Where there is injury, pardon
> Where there is doubt, faith
> Where there is despair, hope
> Where there is darkness, light."

Each rally began with walks around the courthouse. Participants held signs like "Faith, Hope, Love, but the Greatest of These Is Love" and "With Malice toward None, with Charity for All."

Sometimes on courthouse steps, other times on the lawn, Poshard stepped back from the crowd so he could safely remove his mask, worn due to the pandemic. In unfolding Lincoln's Gettysburg Address, Poshard first cited a Lincoln speech, given in 1838, in which the future president warns that the greatest threat to our way of life is from within: "If destruction be our lot, we must ourselves be its author and finisher." Poshard further quotes Lincoln as saying that as a country of free men, we will "live forever or die by suicide."

Poshard recited from memory the 272-word Gettysburg Address that Lincoln wrote on the train en route to his secondary speaking role in dedicating the national cemetery. Poshard walked his audience through each part of the speech, noting that Lincoln's opening referred to the eighty-seven-year-old Declaration of Independence, which says in part, "We hold these truths to be self-evident, that all men are created equal, that they are endowed by their Creator with certain inalienable Rights, that among these are Life, Liberty and the pursuit of Happiness."

Poshard emphasizes these words that Lincoln spoke at Gettysburg: "We cannot dedicate—we cannot consecrate—we cannot hallow—this ground. The brave men, living and dead, who struggled here, have consecrated it, far above our poor power to add or detract. The world will little note, nor long remember what we say here, but it can never forget what they did here. It is for us the living, rather, to be dedicated here to the unfinished work which they who fought here have thus far so nobly advanced. It is rather for us to be here dedicated to the great task remaining before us—that from these honored dead we take increased devotion to that cause for which they gave the last full measure of devotion."

"What is this unfinished work, this great task remaining before us?" he asked his audience. "Namely this," Poshard says. "When any citizen is denied life, liberty, and the pursuit of happiness, we remind our people who we are, what we stand for, and we act. The 'unfinished work, this great task remaining before us' is the responsibility of every generation of Americans."

Poshard underlines the theme of a forward-looking, healing approach as he moves to Lincoln's second inaugural address. Thousands came expecting the president to advocate crushing the South after the Civil War. Poshard stomps his foot to the ground for effect to show what people thought Lincoln would say. "What did they hear?" Poshard asks.

"With malice toward none; with charity for all . . . let us strive on to finish the work we are in; to bind up the nation's wounds; to care for him who shall have borne the battle . . . to do all which may achieve and cherish a just and a lasting peace among ourselves, and with all nations."

Then Poshard moves forward to President Kennedy's only inaugural address. "We dare not forget today that we are the heirs of that first revolution." Later, Kennedy speaks the famous words: "And so my fellow Americans, ask not what your country can do for you—ask what you can do for your country."

"As the heirs of that first Revolution, what are we called on to do?" Poshard again asks. He repeats, taking time for pauses to emphasize: "When . . . any citizen . . . is denied life . . . liberty . . . and the pursuit of happiness, it reminds us of the unfinished work that remains before us as the heirs to the Declaration. We march. We protest. We stand against injustice. Peaceful protest is honorable. But violence is never the solution."

Reflecting on the marches, Poshard turned to poetry, reminding people of the words of warning from Jefferson, Lincoln, and John Lewis. Poshard captured the message of the marches in a poem he wrote, reflecting on the words of warning from Jefferson, Lincoln, and John Lewis about subjecting the country to division and violence.

### *A REMINDER*

*Thomas*
*Are we not a nation that's free?*
  *Not when you forget the Declaration's decree.*

*Abraham*
*It seems the nation does mourn!*
  *Small wonder when charity is forlorn.*

*Abraham*
*What wisdom to impart*
*A nation so divided and torn?*
  *Strive on to finish the work you are in*
  *A just and lasting peace among yourselves reborn*

*John*
*Must violent words fly*
*Another war to fight?*
  *Only love and forgiveness unite*

*John*
*You were broken on the bridge*
  *I forgave, I carried on.*
*What legacy do you leave us now*
  *March on, March on!*

Hundreds joined them in their peaceful marches for nonviolence. The Poshards were uniquely positioned to bring people together with a hopeful message at a time when the threats of violence ran rampant in America.

Likewise, they were uniquely positioned to brighten children's lives across southern Illinois. On multiple occasions when Poshard's colleagues at SIU recounted his days as SIU president, the session ended with an unsolicited remark along these lines. "Glenn and Jo Poshard are the only ones who could have put together the Foundation that has done unbelievable work."

From another: "Their Foundation has done work that's had major impact on saving children from lives of abuse and neglect."

From an intimate living room conversation the day after a heartbreaking political defeat comes this richness of their many life experiences to the benefit of those most in need. It is a way for the Poshards to positively address the question posed in 1949 in the inaugural address by SIU president Delyte Morris.

"To what are our children born?"

APPENDIXES

NOTES

INDEX

# APPENDIX A

### *Constituent Issues, 1993–94*

Poshard and his staff regularly interacted with leaders in communities he served. He also regularly hosted town halls, office hours, and other times for anyone to communicate with his staff. He considered it fundamental to his work in Congress to advocate for and deliver on initiatives important to constituents. Below are further examples from chapter 13 of ways in which he responded to identified needs in his early years of representing the Nineteenth District.

In December 1993 he announced a $1.65 million federal grant to retrain coal miners who lost jobs after passage of the Clean Air Act.[1] "This is the first major step forward in putting people who lost their livelihood because of this bill back to work," he said. Much of the retraining was delivered by community colleges. Earlier in the year, Illinois Eastern Community College received a $170,000 grant to help keep low-income and disabled students in school, and Shawnee Community College, in Ullin, received $165,523 for students with special needs.[2]

"The community colleges have the flexibility and know-how to respond to immediate needs such as job training," Poshard said. "They fulfill a great mission in preparing workers for our regional economy. They are unsurpassed in responding to community needs, and central and southern Illinois are blessed to have such a great network of these fine institutions."

His central Illinois work included help with an $800,000 transit facility in Decatur; $300,000 for watershed management along the Embarras River; $50,000 for a rural primary care network based in Richland County; improvements at the Decatur airport; $251,000 for patrols at the Decatur Housing Authority; a $400,000 loan to help finance a rubber-mixing facility for the Wayne-White Electric Cooperative; $300,000 to address erosion along the Embarras River in Jasper County; $491,000 for a water-and-sewer plant in the city of Newton; $3 million in federal support for the Hardinville Water

Company; a grant-and-loan project for the Millstone Water District; a $1.25 million loan guarantee for a rural water system near Mattoon; $2.87 million sewer-and-water line extension in Coles County; a $4.3 million grant-and-loan package for the Effingham/Jasper County Water Corporation, based in Dieterich.[3]

In southern Illinois, projects included the Upper Crab Orchard Creek flood control project in Marion, which solved a long-standing problem of flooding in southeast Marion; repair of the Rend Lake subimpoundment dams, which were critical to sustain water delivery to over twenty-five communities; improvement projects at the Williamson County airport; millions in improved public housing throughout his entire district; a $105,000 grant for a sewage treatment plant in Golconda; $348,000 for a sewer plant in the Village of West City; a grant to upgrade the sewer system in Herrin; a $1.9 million loan for an expansion-and-improvement project at Marion Memorial Hospital; and $240,000 for the Saline Valley Conservancy water system.[4]

Poshard helped ensure a $3.4 million contract between the Army and the Olin Corporation to dismantle and recycle 20-mm ammunition for other uses, a move that protected jobs in Marion. He worked to keep the U.S. Forest Service office in Harrisburg and to develop a visitor center rather than move the office near Interstate 57. He supported a grant for Shawnee Community College that promoted distance learning. He worked to secure funding for a $5.6 million purchase of 1,103 acres for the Shawnee National Forest and 7,700 acres to fill in more of the boundary for the Cypress Creek Refuge. He worked to pass legislation to help coal miners who suffered from black lung disease by loosening requirements to qualify for benefits.[5]

Across his entire district, he promoted support for four highways—US Route 36, US Route 51, Illinois Route 1, and US Route 50—as national highways eligible for additional funds for construction, resurfacing, and other improvements. He helped pass the Family Leave Act, which included job security and up to twelve weeks of unpaid leave for birth of a child or family health emergency. He consistently supported funding for the Head Start program, which helped numerous children in his district better prepare for school-age years.

# APPENDIX B

### *Constituent Issues, 1995–96*

In the years covered in chapters 14 and 15, Glenn Poshard was involved in delivering on multiple other projects that were bread-and-butter issues in large and small communities throughout his district. Examples include a $1.4 million federal grant that was designed to help 134 coal miners who lost jobs owing to the Clean Air Act to find new work. Poshard criticized Republican efforts to gut legislation that protected health benefits of about one hundred thousand miners whose employers either closed their doors or sold their businesses. Likewise, Poshard opposed their efforts to defund black lung clinics. "These clinics were keeping alive people who had spent a lifetime in the coal mines, having breathed in the coal dust for years, and we had to fight to keep the clinics open. To treat people this way, people who had gone down into the belly of the earth and sacrificed their health to provide for the energy needs of this country, was a shameful chapter in the history of Congress," he said.

Poshard helped Rend Lake and Shawnee Community Colleges receive federal matching dollars of $500,000 and $300,000 respectively as two-for-one matching donations to the colleges' endowment funds. The Illinois Eastern Community Colleges received $300,000 to link video and teleconferencing equipment among campuses in Fairfield, Robinson, Olney, and Mt. Carmel.[1] The technology opened the door to distance-learning courses in health care and teleconferencing for local businesses. An AmeriCorps grant involving six community colleges placed AmeriCorps members in elementary classrooms to help at-risk students. Poshard had carried all the appropriations bills for community colleges in the Illinois Senate, and his support of them was an important part of his work in Congress.

"I believe the community colleges are on an equal footing with our private and public universities. They're flexible and can adjust to community and economic needs at a moment's notice, whether it's job training for local industries and businesses that require cutting-edge automotive or other technologies, preparing students for emerging trends in areas such as cybersecurity, or getting them ready for the university. They are America's most effective 'bang for the buck' when it comes to higher education."

In May 1995, Poshard dealt with a trade issue that impacted an employer in his district. Roadmaster employed more than two thousand people in producing bicycles at facilities in Olney and Effingham. Those jobs became at risk when China began "dumping" bicycles on the American market. The International Trade Commission agreed with Roadmaster and Poshard, finding a "reasonable indication" that bicycle production in the United States was threatened or injured.

In October, Poshard announced a federal grant to provide mental health services to farm and coal families whose livelihoods had been impacted by a difficult farm economy. Poshard said many farm and coal families were reluctant to seek counseling. The Farm Resource Center was designed to make it easier and more comfortable for people to accept help. "Having grown up on a small family farm, I know the risks farm families face every year. Inclement weather conditions, unstable markets, escalating energy costs, and many other variables caused the loss of thousands of family farms during the eighties and nineties. Farm families are independent. Even when they face the loss of a farm that's been in the family for generations and the stress that comes with that tragedy, they are reluctant to seek mental health services. There is still a stigma attached to seeking help, which is considered a sign of weakness. We had to find a way to bring the services to them, where they lived, and that was the purpose of the Farm Resource Center. I believe the workers in that center saved a lot of people's lives."

In the fall of 1995, Poshard was among the farm state lawmakers who successfully lobbied the House Ways and Means Committee to restore incentives for ethanol production. "There is probably no more important issue for our farm families and the rural economy as a whole than the continued and expanded use of ethanol," he said at the time.

There were other issues on which he provided leadership:

- pushing, as cochairman of the Oil and Gas Caucus, legislation that provided a tax credit to preserve domestic oil and gas production from marginal wells and to promote new drilling

- helping to preserve Amtrak service from Chicago to Carbondale and points in between, including Mattoon. The service was particularly important for students at Eastern Illinois University and Southern Illinois University
- taking a balanced approach to clean water legislation. Farmers pushed against what they considered overregulation that may devalue their property

Water and sewer projects were the most time-consuming. Some of those included a $1 million federal loan to the Saline Valley Conservancy District announced in June 1995. There was a $440,000 loan and $203,000 grant to the Burnside Water District for extension of a rural water district; $242,000 for erosion protection along the Wabash River; $32.1 million for the Olmsted Locks and Dam along the Ohio River; $6.3 million for Lake Shelbyville; $3.4 million for Rend Lake operations and another $300,000 to address deficiencies at the Rend Lake subimpoundment dams; a $568,000 grant for an elevated water tank and water line extension in Benton; a $650,000 grant-and-loan package for a sewer system in Whiteash; $252,000 for sediment control around Lake Shelbyville; $572,000 for a water tower in Herrin; $2.8 million for a flood control project in Marion; a $3.2 million grant and $3 million loan to the Southwater rural water district; and a $12,000 grant for recreational riverfront development in Hardin County along the Ohio River. Working with local governments to identify priority projects and getting those projects funded by the federal agencies, Poshard helped many local communities meet their pressing infrastructure needs.

Millions of dollars flowed into public housing grants throughout his district, including $1.3 million for transitional housing for the homeless in which Poshard took a special interest. Combined with a $2.4 million federal block grant for a summer jobs program in Decatur, the quality of life for lower-income citizens could see some improvement in the largest urban center in his district.

Poshard worked with Republican congressman Ray LaHood of Peoria to keep the Small Business Administration Office in Springfield open. The office had been slated for closure. Poshard said the Illinois delegation met monthly to discuss issues and often worked in a bipartisan way to help with issues across the state.

Road projects across his district were supported by Poshard as a member of the Transportation and Infrastructure Committee, including $1.7 million for the Raney Street overpass in Effingham, $257,000 to extend Sloan Street and thus accommodate the Harrisburg Medical Center, and $700,000 for road improvements to the Garden of the Gods blacktop, just a few of the many road improvements that he helped bring to his district in 1995.

He visited the Big Brothers Big Sisters program in Decatur at the invitation of executive director Jeanne Stahlheber, after attending the organization's convention in Washington, D.C. Organizations throughout his district, particularly those that served the needs of the young and the old, found Poshard to be a frequent visitor.[2]

Poshard worked with a broom manufacturer in Greenup for reinstatement of tariffs to level the playing field between companies in Mexico and the United States. The move to reinstate the tariffs reversed dynamic growth by 10–40 percent for Mexico-produced brooms.[3]

As cochair of the Oil and Gas Caucus, Poshard was among a group of lawmakers advocating for a middle-ground regulatory approach to domestic oil and natural gas exploration. Costly and sometimes duplicative regulations challenged domestic producers to compete with other oil-rich nations, and Poshard wanted to level the playing field as much as possible.

As cochair of the Rural Health Care Caucus, Poshard promoted rural health legislation designed to help struggling hospitals stay open. In many cases, rural hospitals lacked the volume to offer the range of services that were the norm. But these hospitals played an important role in their communities. Thus they needed flexibility to adjust their structure, and they needed the same reimbursement as urban hospitals.

In Decatur, Olney, and Johnson County, Poshard worked with local officials on safe drinking water initiatives. Nitrate levels in Lake Decatur led to action by Poshard and county and city officials. Poshard told local officials he hoped that Decatur would become a good example for other cities across the country which wanted to develop an aggressive action plan for resolving agricultural chemical runoff into drinking water sources. The Safe Drinking Water Act, cosponsored by Poshard, included money for a water tower in Olney and water line extension in Johnson County.[4]

Poshard helped secure a $340,421 federal grant for improvements at the Williamson County Regional Airport.[5] He also worked with local officials who successfully advocated for continuing tower operations by proving the economic benefits at a time when the Federal Aviation Administration was cutting back on tower funding at smaller airports around the country. His seat on the Aviation Subcommittee of the Transportation Committee was helpful to airports all over his district. James Oberstar, chairman of the Aviation Subcommittee, visited his district and helped Poshard gain critical funding.

In two different news releases, Poshard announced that twenty-five different police agencies hired forty-three officers through the COPS (Community Oriented Policing Services) grants for a total of more than $2.5 million of federal assistance.[6] "Putting additional officers on patrol is an effective way of keeping our communities safe places to live and work," he said.

Infrastructure projects included study of the Embarras River watershed; a low-interest loan for a rural water project in Wayne County; a federal loan and grant for sewer system upgrade in rural Edwards County; a $70,000 grant for Pana to improve its industrial park; $100,000 for a road connecting Illinois Route 1 with a barge-loading facility in Hardin County; continued funding of the Olmsted Locks and Dam project; housing authority improvements; increased funding for operations at Rend Lake and Lake Shelbyville; a financing package for the Effingham-Jasper rural water district; a $190,000 loan for a sewage treatment plant in Thompsonville; $1 million to improve the sewer system in Parkersburg; a grant and loan for a sewer system in Eddyville; hundreds of thousands for high-water boat ramps at Lake Shelbyville; and a water tower project in Assumption.

Poshard supported a bill that raised the minimum wage from $4.25 to $4.75 an hour while also offering tax breaks to small businesses such as expanding contribution levels to individual retirement accounts, creating 401(K) retirement accounts, and increasing deductions for business-related equipment.

He supported federal disaster declarations after an April tornado in the Decatur area and May floods in southern Illinois. Economic development remained a priority as he announced the Mid-South Regional Partnership Coalition receiving a competitive grant for a school-to-work program. Another education effort was the release of

$1.9 million to help retrain coal miners who lost jobs because of the Clean Air Act.[7] In February 1996, Poshard hosted U.S. Education Secretary Richard Riley, who made one of his stops Jo Poshard's third-grade classroom in Carterville. In an all-school assembly, Riley encouraged the students to pick up a book rather than turn on the TV and to not let a lack of money deter them from going to college.[8]

Poshard supported the 1996 Farm Bill that moved away from subsidies. In one of many interviews, he described the bill as 60 percent favorable to his district. "On balance," he said, "it's worth supporting." Poshard hosted meetings during the federal government shutdown in late 1995 and January 1996. He had more than one thousand federal workers in his district, including employees of the Marion VA Hospital and the Marion Federal Prison. "The shutdown was totally unnecessary—very difficult to explain to hard-working federal employees. It hurt a lot of families. It happened because people in Congress wouldn't compromise, and it caused a lot of people to lose faith in their government."

He supported language in the Department of Defense funding bill that required domestic purchase of items such as gloves manufactured at family-owned businesses in Effingham, Harrisburg, and Metropolis.

# APPENDIX C

### *President Emeritus Citation*

Below is the citation, passed unanimously by the SIU Board of Trustees, establishing Poshard as SIU President Emeritus.[1]

*Whereas*, Glenn Poshard is a three-degree graduate of Southern Illinois University Carbondale; a veteran of the United States Army; entered SIU on the G.I. Bill where he earned a bachelor's degree in secondary education in 1970; a master's degree in health education in 1974, and a Ph.D. in higher education administration in 1984; and

*Whereas*, following his service in the Illinois Senate and the United States Congress, he was appointed Vice Chancellor for Administration for the Carbondale campus of SIU in 1999; he was appointed to the Board of Trustees of Southern Illinois University in January 2004 and eventually elected Chair of the Board until declaring his candidacy for President of the university system; and became President of SIU in January of 2006; and,

*Whereas*, under his leadership, each year he and the SIU Board of Trustees agreed upon a set of goals and objectives to move the system forward toward the 2020 Vision Statement working closely with the chancellors, assuring the presidential as well as the campus goals were achieved; and,

*Whereas*, under his leadership, and despite economic hardship in the State of Illinois, he held tuition at each campus the lowest among peer groups for each university; and,

*Whereas*, under his leadership, he was a leading voice before the legislature in getting Amtrak service expanded to SIU and as a result of his efforts, a new Saluki train was added to complement the Illini, and additional trains were added to the Chicago–St. Louis route with a stop in Edwardsville; and

*Whereas*, under his leadership, and despite economic hardship in the State of Illinois and in the nation, he secured increased funding from state and federal agencies to help programs including the SIU School of Pharmacy, National Corn to Ethanol Research Center, SIU Dental School, Broadband Access and Mapping Grants, SIUC Autism Grant, and the Simmons Cancer Institute; in just four years SIU received over $51 million; his leadership in light of the dire financial crisis facing higher education in Illinois kept the university financially strong; and,

*Whereas*, under his leadership, he was appointed by the Governor to oversee a capital bill for the state which brought in $168,265,800 for the system allowing monies for the SIU-C Transportation Education Center, the SIU-E Science building, Renovation and Deferred Maintenance for the campuses; and

*Whereas*, under his leadership, he strengthened the ties between the SIU state and federal legislators; he successfully led a statewide effort to reinstate MAP funding and worked successfully to increase PELL grant funding at the federal level; and,

*Whereas*, Dr. Poshard is a past recipient of the Lindell W. Sturgis Memorial Public Service Award and the SIU Distinguished Alumni Award and is a member of the SIU-C College of Education and Human Services Hall of Fame; and

*Whereas*, Glenn Poshard is the second-longest serving President of SIU; Dr. Poshard excelled as a leader for SIU; in his tenure he quickly became one of the most respected voices in the state for higher education; he was called upon consistently to assist state government with critical needs and issues; and, he led SIU into a new era of regional and economic cooperation which enlarged SIU's role of service to the region; Dr. Poshard showed extraordinary leadership in working with the legislature and state agencies to effectively manage SIU's budget and cash flow needs; and,

NOW, THEREFORE, BE IT RESOLVED, by the Board of Trustees in regular meeting assembled, that the Board expresses its profound gratitude and appreciation to Glenn Poshard for his years of distinguished and invaluable service and contributions to Southern Illinois University, to its constituents, its students, and to the region; and,

BE IT FURTHER RESOLVED, that the title of President Emeritus be conferred upon Glenn Poshard effective December 5, 2019, and,

BE IT FURTHER RESOLVED, That the members of this Board, individually and as a group, offer Dr. Poshard their best wishes and gratitude for his service to Southern Illinois University.

*J. Phil Gilbert, Chairman*
*Southern Illinois University Board of Trustees*

# NOTES

## *1. White County Hills*

1. Glenn Poshard, document from personal files.
2. Ed Poshard, interview by author, Carmi, Illinois, May 5, 2017.
3. Poshard, personal files.
4. Poshard, personal files.

## *2. A Quiet Country Kid at the Front*

1. Jim Endicott, interview by author, Carmi, May 5, 2017.

## *3. Military Life in Missouri, Korea, Indiana, and New York*

1. Poshard, personal files.

## *6. Working for an Opponent*

1. Ed Smith, phone interview by author, February 6, 2019.
2. Ron House, interview by author, John A. Logan College, November 15, 2019.
3. House, interview.
4. Larry Woolard, phone interview by author, August 13, 2020.

## *7. At Home in Lincoln Land*

1. Brenda Kirkpatrick, "Group to Compile Industrial Development Book," *Marion Daily Republican*, July 12, 1985.
2. Tim Landis, "Silent Goforth Kept His Campaign Pledge," *Southern Illinoisan*, August 28, 1985, 1.
3. David Phelps, phone interview by author, October 7, 2020.
4. Tim Landis, "Jabr Hands Thompson Keys to Du Quoin Fair," *Southern Illinoisan*, December 20, 1985, 1.
5. Tim Landis, "Hopes, Fears Travel Proposed River-to-River Road," *Southern Illinoisan*, October 8, 1985, 1.
6. *Benton Evening News*, June 6, 1986.
7. Beth Haller, "No Hope for Cairo Center," *Southern Illinoisan*, August 2, 1988, 1.

8. News release published in local newspapers, "Poshard Hails Unemployment Bill," 1987.
9. House, interview.

### 8. *On the Issues, a Race for Congress*

1. Emeritus/retired faculty biography of Patrick J. Kelley, Southern Illinois University School of Law webpage, accessed August 2, 2020, https://law.siu.edu/faculty/emeritus-faculty/kelley.html.
2. John Jackson, email to author, August 2, 2020.
3. Tim Landis, "Kelley, Poshard Steal Spotlight in Mt. Vernon," *Southern Illinoisan*, October 19, 1988, A6.
4. Jane Davison, "Kelley, Poshard Square Off in Pinckneyville Forum," *Du Quoin Evening Call*, August 10, 1988, 1.
5. David Belcher, "Kelley and Others Protest Visit," *West Frankfort Daily American*, October 8, 1988, 1.
6. Full-page ad, *Daily Egyptian*, November 4, 1988, 11.
7. "22nd Congressional District," *Southern Illinoisan*, October 21, 1988, 22.
8. "Congressional Race Sticking to High Road," *Daily Egyptian*, October 26, 1988, 4.

### 9. *Not All about the Money*

1. Glenn Poshard, personal files.
2. Cindy Humphreys, "Agreement to Paint Chester Bridge Finally Reached," *Southern Illinoisan*, April 1, 1989, 1.
3. Beth Pierce Wright, interview with author, August 13, 2020.
4. Brian Matmiller, "Poshard Satisfied with Navy Probe," *Southern Illinoisan*, July 9, 1989, 1.
5. Marta Brautigam, "Pittston Treated Miners Unfairly, Panel Says," *Southern Illinoisan*, September 2, 1989, 3.
6. Marcy Burstiner, "Poshard Seeks Investigation of Post Office," *Southern Illinoisan*, October 7, 1989, 1.
7. Tim Landis, "Committee to Study Poverty along River," *Southern Illinoisan*, February 17, 1989.
8. Cindy Humphreys, "Lock, Dam Could Pay Dividends," *Southern Illinoisan*, March 5, 1989, 1.
9. Anne Marie Obiala, "Local Jobs in Jeopardy at Olmsted," *Southern Illinoisan*, May 31, 1993, 1.

10. David Zoeller, "Officials Applaud Completion of $3 Billion Olmsted Project," *Paducah Sun*, August 31, 2018, 1.
11. Ed Smith, interview.
12. Kristen Poshard, Glenn Poshard's personal files.
13. Teryl Franklin, "Cache Swamp Links Region to Its Past," *Southern Illinoisan*, May 19, 1991, 1.
14. Norm Heikens, "Poshard Outlines His Wilderness Area Legislation," *Southern Illinoisan*, October 15, 1989, 1.
15. Wright, interview.
16. Poshard, news release on PACs, August 1989.

### *10. A Change of Heart*

1. Norm Heikens, "Poshard Seeks Time, Grant for PCB Study," *Southern Illinoisan*, November 28, 1989, 1.
2. Brian Matmiller, "Industry Urged to Do More to Battle Illiteracy," *Southern Illinoisan*, February 6, 1990, 1.
3. Jim Kirkpatrick, interview with author, John A. Logan College, December 2, 2019.

### *11. Worth the Fight*

1. Glenn Poshard, personal files.
2. Jon Baron, phone interview with author, November 24, 2020.
3. Roll Call, cited in Poshard news releases.
4. Brian Mattmiller, "Poshard Blames Harrisburg Board for Delay in Talks," *Southern Illinoisan*, September 25, 1992, 1.
5. Brian Mattmiller, "Southern Illinoisans Bargain to Give Sanctions More Time," *Southern Illinoisan*, January 10, 1991, 1.
6. Curtis Winston, "After 40 Years or So, Funds Released for Making Route 13 Four Lanes," *Harrisburg Daily Register*, May 6, 1992, 1.
7. Heidi Hildebrand, "Marion V.A. Hospital to Get Outpatient Clinic," *Southern Illinoisan*, July 31, 1992, 4A.
8. Tom Woolf, "Court Rejects Southern Illinois Remap Proposal," *Southern Illinoisan*, October 22, 1991, 1.

### *12. Redistricting and a New Constituency*

1. Gary Minich, "Staley Locks Out AIW," *Decatur Herald and Review*, June 28, 1993, 1.

2. Teryl Franklin, "Poshard, Bruce Battle over Vote on Clean Air," *Southern Illinoisan*, March 8, 1992, 2D.
3. "PACS Become Focal Point," *Southern Illinoisan*, March 8, 1992, D1.
4. Rob Wick, "Prominent Macon County Democrats Endorse Poshard," *Harrisburg Daily Register*, 1992, 1.
5. Reid Magney and Teryl Franklin, "Poshard Whips Challenger," *Decatur Herald and Review*, November 4, 1992.
6. Linda Sickler, "Details of Nuns' Deaths Revealed," *Southern Illinoisan*, November 11, 1992.

### *13. Welcoming Central Illinois*

1. "Top U.S. Agricultural Exports in 2017," U.S. Department of Agriculture, March 23, 2018, https://www.fas.usda.gov/data/top-us-agricultural-exports-2017.
2. Judy Hampton, interview with author, John A. Logan College, December 2, 2019.
3. Glenn Poshard, "A Staley Proposal," *Decatur Herald and Review*, March 2, 1993, A8.
4. Glenn Poshard, personal files.
5. Glenn Poshard, news release, March 11, 1994.
6. Glenn Poshard, personal files.
7. Scott Clem, "Poshard Abandoned His Supporters," *Southern Illinoisan*, August 31, 1994, 7A.

### *14. Trusting Only America*

1. David Gillies, phone interview with author, August 14, 2020.
2. Press releases, "Poshard Again Earns Concord Coalition Honor Roll," January 7, 1997, and "Poshard Honored by Concord Coalition for Fiscal Responsibility," June 28, 1998, the second based on "Concord Releases 1997 Scorecard Scoring Members of Congress on Fiscal Responsibility," *Concord Coalition*, March 16, 1998, https://www.concordcoalition.org/press-releases/1998/0317/concord-releases-1997-scorecard-scoring-members-congress-fiscal-responsibil.
3. Ronald Brownstein, "Christian Coalition in a Good Spot to Show It's More Than Just a GOP Arm," *Los Angeles Times*, April 10, 1995, A5.

4. David Gillies, interview.
5. Dave Moore, "Labor Woes Gain National Ear," *Decatur Herald and Review*, January 11, 1995, 1.

### *15. Keeping a Promise*

1. Chris Mortell, "Poshard Rolls to Re-election for a Fifth Term in Congress," *Mattoon Journal Gazette*, November 6, 1996.
2. Bill Hamel, "Glenn Poshard Should Be Re-elected as Congressman," *Mattoon Journal Gazette*, October 26, 1996, 4.
3. "Re-elect Poshard," *Decatur Herald and Review*, October 29, 1996, 11.
4. Russell Darby, "Poshard Saves $1.2 Million on Office Costs," *Marion Daily Republican*, July 11, 1996, 1.
5. Dawn Schabbing, "At a Distance, Poshard Links Up with High Schools through Network in Teleconference," *Mattoon Journal Gazette*, April 11, 1996, 1.
6. Glenn Poshard, personal file.
7. John C. Patterson, "Big Tent All Their Own," *Decatur Herald and Review*, February 16, 1996, 4.
8. Chris Mortell, "Union Approves Contract," *Charleston Times-Courier*, July 2, 1996, 1.
9. Bill Lipinski, phone interview with author, October 8, 2020.
10. Jerry Costello, phone interview with author, October 20, 2020.

### *16. Pitching Lunch Bucket Populism*

1. "Campaign Finance Reform Is an Issue That Won't Go Away," *Southtown Star*, June 5, 1997, A-6.
2. Thomas Beaumont, "Poshard Kicks Off His Campaign for Governor with 5-City Swing," *Southern Illinoisan*, May 11, 1997, 1.
3. John C. Patterson, "Party Chairman Backs Poshard," *Quad City Times*, May 6, 1997.
4. Shannon Woodworth, "Will Glenn Poshard Run for Governor?" *West Frankfort Daily American*, February 15, 1997, 1.
5. Steve Neal, "Downstater Starts Uphill Battle Here," *Chicago Sun-Times*, March 10, 1997.
6. Carla Eskew, "Local Dems Rush to Support Poshard," *Decatur Herald and Review*, March 11, 1997.

7. Bill Grimes, "Poshard Seeing Things Differently in Tour of State," *West Frankfort Daily American*, April 14, 1997.
8. Carl Walworth, "Poshard Pulls Crowd at Rally," *Mattoon Journal Gazette*, June 30, 1997, 1.
9. Brownstein, "Christian Coalition in a Good Spot."
10. Robert F. Kennedy, "'Freedom and Democracy': University of Cape Town, Cape Town, South Africa," box 2, speeches and press releases, Senate papers, papers of Robert F. Kennedy, John F. Kennedy Presidential Library, Boston.
11. Associated Press, "Poshard Endorsed by AFL-CIO," *Carmi Times*, January 10, 1998, 1.
12. John Kass, "Schmidt's Negative Ads Hint at the Kind of Leader He'd Make," *Chicago Tribune*, March 16, 1998, 3.
13. Rick Pearson, "Poshard, Schmidt Spar over TV Spots," *Chicago Tribune*, March 14, 1998, 1.
14. "Meet Democrat Glenn Poshard," flyer for governorship campaign, 1997.

### *17. Liberal Fallout, Lost Opportunity*

1. Thomas Beaumont, "Poshard Staff Argues Points," *Southern Illinoisan*, September 21, 1998.
2. "Glenn Poshard for Governor, 1998 Bus Tour," internal campaign folder.
3. Thomas Beaumont, "Chicago Mayor Preaches Party Unity," *Southern Illinoisan*, June 3, 1998, 1.
4. Glenn Poshard, handwritten note, personal files.
5. Poshard, handwritten note.
6. Jo Poshard, interview with author, John A. Logan College, December 3, 2019.
7. Jo Poshard, interview.
8. "Progressives Denounce Ryan's Tactics," October 12, 1998, governorship campaign materials.
9. Rick Garcia to Jan Schakowsky, April 15, 1998, Poshard's personal files.
10. Rogers Worthington, "Poshard's 3rd-Airport Comments Draw Fire from Party Members," *Chicago Tribune*, April 30, 1998, section 2, 7.

11. Rick Pearson and Susan Kuczka, "No Debate about It; This Isn't News, It's History," *Chicago Tribune*, October 16, 1998.
12. Scott Fornek, "Schmidt Drops Rivalry, Stumps for Poshard," *Chicago Sun-Times*, September 2, 1998.
13. George Will, "An Endangered Species in Illinois: Conservative Southern Democrat," *Centralia Sentinel*, September 21, 1998, 5A.
14. Steve Neal, "Liberal Democrats Rally to Poshard's Defense," *Chicago Sun-Times*, September 21, 1998.
15. Neal, "Liberal Democrats Rally."
16. Scott Fornek and Dave McKinney, "Poshard Ads Rip Ryan on License Scandal," *Chicago Sun-Times*, September 18, 1998.
17. "Poshard Turns Tragedy to His Benefit," *Chicago Tribune*, October 6, 1998, 12.
18. "The Toll of the License Scandal," *Chicago Tribune*, March 8, 2000, 20.
19. Associated Press, "Poshard: Photo Shot from 'Ambush,'" *Southern Illinoisan*, November 2, 1998.
20. Matt O'Connor and Ray Long, Ray, "U.S. Says Ryan Fund Got Money in License Scam," *Chicago Tribune*, October 7, 1998, 1.
21. Poshard for governor news release, October 1998.
22. Scott Fornek, "Ryan's Big Lead Vanishes," *Chicago Sun-Times*, October 22, 1998, 1.
23. John Kass, "Poshard's Character Brings Integrity to His Candidacy," *Chicago Tribune*, November 2, 1998.
24. Glenn Poshard, concession speech, November 4, 1998.
25. LarryWoolard, interview.
26. Robert Davis and Sue Ellen Christian, "New Session, Familiar Rivals in Springfield," *Chicago Tribune*, January 9, 1997, 1.
27. John Jackson, interview with author, December 2, 2019.
28. Marilyn Halstead, "Rednour Home Is a Showpiece of the Du Quoin State Fair," *Southern Illinoisan*, August 30, 2015.

### *18. Meeting the New Governor*

1. Glenn Poshard to Governor George Ryan on John A. Logan College letterhead, March 29, 1999, Poshard's personal files.
2. Tracy James, "OK for John A. Logan," *Southern Illinoisan*, April 14, 1999, 1.

3. Capitol Fax, January-June 1999, Capitol Fax newsletter collection, University of Illinois Springfield, Archives and Special Collections, box 1, folder 4, MC99, accessed July 5, 2021, https://research.archivesspace.uis.edu/repositories/2/archival_objects/55151.
4. Glenn Poshard to Capitol Fax, 1999, personal files.

### *19. Vision and Action on Campus*

1. "Poshard Is a Man of Action," *Daily Egyptian*, October 7, 1999, 4.
2. Karen Binder, "Touch of Nature, Administration Putting Plan into Action to Improve SIUC's Environmental Center," *Southern Illinoisan*, September 3, 2000, 1C.
3. "Poshard's Decision to Stay Brings Stability to SIUC Infrastructure," *Daily Egyptian*, August 23, 2000, 4.
4. Phil Gatton, phone interview with author, March 24, 2020.
5. Gatton, interview.
6. Gatton, interview.
7. "Poshard's Decision to Stay Brings Stability."
8. 2020 Vision Committee, "Report and Recommendation," September 2002, Glenn Poshard's personal files.
9. Jim Muir, "It's Time for Me to Tell My Story," *Southern Illinoisan*, March 2, 2003, 1.
10. Matt O'Connor and Rudolph Bush, "Ryan Guilty," *Chicago Tribune*, April 18, 2006, 1.
11. Jim Muir, "Back to School in Benton," *Southern Illinoisan*, September 23, 2003, 1.

### *20. Trustees Turning Inward*

1. Ed Hightower, phone interview with author, February 21, 2020.
2. Hightower, interview.
3. Caleb Hale, "It's Official: President Poshard," *Southern Illinoisan*, September 29, 2006, 1.
4. Robert Frost, "Reluctance," *Poets.org*, Academy of American Poets, accessed September 1, 2022, poets.org/poem/reluctance.
5. John Haller, interview with author, Morris Library, December 2, 2019.
6. John S. Haller Jr., "The Illinois Board of Higher Education and the Office of the President," in John S. Jackson, ed., *Southern Illinois*

*University at 150* (Carbondale: Southern Illinois University Press, 2019), 72.

7. Paula Keith, interview with author, Stone Center, SIU Carbondale, December 12, 2019.
8. Vaughn Vandegrift, phone interview with author, May 1, 2019.
9. Dave Gross, interview with author, Springfield, December 6, 2019.
10. Vandegrift, interview
11. Vandegrift, interview.
12. Written performance review as SIU president, Glenn Poshard's personal file.
13. "Attitudes Are Contagious," *Daily Egyptian*, January 22, 2007, 6.
14. Glenn Poshard, personal files.
15. Glenn Poshard, personal files.
16. Jerry Blakemore, phone interview with author, March 23, 2020.
17. Two-page ad, "Southern Illinois University," *Southern Illinoisan*, July 1, 2007, 4B–5B.
18. John D. Homan, "Poshard: No Complaining, Time to Compete for Students," *Southern Illinoisan*, February 16, 2007, 1.
19. "Talking Points for Official Opening of SIU System Service Center," September 12, 2007, Glenn Poshard's personal files.
20. Gus Bode, "Wendler Ousted," *Daily Egyptian*, December 13, 2006, 1.
21. Ashley Wiehle, "SIUC Finds Its New Man," *Southern Illinoisan*, May 23, 2007, 1.
22. Caleb Hale and Scott Fitzgerald, "Door Could Be Closing on Trevino," *Southern Illinoisan*, March 18, 2008, 1.
23. Sam Goldman, interview with author, December 12, 2019.
24. John Simmons, phone interview with author, August 19, 2020.
25. Blakemore, interview.

### *21. Not a Job*

1. Jeff Coen and Bob Secter, "14 years for Blagojevich," *Chicago Tribune*, December 8, 2011, 1.
2. Kurt Erickson, "Heavy Hitters May Aid Blagojevich," *Decatur Herald and Review*, March 4, 2008, 1.
3. Mike Riopell, "It's Official: Quinn Signs $31 Billion Capital Bill," *Decatur Herald and Review*, July 14, 2009, 1.

4. John Jackson, interview.
5. Kevin Bame, interview with author, Stone Center, December 12, 2019.
6. Duane Stucky, interview with author, Stone Center, December 12, 2019.
7. Paula Keith, interview.
8. Dave Gross, interview.
9. Keith, interview.
10. Gross, interview.
11. Bame, interview.
12. Haller, interview.
13. Roger Tedrick, phone interview with author, April 2020.
14. Jodi Cohen, "Words Coming Back to Haunt SIU," *Chicago Tribune*, July 19, 2006, section 2, 1.
15. Jordan Wilson and Joe Crawford, "Poshard Defends Dissertation against Plagiarism Accusation," *Daily Egyptian*, August 30, 2007, 1.
16. Scott Fitzgerald, "AFAC Embraces Whistleblower Role," *Southern Illinoisan*, September 10, 2007, 1.
17. Haller, interview.
18. Keith, interview.
19. Stucky, interview.
20. Haller, interview.
21. Blakemore, interview.
22. Goldman, interview.
23. "Harrisburg Physician Appointed to SIU Board of Trustees," *Harrisburg Register*, April 2011, 1.
24. Stucky, interview.
25. Jeff Denneen and Tom Dretler, "The Financially Sustainable University," *Bain and Company*, July 6, 2010, https://www.bain.com/insights/financially-sustainable-university/.
26. Glenn Poshard, handwritten note, personal files.
27. "SIU President Glenn Poshard to Retire," Illinois Public Media website, July 25, 2013, will.illinois.edu/news/story/siu-president-glenn-poshard-to-retire.
28. Brian Munoz, "Dunn Removed as SIU President after Attempt in Dissolving University System," *Daily Egyptian*, July 13, 2018, 1.
29. Stucky, interview.

### *22. The Right to Rise?*

1. "About" webpage, City Club of Chicago website, accessed 2021, https://www.cityclub-chicago.org/about.
2. Glenn Poshard, speech to City Club, October 2, 2013, City Club of Chicago, https://www.cityclub-chicago.org/video/856/glenn-poshard.
3. Illinois Board of Higher Education, "The Illinois Public Agenda for College and Career Success," 2008, https://www.ibhe.org/assets/files/ExecutiveSummary.pdf.
4. Robert Gates and David Boren, "Public Colleges Boost Economic Growth," *Wall Street Journal*, August 26, 2013.

### *23. Professional Baseball in Southern Illinois*

1. Owner bio, Southern Illinois Miners, accessed July 22, 2022, https://southernillinoisminers.com/information/directory/bios/Jayne_Simmons?view=bio.

### *24. Rend Lake Turnaround*

1. "Inter-City Water Fund," Rend Lake Conservancy District, accessed July 22, 2022, https://rendlake.org/?page_id=13.
2. Jim Muir, "Audit Blames RLCD Problems on Board," *Southern Illinoisan*, September 24, 2004, 1.
3. Jeff Mark, phone interview with author, June 18, 2020.
4. Mark, interview.
5. Blakemore, opinion on Illinois Health Facilities Planning Board.

### *25. Faith and Politics*

1. Luke 20:25, American Standard version, Bible Hub.com.
2. Faith and Politics Institute, July 2021, http:www.faithandpolitics.org.
3. "Cairo Calm after Bombs," *Southern Illinoisan*, July 18, 1967, 1.
4. Joe Eldridge, phone interview with author, November 30, 2019.
5. Eldridge, interview.
6. W. Douglas Tanner Jr., *The Truth Can Set Us Free: Toward a Politics of Grace and Healing* (Kalamazoo, MI: Fetzer Institute, 2007).

7. Bruno to Glenn Poshard, summer of 1991 or 1992, Poshard's personal files.
8. Glenn Poshard, personal files.

### *26. The Shadow Side of Leadership*

1. Parker Palmer, *Leading from Within: Reflections on Spirituality and Leadership* (Washington, D.C.: Servant Leadership School), 1990.

### *27. Poshard Foundation and Beyond*

1. Jo Poshard, interview.
2. Jo Poshard, interview.
3. Jo Poshard, interview.
4. Jo Poshard, interview.
5. Jo Poshard, interview.

### *Appendix A*

1. Poshard news releases.
2. Poshard news releases, 1993.
3. Poshard news releases, 1993.
4. Poshard news releases, 1993.
5. Poshard news releases, 1994.

### *Appendix B*

1. Poshard news releases.
2. Billy Tyus, "Poshard Stumps for Big Brothers/Sisters," *Decatur Herald and Review*, July 9, 1996.
3. Dawn Schabbing, "Broom Makers Ask Trade Protection," *Mattoon Journal Gazette*, September 18, 1996.
4. Poshard news release, "Drinking Water Bill Includes Aid for 19th District," June 25, 1996.
5. Poshard news release, "Durbin, Moseley-Braun, Poshard Announce Decatur, Williamson County Airport Improvement Grants," May 1, 1997.
6. Poshard news release, "19th District Adds Police Manpower Thanks to Crime Bill Program"; news releases dated May 14 and December 17, 1996.

7. Poshard news release, "Congressmen Announce Miner Retraining Grant for Franklin, Perry Counties," 1996.
8. John D. Homan, "U.S. Secretary of Education Visits C'ville," *Herrin Spokesman*, February 21, 1996, 1.

### *Appendix C*

1. "Recognition of Glenn Poshard Resolution," in "Agenda, Meeting of the Board of Trustees, Southern Illinois University," December 5, 2019, AA-1–AA-2, SIU System, https://siusystem.edu/board-of-trustees/meetings/2019/1219agenda-website.pdf.

# INDEX

**Glenn Poshard** has been at the forefront of educational and economic development initiatives at the regional, state, and national level for more than five decades. His lengthy service-oriented career has included time as a soldier, teacher, Illinois state senator, a member of the U.S. Congress, chairman of the Southern Illinois University Board of Trustees, and President of the SIU system. The Poshard Foundation for Abused Children, a volunteer organization founded by Poshard and his wife, Jo, has served the needs of vulnerable children in Southern Illinois for nearly 25 years.

**Carl Walworth** worked for thirty-one years as a reporter, editor, and, later, publisher in the newspaper industry in Illinois. He currently is the library director at the Mattoon Public Library. He is the author of *The Mayor of Moultrie Avenue* and a researcher for *Lake Sara, the Hidden Jewel in America's Heartland.*